D0452140

Praise for *A Spiritual Approach to Parenting: Secrets of Raising the 21st Century Child*

"As we welcome the Indigo and Crystal children who are our future leaders, Dr. Barrick has written a valuable and timely book. Drawing on ancient wisdom and personal experience, she offers sound advice to help parents support the growth and creativity of these wonderful young people."

—CHRISTINE PAGE, M.D.,
media presenter and author of *Spiritual Alchemy: How to Transform Your Life*

"Filled with remarkable insights into the psychology of the child's soul, this book goes way beyond current parenting approaches. By exploring children's deep spiritual needs through their developmental stages and ways to raise up the Inner genius, A Spiritual Approach to Parenting *offers real healing and hope to the many sensitive, bright children that have been mislabeled as 'learning disabled' or 'problem' children."*

—DR. JOYE B. BENNETT,
child psychologist and co-editor of
Nurturing Your Baby's Soul: A Spiritual Guide for Expectant Parents

"Drawing from a rich background in psychology and religion, as a former professor at a major university, a practicing clinical therapist and a minister of many years' standing, Dr. Barrick has written with great clarity a profound book that couples wise insights with practical applications for everyday life.

"This is a must book for the Aquarian age families who are raising the advanced souls coming in as children today. Dr. Barrick's explanation of the developmental stages of life is priceless and unique in its depth of spiritual and psychological understanding. I love the book and highly recommend it."

—REV. E. GENE VOSSELER,
writer, spiritual counselor and former director of social service programs for
disadvantaged youth

Praise for *Soul Reflections: Many Lives, Many Journeys*

"Marilyn Barrick fervently believes in the power of lifting up deep, inner compassion as a potent tool for healing human sorrow and suffering. She offers us the possibility—nay, the promise—of spiritual companionship and support the moment we honor our brief time on earth as a gift to be opened, rather than as a problem to be solved.

"Dr. Barrick offers kindness, healing and hope to anyone who reads this book. She helps us heal the past while creating a luminous future for ourselves and for the family of the earth."
—WAYNE MULLER,
N.Y. Times best-selling author of *Legacy of the Heart*

"Soul Reflections takes you on a journey into your own inner dimensions of being, to a place of healing and light. Dr. Barrick has outlined a clear path for your soul's homeward journey, illumined by her many years of experience in guiding souls through life's difficult moments.

"A handbook for those whose hearts yearn for soul liberation. The reader will greatly benefit from the spiritual exercises and case histories in the book."
—DR. NEROLI DUFFY,
lecturer, medical doctor, counselor and co-author with Dr. Marilyn C. Barrick of
Wanting to Live: Overcoming the Seduction of Suicide

"In Soul Reflections: Many Lives, Many Journeys, *Dr. Barrick blends profound wisdom and keen psychological insights with practical tools and exercises for personal application of the truths revealed.*

"This book is a must-read for any serious seeker who hungers for knowledge of the path that can lead to enlightenment, God-realization and the ascension in the light."
—REV. E. GENE VOSSELER,
public speaker, writer and spiritual counselor

Praise for *Emotions: Transforming Anger, Fear and Pain*

"Marilyn Barrick is on the mark. While we search for the understanding of our physical, mental and spiritual selves, we often forget the source of the balance between all of them—our emotional self. This book addresses the issue magnificently. Read it and grow."

—DANNION BRINKLEY,
N.Y. Times best-selling author of *Saved by the Light* and *At Peace in the Light*

"Emotions is a wise, heartfelt and deeply spiritual path that can lead you from fear to courage, anger to joy, and helplessness to effectiveness—whatever challenges you may be facing. I have found it tremendously helpful."

—MARTIN L. ROSSMAN, M.D.,
author of *Guided Imagery for Self-Healing*

"Written in an easily understandable style, Emotions: Transforming Anger, Fear and Pain *offers a wealth of information.* Dr. Barrick provides excellent methods for freeing ourselves from some of our most destructive emotions—thus opening the door to improved health at all levels. This book is deserving of wide reading and rereading."

—RANVILLE S. CLARK, M.D.,
psychiatrist, Washington, D.C.

Praise for *Dreams: Exploring the Secrets of Your Soul*

"This unique book on dreams integrates the soul's development on the spiritual path with personal dream work.... It invites us to consider a greater potential of the self beyond life's ordinary conflicts and helps us open up to a greater understanding of the purpose of life."

—RALPH YANEY, M.D.,
psychiatrist/psychoanalyst and author of *10,001*

Praise for *Sacred Psychology of Change:*
Life as a Voyage of Transformation

"This book asks us to 'focus our attention on the higher intelligence of our heart' and then describes in loving detail ways of doing just that. Those interested in the heart's ability to heal will find encouragement in these pages."

—RUTH BLY,
licensed psychologist, Jungian analyst, author

"A profound treasure of spiritual truths and their practical application based on the author's many successful years of personal and professional experience. Written in the language of the heart and with remarkable clarity and sensitivity, this book will lead you, chapter by chapter and step by step, to a profoundly healing dialogue with yourself—and through an exciting spiritual and psychological journey of change."

—KENNETH FRAZIER, L.P.C., D.A.P.A., A.C.P.E.

Praise for *Sacred Psychology of Love:*
The Quest for Relationships That Unite Heart and Soul

"A wonderful marriage of the mystical and practical, this soul-nourishing book is beautiful, healing and thought-provoking."

—SUE PATTON THOELE,
author of *Heart Centered Marriage*

"In our search for the Beloved, whether inner or outer, we seek that mysterious blend of beauty and practicality which Dr. Marilyn Barrick masterfully conveys on every page. Synthesizing her knowledge of sacred text, her clinical expertise and her life's wisdom, she has written a book for anyone seeking to love or to be loved. With compassion and humor, she gives us an important tool for enriching relationships."

—ANNE DE VORE,
Jungian analyst

A SPIRITUAL APPROACH TO

PARENTING

Secrets of Raising the 21st Century Child

Other Books in the Sacred Psychology Series
by Marilyn C. Barrick, Ph.D.

Sacred Psychology of Love:
The Quest for Relationships That Unite Heart and Soul

Sacred Psychology of Change:
Life as a Voyage of Transformation

Dreams:
Exploring the Secrets of Your Soul

Emotions:
Transforming Anger, Fear and Pain

Soul Reflections:
Many Lives, Many Journeys

A SPIRITUAL APPROACH TO

PARENTING

Secrets of Raising the 21st Century Child

Marilyn C. Barrick, Ph.D.

SUMMIT UNIVERSITY PRESS

A SPIRITUAL APPROACH TO PARENTING:
Secrets of Raising the Twenty-First-Century Child
by Marilyn C. Barrick, Ph.D.
Copyright © 2004 by Marilyn C. Barrick and Summit University Press

All rights reserved

No part of this book may be reproduced, translated, or electronically stored, posted or transmitted, or used in any format or medium whatsoever without prior written permission, except by a reviewer who may quote brief passages in a review. For information, contact Summit University Press, PO Box 5000, Corwin Springs, MT 59030-5000. Tel: 1-800-245-5445 or 406-848-9500. www.summituniversitypress.com

Library of Congress Control Number: 2004103930
ISBN: 0-922729-96-4

SUMMIT UNIVERSITY ❧ PRESS®

The Summit Lighthouse is a trademark registered in the U.S. Patent and Trademark Office and in other countries. All rights reserved

08 07 06 05 04   5 4 3 2 1

I dedicate this book on the Aquarian family
to our families, children and youth,
who are the creators of the world of tomorrow.

May the family be a harbor of peace and harmony
and our children and youth richly blessed.
May life be bright with expectancy
and each one's talents marked for success.

May the soul be graced with courage
to overcome hazards on the road of life.
May each of us strive for excellence
and be victorious midst the strife.

When we meet the foe we call adversity,
may we overcome its ploy.
And when life is bright with promise,
let us celebrate our joy.

May the peace of God be with us,
and with God's love as sunlight's ray,
let us forge our daily victories,
as our guardian angels lead the way.

Contents

Acknowledgments

It is with a grateful heart that I acknowledge my family and friends who have provided the foundation for this book. And I bless the day that I met my spiritual teacher, Elizabeth Clare Prophet, who has guided my spiritual journey and introduced me to my inner teachers, the ascended masters.

I am forever grateful to my Lord and Savior Jesus Christ, who has helped me to "walk in his footsteps" throughout my childhood and youth and in the years beyond. And I offer my love and gratitude to Kuthumi, my spiritual mentor, who inspired me to write the spiritual psychology series. His inner guidance has been invaluable in bringing each of the books to fruition.

To my clients I owe a debt of gratitude for the inspiration and teaching I have received in the hours we have spent together. And some of you appear in this book, disguised in detail and appearance, of course. You have been key to furthering my understanding of family and children.

I am especially grateful to the special people who have helped me complete and publish this book: Dr. Joye Bennett, for her expertise in child psychology; Karen Gordon, my skillful and enduring editor; James Bennett, for the beautiful cover design; and Nigel Yorwerth, for his valuable sales and marketing input.

Preface

Long were you a dream in your mother's sleep,
and then she woke to give you birth.

–KAHLIL GIBRAN
Sand and Foam

As I contemplated writing this book on the Aquarian age family, I reflected on the extraordinary cultural shifts that have occurred since the turn of the century. We rang in the new age on New Year's Day 2000, and our lives changed dramatically less than two years later with the shocking events of September 11, 2001. It's been a time of fast-moving change ever since. And parents have concerns: How do we prepare our youth and children to feel secure and find their way in a crazy world? That's what the information and case examples in this book are all about.*

Fortunately, we also have good news! Amazing new souls are coming into embodiment and changing the complexion of family life. Even as families are running full speed ahead to keep up with cultural change, the Indigo, Crystal and "spirited" children are providing inspiration and inducing everyone to take lightning steps forward. Many of these children are advanced souls who know that they are here for a cosmic purpose.

---

*In the case examples in this book, names, places and details have been changed to protect the anonymity of the individuals whose stories are included.

They are coming in while we are at a spiritual crossroads in both planetary and personal life. We will either take a stand for higher values or stay stuck in the quagmire of political and economic turmoil, international conflict, terrorist attacks and the ever-present threat of nuclear war.

In the midst of worldwide unrest the Aquarian energy is prompting us to explore the facets of our Higher Self and to forge a higher destiny. And the family as the cradle of love and hope is where it all begins.

While we do not remember every detail of our growing-up years, every encounter has left its impression. Our character is molded by these formative experiences. Our opinions are developed within family norms and our habits installed in the family circle. Indeed, we are molded, for better or for worse, by who we are genetically and who we become as the result of early life experiences. Are these characteristics indelible? No, but they definitely influence us both consciously and subconsciously.

Life itself is the greatest teacher, and the lessons of life are typically a mix of ups and downs. Children are born with a sense of wonder and delight about exploring life. And the task of the family is to ready young people to meet life's challenges. Thus we are called to nurture, mentor and lend a helping hand as needed.

Some Teachers We Never Forget

When we reflect on our upbringing, we realize we had a few outstanding teachers who helped us take giant steps forward in our education and life skills. Do you remember a sterling teacher who touched your life in a profound way? What were the special qualities of that person? Why was he or she such a good teacher?

I realize that the teachers who helped me jump forward in my education were those who knew their subject backwards and forwards. They ignited my interest, related the subject to life experience, appreciated my talents, encouraged my efforts and rewarded my achievements. And they also shared a respect for young people, which helped to bring out the best in their students.

Actually these teachers were transformational mentors who helped us take a successful leap into the unknown. They were supportive, a sounding board for our ideas, and a source of help and encouragement when we were confused or downhearted. Their example and support helped us expand our minds and establish positive attitudes and skills for lifelong learning.

The most profound mentor I ever had is Elizabeth Clare Prophet, whose husband Mark L. Prophet founded The Summit Lighthouse, a worldwide organization that draws on the teachings of the world's great spiritual traditions. She has been an inspiration to me, and her wisdom is the foundation of much of the spiritual teaching in this book on family and children.

I remember the first time I met her, in 1973. It was at La Tourelle, a stately mansion in Colorado Springs, Colorado, where she and her husband had established The Summit Lighthouse headquarters.

I had driven down from my home in Boulder, Colorado, to pursue what was to become a life-changing journey. I looked up as I drove through the gates and saw a woman standing at a floor-length window on the second floor. What caught my attention was the glow of white light that surrounded her. In my heart I knew this was a magnificent woman I needed to get to know.

As I parked the car I reflected on my initial acquaintance with the teachings of The Summit Lighthouse. I felt the excitement all over again and laughed to myself as I remembered what had happened. I had been busy raising my three teenage children, keeping up with my private practice, and working at the University of Colorado as a clinical psychologist—counseling students and teaching graduate-level psychology courses. I was seeking enlightenment in my own way, but I wasn't chasing around looking for a spiritual teacher as a lot of the students were doing.

My friend Vickie and I had gone out to dinner at a little Mexican restaurant we both enjoyed. She began telling me about her experience at a spiritual conference that Elizabeth Clare Prophet had just conducted close to Colorado Springs. She had scarcely said a few dozen words when I lit up inside. I began to feel exhilarating energy pouring through me. And I started asking questions a mile a minute.

I don't remember the exact details of our conversation, but I knew I had to meet Mrs. Prophet and learn more about these teachings from the ascended masters, whoever they turned out to be. It was an instantaneous recognition of my next step on the spiritual path and a fitting prologue for the next thirty years of my life.

As I walked toward the front door of La Tourelle and looked up at the window again, the woman was no longer there. An attractive young woman, Marla, welcomed me at the front door. I was impressed with her graciousness and the beauty and vibration in this lovely place.

After an uplifting presentation, during which I have to admit I was enjoying the vibes more than taking in specific information, Mrs. Prophet greeted me with a big smile. And I had a humorous experience with my spiritual teacher-to-be.

She walked over to a table on which sat a huge pile of posters and proceeded to offer a large stack to me. "I would be so pleased if you would put these posters up for me in Boulder," she suggested cheerfully. I was a bit surprised but found myself saying, "Of course, I'll be happy to." And that was the beginning of my relationship with Elizabeth Clare Prophet.

Yes, indeed, I put up the posters around Boulder and attended the event they were advertising. In those days posters were everywhere in Boulder because in addition to business announcements and university happenings, many young people were seeking enlightenment. And posters were the way most of us found out about interesting events.

Over the years since then I have occasionally remembered our first encounter and chuckled over it. Elizabeth Clare Prophet became my mentor on the quest for enlightenment and we have been friends and colleagues for many years. She has been a guiding spiritual light and I have had the privilege of sharing my expertise in psychology with her.

Mark and Elizabeth raised children of their own, and Elizabeth has always had a special interest in family and children. She has loved spending time with young people, answering their questions and supporting their projects. She has been a mentor to many who are moving on successfully in their adult lives.

Each of us can strive to become a mentor to the next generation. To do so we need to accent our spiritual strengths, continue a process of self-transformation, and focus on thinking out of the box. We can thereby make a worthy contribution to society and offer a legacy of love to our children and youth.

Mrs. Prophet introduced me to the ascended masters,

whom I came to know as advanced souls who lived on Earth, achieved enlightenment and made it home to the heaven-world. Her esoteric perspective combined nicely with my transpersonal psychology approach, which has been vastly enriched since I walked through the door of La Tourelle so many years ago. She has been a loving champion of my soul.

Kahlil Gibran "On Children"

Many people love the writings of Kahlil Gibran. In his stirring poem "On Children," the understanding of the role of parent strikes a chord in our hearts. Gibran's profound message can be our inspiration as we guide young people to fulfill their higher destiny.

> You are the bows from which your
> children as living arrows are sent forth.
> The archer sees the mark upon the path
> of the infinite, and He bends you with His
> might that His arrows may go swift and far.
> Let your bending in the archer's hand
> be for gladness;
> For even as He loves the arrow that flies,
> So He loves also the bow that is stable.[1]

Introduction

The more intensively the family has stamped its character upon the child, the more it will tend to feel and see its earlier miniature world again in the bigger world of adult life.

—CARL GUSTAV JUNG
The Theory of Psychoanalysis

In early twentieth-century America a child was nurtured in the protective and comforting cocoon of family and community during his growing-up years. Perhaps he lived in a little village in central New York, went to school there, played with the neighborhood kids and knew his parents' friends. He was friends with the grocer, the doctor, the paperboy and all the people who made up the community.

If he got an A on a test, the extended family rejoiced. If he skinned his knee in a scuffle, someone he knew quickly took care of it. On the weekend he and his family went to the movie on the corner of Main Street. As they took their seats they said hello to people sitting around them. People chatted about their kids, the weather and breaking news such as Charles Lindbergh's and Amelia Earhart's flights over the Atlantic.

To a large extent the innocence of the soul was protected in the bosom of family, church and community. Children played in the security of a neighborhood they knew and families who knew them. When they came home from school, mom was there and they likely had chores to do. Dad came home a little later and the family had dinner together. On Sunday most families went to church to worship and have fellowship with one another.

Of course there was usually a neighborhood bad boy, but he was the exception, not the rule. Families lived by the values of their parents and grandparents, and these were days of love of God, family and country. To most children and youth the future was full of hope and promise.

Little boys dreamed of becoming inventors like Thomas Edison, ballplayers like Babe Ruth, aviators like Charles Lindbergh or explorers like Lewis and Clark. Little girls dreamed of being a teacher like Laura Ingalls Wilder (author of *Little House on the Prairie*), a social reformer like Carry Nation, a battlefield nurse like Clara Barton, or marrying their true love and living happily ever after.

Family Life: Yesterday and Today

In the United States and all over the world, family life has changed radically from the way it was when many of us grew up. Modern technology has advanced to the point where we are instantaneously aware of world events courtesy of the news networks. And these events are often unsettling, particularly to families.

Many of the changes have been exciting, mind expanding and culturally broadening. Yet we retain fond memories of our childhood in a time and place that was less complex and closer to nature. We were raised in an environment that was considerably safer and fostered our imagination.

In the 1930s and 1940s families relied on the radio for news and drama, which was great for imagining. I remember how I would see the action in my mind's eye as I listened to the Lone Ranger galloping along on his horse shouting "Hi-Yo, Silver!" with faithful Tonto at his side. I didn't wonder about the reality of what I was envisioning, and my creativity blossomed.

After school, children played alone or together with neighbors, and when it got dark they disappeared into their own houses. In the summer we kids would sleep on the roof of our hacienda-style house, and my father would point out the constellations. I remember wishing I could touch the stars that were so clear and bright in the Arizona sky.

Children in the country took a bus that slowly made its way to school or they walked or rode their bikes those several miles. I usually had my nose in a book if I rode the bus—and sometimes even when I was walking. Absorbing information from books was exciting to me and most of us learned about people in other parts of the world through literature. We daydreamed and sometimes playacted the characters and scenes in the books. And, as you might guess, all of this was foundational to my work as a writer today.

My father and mother loved books and passed that quality on to me. I remember when I was five my mother thought I had learned to read even though I hadn't yet gone to school. She was very excited about it. Then one day she found me reading out loud with the book upside down. Oops! I had memorized the book from listening to my dad read the stories out loud. After that, Mother taught me how to sound out and read the words from the book. That was much more satisfactory to all concerned, and a whole world opened up—the world of literature.

Play was very important when we were growing up, and naps became the bane of our childhood existence. I have a clear memory from kindergarten of lying on my mat for nap time, willing it to be over so we could play. I'd shut my eyes when the teacher came around, but I don't remember ever napping.

I have an amusing memory of my mother trying to get my sister and me to take a nap at home. As usual we were playing instead of napping, but when we heard Mother coming we pretended to be asleep. She figured it out and tickled our feet with a feather. Of course we giggled and then she reminded us we needed to take a nap. And I wondered, why?

Everyone in my generation remembers the "ice man" who would drive up in his wagon and put a large chunk of ice in the icebox, the refrigerator of the day. And the farmer would come by with fresh vegetables—they tasted really good, especially the corn on the cob. And best of all, the ice-cream man would make his way through the neighborhood with children excitedly chasing after him once they had talked their parents into a nickel for ice cream.

I remember pictures of my dad's shiny black Model T from the '20s, which would be left in a cloud of dust on the roads today. I was reminded of it recently when I found a picture of Henry Ford driving his Model T with Thomas Edison in the passenger seat.[1] My dad kept up with the times and regularly traded in his car for whatever new model was popular. From the point of view of us kids, the biggest adventure with the car was driving into Phoenix to see the bright lights of the city. And those lights seemed magical!

Do you remember how Ringling Brothers' circus used to come to town? I remember watching the long train of railroad cars and being amazed at how the elephants and their trainers unloaded everything. The circus was an adventure for children and parents alike, especially watching the trapeze artists, who leapt from trapeze to trapeze high up in the tent above us as we sat mesmerized.

I used to like going for walks with Uncle Henry, who wasn't really an uncle but the man who did our yard work, and feeding apples to horses in neighboring fields. And I remember riding with my friend on her pony out into the desert and riding my bike for miles and miles along the canals and orange groves. I can remember the sun glinting off the water and the fragrance of the orange blossoms. When I think about the life we lived, it was much simpler than life is today. And there was plenty of time for daydreaming and imagination.

Yet we had our early twentieth-century traumas. I remember my dad talking about the Great Depression and how banks and businesses failed and people were out of work. It was horrifying to learn that some people got so scared they jumped off buildings and killed themselves. I wondered what happened to their families.

I remember when Pearl Harbor was bombed in 1941. Everyone stayed glued to the radio for news. We kids collected newspapers for the paper drive and practiced ducking under our desks in case a bomb dropped. It was a time of national mobilization and family tension. All of us were excited as we joined in the victory celebrations when the war was over. We thought that would be the last war ever.

But that was short-lived. There was Korea, Vietnam and the Gulf War. And since the turn of the century we have had the terrorist attacks of September 11, the wars in Afghanistan and Iraq, the railroad bombing in Spain and suicide bombers in Israel, Turkey, Saudi Arabia, Russia, Indonesia and other countries. Today's youth and children see war and terrorism as a part of life, and that breeds an underlying sense of fear and uncertainty.

Creating Security in an Insecure World

Families today experience a certain sense of insecurity, and not just because of what is happening on the other side of the world. Many neighborhoods are not necessarily safe places for children to play and explore. Schools are not so safe either. High school staffers are using metal detectors to screen for kids carrying guns or knives. And children can be exposed to violence on the playground or to gangs waiting around the corner.

Many parents drive their kids to and from school or escort them to the school bus for safety reasons. They set up after-school activities to limit neighborhood problems or their children roaming the streets. A number of parents limit their kids to TV channels that are wholesome for children, such as Disney, Travel, History or National Geographic, particularly when the parents aren't home.

We all realize it isn't practical to cushion young people to the point where they are not prepared to deal with what is happening in the world. Family and school discussions can help young people put into perspective what they see on TV and the Web or read about in newspapers and magazines. Whether it's war, crime, abduction, drugs, alcohol or date rape, we have a responsibility to teach our youth about the down side of life so they are not taken in by it.

We can also focus our attention on the up side of life. We can teach our children to choose friends and activities that are healthy and upbeat. And the family can make it a point to watch inspiring or amusing movies that remind us that good things happen too.

Families ask me questions such as: "How can we preserve our children's faith and values in a world where moral imperatives are often replaced with expediency? How do we keep ourselves informed without our children being shocked by horrific happenings? How can we help children and youth feel secure in the middle of an insecure world?"

These are meaningful questions to which there are positive answers. Children follow the example of people they respect, particularly mom and dad. They notice what we do and how we do it; they model themselves after us. This is how they learn to be a good friend or neighbor. When we visit a friend who is sick, help a neighbor with shopping, take our turn in the car pool, sponsor a worthy cause, umpire a kids' softball game, we feel good about ourselves. And our children and youth notice and learn.

Young people are growing up quickly in terms of access to information that in the past was reserved for adults, and they need to learn how to assimilate and find a constructive purpose for what they learn. Otherwise, they can feel overwhelmed by shocking events and complicated information. And that's where parents and teachers can give a helping hand.

Throughout this book we will examine family issues, psychologically and spiritually, including the impact of the information explosion and how parents and teachers can help young people be true to higher aspirations in the face of changing cultural norms.

Life in the Global Village

Children and youth today live in a global village. They are aware of major events as they happen everywhere in the world. Many young people live in urban neighborhoods and come home from school ahead of working parents. They have instructions to get started on homework but are tempted to turn on the TV instead.

When the news comes on they see a confusing and often scary side of life, with commentators analyzing the dramas: international unrest, scenes of war or terrorist strikes, criminal trials, families who have lost loved ones, corporate corruption, serious accidents or international health scares. And sometimes, as with the World Trade Center disaster, they see disturbing images over and over again. When they turn to sports or educational channels, they get a more upbeat perspective on the world. And that is a welcome relief to the soul.

Parents can mitigate problematic TV, magazine or newspaper images by reminding children that these events are happening in another city or country and that doctors and nurses are there to help people who get hurt. Parents can ask their children if they have questions and answer those questions simply and reassuringly. When the family discusses whatever they are concerned about, young people feel reassured and supported.

We can help younger children understand that when bad things happen they aren't happening to everybody all the time. We can explain that images on the TV screen are often blown out of proportion. Although it looks like terrible events are happening over and over again, many times it's one event being shown and analyzed over and over again by different newscasters.

We can answer the questions they have, discuss potential solutions, and reassure young people that the world is not falling apart. It just seems that way from the constant media bombardment. Although the world is in a state of chaos, out of chaos comes order. And order can herald a rebirth of civility.

Another essential task for parents today is to help young people pinpoint what they need to learn out of the ever-growing stacks of information. Not only is there a wealth of knowledge but also multiple avenues of discovery: traditional schooling, home-schooling, schoolbooks, libraries, encyclopedias, and worldwide communication via travel, cell phones, the Web, chat rooms and e-mail.

In fact, there are so many ways to expand knowledge that the learning process itself can be overwhelming. Then it's time to take a quick breather: go for a walk, a run with the dog or whatever is the young person's favorite physical activity.

As young people explore, discover and become knowledgeable about the world's cultures and literature, historical events, scientific advances and modern technology, they ready themselves to make their contribution to the world. And as they interact electronically with young people from different countries, the world becomes their neighborhood.

Generations on the Move

Today's young adults and youth, known respectively as Generations X and Y,* are involved in diverse creative projects, scientific pursuits and humanitarian endeavors. And what they all share is an excitement about exploring the universe. Is there anyone who isn't fascinated by space exploration or pictures of an eclipse of the moon? Youth are typically glued to the screen watching space shuttle takeoffs. Many of them imagine themselves in space, and some will actually go through the rigors of becoming astronauts.

These young people's goals and vision of the future have been shaped by recent cultural, scientific and technological changes. Consider the world as they see it:

---

*Generation X refers to those born between approximately 1961 and 1982. Generation Y, the Millennial generation, are those born from approximately 1982 to the present time.

- A woman has always served on the U.S. Supreme Court.

- Computer games have always been a leisure activity.

- ATMs have always been a money source.

- Home movies don't require slide projectors and screens.

- Post-it Notes and Velcro are staples of life.

- Millennials look at the '60s historically—not nostalgically.

- Tattoos aren't gender based and there's more to pierce than your ear.

- Remote controls make it unlikely that they'll ever manually change a TV channel.[2]

Exchange students, sports enthusiasts, business people, tourists and families make regular treks to other countries. And many young people travel via television, movies and the Web. The world neighborhood seems somehow closer and more familiar. And the benefits of worldwide personal and cultural exchange are evident in the lives of young people today.

In my own family my son, his wife and children have had the opportunity to travel all over the world because of my son's business and his wife's church choir tours. The fruits of travel have been rich, including a deep friendship with a man in Poland and extensive first-hand knowledge of European culture.

Their daughter, fascinated by Japanese culture, qualified for a graduate-school program of technical communication in Japanese and a six-month internship in Japan. And their son, who experimented with his own business for a time, is now pursuing a college degree to top off his computer and business skills. Their choices illustrate a breadth of interest and pursuit of knowledge that is typical of today's young adults, whether we identify them as X or Y.

Education through travel and life experience is not restricted to the youth of America. Many European young people, known as Generation E (for Europe), are multilingual and travel extensively. They are just as apt to take a quick trip from Sweden to Spain as New England students are to take a spring break in Florida. Young people everywhere are crossing borders to study and work, multiply their language skills and chip away at national stereotypes.

What does the future hold for these leaders of tomorrow? Will they create peace on Earth and goodwill toward men? I believe that much depends on the family because the family is the cradle of civilization.

Although today we live in a world of unrest, I see the future as bright with promise. Our youth and children are on the move. They view life as a challenge and the future as an unfolding drama in which they plan to play a major role. We as parents and mentors are learning how to champion their journey with love, support and guidance. And that is what this book is all about.

PART ONE

The Aquarian Family

1

Indigo, Crystal and Spirited Children

A little child shall lead them.

—ISAIAH 11:6

We are living in what is known astrologically as the Aquarian age, an age when souls with special gifts are being born to help the evolutions of Earth fulfill their divine destiny. These souls are advanced in wisdom and compassion and have high energy. I believe they are here to help us calibrate our consciousness so that we function in a more attuned way and recognize our inner oneness with God.

Although many of these souls are highly evolved spiritually, they need loving adults to help them develop their gifts and talents. Parents, families and teachers are meant to guide and support these children so that they will fulfill their mission.

Intuition and Wisdom: The Indigo Children

Have you heard about the "Indigo Children"? They are souls of light, children whose special nature is signified by the deep violet-blue in their aura.[1] The Indigos started arriving in droves in the 1980s and range anywhere from seven to twenty-five years of age today. They are intuitive, active and wise beyond their years.

I believe the Indigos are the precursors of the seventh root race, which spiritual teachers believe is to begin embodying during the age of Aquarius. The Indigos themselves, by their own understanding, are ancient souls who have embodied again to prepare the way for a spiritually enlightened age.

These children may talk about having lived before—or even on a different planet. They are inherently spiritual and humanitarian. They know they are here for a spiritual purpose and can get very frustrated with people unconcerned about fulfilling that purpose. The Indigos are described as having been "born knowing." When they are treated with respect, they flourish. When they are laughed at, ridiculed or disrespected, they withdraw or burst out in anger.

They can be likened to an emotional rollercoaster, going from elated to crestfallen in seconds, many times a day. Because of this they are often seen as difficult by normal standards and are sometimes ostracized by their peers.

Lee Carroll and Jan Tober, in their book *The Indigo Children: The New Kids Have Arrived*, describe ten of the most common behavioral traits of these wonderful, creative, and at times exasperating children:

1. They come into the world with a feeling of royalty (and often act like it).

2. They have a feeling of "deserving to be here," and are surprised when others don't share that.

3. Self-worth is not a big issue. They often tell the parents "who they are."

4. They have difficulty with absolute authority (authority without explanation or choice).

5. They simply will not do certain things; for example, waiting in line is difficult for them.

6. They get frustrated with systems that are ritual-oriented and don't require creative thought.

7. They often see better ways of doing things, both at home and in school, which makes them seem like "system busters" (nonconforming to any system).

8. They seem antisocial unless they are with their own kind. If there are no others of like consciousness around them, they often turn inward, feeling like no other human understands them. School is often extremely difficult for them socially.

9. They will not respond to "guilt" discipline ("Wait till your father gets home and finds out what you did").

10. They are not shy in letting you know what they need.[2]

We can see that parents and teachers of Indigo Children have a challenge on their hands. And yet, these children are likely to be the next generation's explorers, inventors and entrepreneurs. They are strong willed but not from an ego stance. Rather, they seem to have an inner North Star to which they attune and set their course in life. They challenge adults from their own awareness of truth. And the amazing fact is they are often right in a most profound way.

These children need to be guided rather than controlled. In fact, trying to control an Indigo child is fruitless in more ways than one. The parent loses patience, the child is discouraged and the moment of truth is lost. On the other hand, when these children are recognized, encouraged and championed for their unique gifts, they can be as bright lights in the family.

Many times the Indigo child relates better to the grandparents than to the parents. In part that is because the grandparents aren't usually involved in the day-to-day interaction and discipline that is necessary in raising any child. The Indigo child also seems to respect the wisdom of the grandparents because that wisdom matches the child's own inner knowing.

When Indigo Children are accepted, loved and guided with a respect for the truths they understand, they become more amenable to discipline. Much of the acting-out of the Indigo child seems to be caused by the frustration of being misunderstood.

When parents respect the child and focus on trying to understand what the child is attempting to express, family life is smoother. These children seem to be born with an acute awareness of subtle energy fields and a hypersensitivity to other people's emotions. They respond intuitively and relate better to adults who treat them as adults. I believe these children to be advanced souls in little bodies.

The Montessori environment, which allows a child to advance at his own speed, is a good place to begin the education of these children. Art and music, both of which speak the language of the soul, are beneficial in the learning process. Perhaps the most important guideline in teaching an Indigo child is to recognize the soul's higher purpose.

Many believe these children are here to take us to another level in our evolution. And those who are raising and guiding them need to have the emotional balance and sense

of self-esteem to give these children the support and understanding they need.

I believe that honoring the soul of the Indigo and the
child's memories of past lives* is a necessary part of educating these children. Some of the Indigos are quite open about
their remembrances of other lifetimes. And they may have a
better grasp of spirituality than their parents and teachers.
Yet their high energy, unless it is channeled appropriately, is
a challenge for the child as well as for parents and teachers.
The trick is how to direct the energy without dampening the
child's spirit.

While many of the Indigo Children seem to be comfortable following their own star, they can become bewildered
and depressed when they do not fit in with their peers. They
are taken aback when their parents do not understand their
past-life recollections. For these children this is simply who
they are. Here is a brief glyph from one wise mother of an
Indigo child:

> Another time, my son told me that he didn't feel his
> name should be Jesse, that in his last lifetime it had been
> Thomas! This led me to start reading about reincarna-
> tion. Many of the things Jesse shared with me have
> changed the way I look at life and at God....
>
> From an early age, Jesse could quite often read our
> thoughts. I feel that he has wisdom way beyond his
> years—at age five and six, he was trying to solve world-
> wide problems such as starvation and housing for
> homeless people. It got to the point where we took him
> to a child therapist because he was so serious and [we]

---

*Our past-life memories are stored in the etheric body, one of the four
energy sheaths of consciousness (physical, emotional, mental and etheric)
that surround the soul.

felt he needed to have more childlike fun. Often he said things like, "Mom, it's okay if we don't have money because we have all the gold in the sun, and that's all we need."[3]

Parenting the Indigo Child

The Indigo Children seem different from previous generations and require careful parenting. They are intuitively aware, emotionally sensitive and intolerant of dishonesty or deceitful behavior.

Many believe that these souls are incarnating at this time to prepare the way for society to advance in spiritual values, integrity and compassion. Most parents of Indigos would agree that their livewire little ones push them to the maximum. They find it absolutely necessary to synchronize with their own higher values in order to relate to their children lovingly and honestly.

These children need to be prepared for their spiritual mission during their formative years. And to do so, parents and teachers are called to guide them by always telling them the truth. We can pray for guidance and speak the truth in a loving way. We can share our feelings with them at the same time that we refrain from shouting or accusing. When we are positive role models to the Indigos, we help them handle their fiery emotions.

To their detriment, some of these gifted children have been diagnosed as ADD (attention deficit disorder) or ADHD (attention deficit, hyperactivity disorder).[4] Doctors may prescribe Ritalin or other medications helpful to ADD or ADHD children but frustrating to the Indigo child. To be medicated to damp down who you really are is not a positive message.

Parents of Indigos soon discover that when they get upset with their children's behavior, they do best to remove themselves from the situation and take a breather to regain their poise. They learn to take calming deep breaths and pray for spiritual intervention from the angels or the ascended masters. Of course, if the child has been indulging in a full-blown tantrum, tearing things up or throwing things around, the parents need to immediately give the child a time-out, and then go about composing themselves.

Some parents envision themselves turning the entire situation over to God. They visualize giving their emotional upset to the angels or their Higher Self for guidance and resolution. Once they feel peaceful, they consider solutions to the problem.

We need to remember that we agreed to bring in these special souls. We met with our spiritual overseers, known as the Lords of Karma, before embodying, and we inwardly understand exactly why we chose to be on Earth during the millennial shift. If we have an Indigo child, we chose to parent that soul. And when we experience our afterlife review in the heaven-world, we will consider the times we were loving and compassionate to our children to be among our greatest victories.

The Entrance of the Crystal Children

Another lifewave of advanced souls coming into embodiment are known as the "Crystal Children." These children, first identified by author Doreen Virtue,[5] are souls of light, often called lightbearers, whose auras radiate an iridescent, multicolored, pastel hue. They are being identified from infancy up to approximately the age of seven, so they have come into embodiment very recently. This is another new generation, and they live up to their name—they are intrigued by crystals and other stones.

These children seem even more advanced than the Indigos and are of a different temperament. The Crystal Children are upbeat, compassionate and forgiving. Idealistic in many ways, they personify the virtues of the Higher Self and point the way for the evolutions of Earth to accelerate spiritually.

Both the Indigo and Crystal Children have qualities that are similar. They both are intuitive, highly sensitive, and have important missions to fulfill. The main difference is their inner nature. I believe Indigos have a "warrior spirit," as Doreen Virtue describes it, because they are here to clear the decks of whatever no longer benefits us. They are here to flag systems in government and society that fail to uphold decency, integrity and honesty. And to do this they need a fiery spirit.

In comparison, the Crystal Children tend to be happy and unruffled. Of course their tempers may flare up from time to time as happens with most children, but as a rule they are compassionate and understanding. The Crystals are the next generation following the Indigos' system busting. Their mission seems to be to raise the consciousness of the earth to a higher vibration. Parents of Crystal Children say their children teach them how to be loving and kind.

Curiously enough, many of these children do not verbalize until age three or four, and therefore their spiritual gifts may be misunderstood. Parents of Crystal Children confirm that they communicate mind to mind, telepathically, with their little ones. The children also use sign language to communicate. The problem is that educational and medical authorities may consider them abnormal or even autistic. It's likely no accident that since the Crystals began coming in, there has been a noticeable increase in the diagnosis of autism,[6] the most severe psychological disorder affecting children.

Yet those who understand Crystal Children and have telepathic capability have no difficulty communicating with them. I do not believe that these children are autistic. The diagnosis of autism includes the criterion of little or no language, either receptive or expressive. The autistic child may be mute, or if speech is present, it is an echo of other people's voices or what he hears on television. In addition, the child behaves as if blind and deaf even though sensory modalities are intact. And autistic children usually do not develop close loving relationships with their parents. In fact, they frequently throw tantrums and exhibit aggressive behavior.

The Crystal Children are quite the reverse. They are loving, concerned, sharing children who are also advanced spiritually. Once they begin talking, they communicate both verbally and telepathically, and they express love, kindness and sensitivity to their families and siblings. Totally unlike an autistic child, a Crystal child will freely embrace others.

In the world of the Crystal Children we will become more aware of our intuitive thoughts and feelings. We will be more compassionate and forgiving toward one another. And our communication will be faster, more direct, and more honest because it will be conducted mentally.

How Did We Forget Who We Are?

In her lovely book *Spiritual Alchemy: How to Transform Your Life*, Dr. Christine Page helps us think about who we really are, which is undoubtedly a part of the mission of the souls of the incoming Crystal Children:

There is a joke that says God created man because she got bored! Well, I certainly imagine we offer ample opportunity for divine and angelic amusement. But seriously, with the development of individual souls for the purpose of self-realization, there has been the tendency to fall asleep to our deeper essence entranced by the physical world we have created and all it has to offer. However, the memory of the Source and the desire to reconnect are inbuilt and hence each lifetime our higher self, the part that maintains the connection, gently nudges us towards unification. . . .

Prior to each incarnation, we are given the opportunity to decide where to direct our attention this time and to make agreements with others to turn up at specific times for particular events and develop a sacred contract. Then, in order to enter this denser environment, our spirit body has to reduce its vibration to match the energy of the three-D world causing varying degrees of *spiritual amnesia* and leading us to ponder:

"Now, why did I come here?"
As the little boy said when he was allowed to be alone
with his newborn sister: "Quick, tell me what it's like
in heaven because I'm beginning to forget."

Today's children are thankfully far less prone to amnesia than their forebears, coming in on a higher vibration and hence retaining their universal connection. Indeed they find it very strange that many adults have forgotten their way, living incongruent lives where heart and head are not communicating with each other. These souls are here to remind us of our planetary purpose and to help us break free of the shackles of our lower mind and truly become multidimensional beings.

They instinctively know that it's through the fulfillment of their purpose they will come to know themselves and generate wisdom, *knowledge in action*. They also know that it's not possible, or indeed useful, to compare the value of one person's life with another as each is unique unto itself and hence to be celebrated. These children wonder at the logic of attempting to evaluate soul growth through the parameters of occupation, wealth, education or wellbeing for they know that none of this matters to our spiritualized self.

For example, a man lying in the gutter staring at the stars may be experiencing his last incarnation with only this one task to complete while those who *tut-tut* as they step over him in their dash to get to work may still have many petals to unfold.*

> *It is not who we are or what we do that matters,*
> *but how we live our life.*

When standing in front of a full-length mirror reflecting on how age, gravity and habits of a lifetime have left their impression on your sagging physical form, it's hard to remember that somewhere inside is a being of light!

However, the primary essence of your soul is pure white light containing all the colors of the rainbow, each vibrating at its own frequency and collectively radiating at the vibration of white light. This vibrating energy source, also known as consciousness, is a synthesis of the wisdom gained from previous lives, the energetic union with other sentient beings, the vibratory blueprint of lives still to be experienced and the eternal connection to

---

*This story reminds me of tales of saints in India who were at a high level of spiritual development and would slip into *samadhi* from time to time. This appeared strange even to some of their devotees, when it was in fact the bliss of nirvana that so many on the spiritual path are seeking.

universal consciousness. When the soul's consciousness is fully expressed, pure white light is seen, an event termed *enlightenment*.

Light is consciousness and consciousness is light.

As our soul enters this incarnation it passes through the "personality cloak" which it has chosen for life with the latter acting as a prism, splitting the white light into its various colors known as the aura, each color representing a different aspect of the soul.

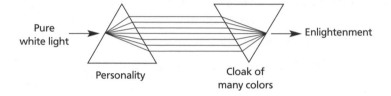

The goal or purpose of our life is to fully explore each feature using the personality provided as the vehicle of expression until a pure, coherent color radiates. When this occurs within all the facets of our being, the completed "cloak of many colors" acts as the second prism recreating the pure white light in the process of enlightenment.

Another way of expressing this is:

Out of the One comes the many expressing the diverse faces of the One and when they are fully expressed they naturally reunite, recreating the One.

You may now start to understand what is meant by the words *we are created in the image of the Divine*, for the journey we take from totality to diversity through experience back to totality is the story of the Creation. However, as with all good esoteric truths, even though day follows night and inspiration follows expiration, in reality there is in fact nowhere to go for despite our numerous excursions we have always been one with the Source![7]

Misdiagnosis of Indigo and Crystal Children

Dr. Page also writes about the risk of misdiagnosis of Indigo and Crystal Children and the deeper lessons to be learned:

> At present there is an alarming increase in the number of children with Autism and ADHD (attention deficit, hyperactivity disorder). Although each of these illnesses exhibits different pathology, there is a common theme that suggests that these children relate strongly to this third function of awareness, i.e., they are able to see in pictures, merge easily with their environment, and often express telepathic tendencies. Most of these children find linear thinking and learning difficult, causing them to feel ungrounded and challenged to fit into social norms. And yet, I sense we are being offered an opportunity to expand our consciousness through these souls who are asking us to meet them in their telepathic, whole-brain thinking rather than insisting on breaking everything down into a language that makes no sense to collective thinkers.
>
> There is also an increase in mental illness reflecting, I believe, more than merely a chemical dysfunction but a change in the functional capacity of neural pathways to accommodate greater interconnectedness and moving us steadily towards our inherent multidimensional existence. Rather than seeing this shift as a problem to be fixed we need to appreciate the magnitude of the change it heralds. We can accelerate its integration by paying

greater attention to the value of the arts which enhance creative inspiration and by increasing tolerance for those who live by a different creed.

It is also important to resolve rhythm in our lives similar to the rhythm of the heart finding time to rest, play and work in tune with a deep inner impulse.

At the same time, the future asks that we should re-establish a healthy co-operation with the planet and, with respect and honor, touch her gently with our hands, feet and humble hearts. It is only when we root ourselves within this world will we be able to withstand the winds of change, for the willingness to go into the depths of our being is directly proportional to the heights we can attain.[8]

Raising a Spirited Child

The Indigo and Crystal Children are not the only children who have been identified as different, who do not match our conventional perspective. Mary Sheedy Kurcinka, in her book *Raising Your Spirited Child: A Guide for Parents Whose Child Is More Intense, Sensitive, Perceptive, Persistent, Energetic*, offers an understanding of other children who do not fit the norms.

Kurcinka gives us an introduction to the "spirited child" and to the challenges to the parents raising these special souls. I believe that in some respects these children have similar characteristics to the Indigo Children we discussed. As Kurcinka's book came out in 1991, well before the first book about the Indigos, she may very well have been describing the early Indigo Children.

Kurcinka tells us:

The word that distinguishes spirited children from other children is *more*. They are normal children who are *more* intense, persistent, sensitive, perceptive, and uncomfortable with change than other children. All children possess these characteristics, but spirited kids possess them with a depth and range not available to other children. Spirited kids are the Super Ball in a room full of rubber balls. Other kids bounce three feet off the ground. Every bounce for a spirited child hits the ceiling.

It is difficult to describe what it is like to be the parent of a spirited child. The answer keeps changing: it depends on the day, even the moment. How does one describe the experience of sliding from joy to exasperation in seconds, ten times a day. How does one explain the "sense" at eight in the morning that this will be a good day or a dreadful one. . . .

Profound statements roll from his mouth, much too mature and intellectual for a child of his age. He remembers experiences you've long since forgotten and drags you to the window to watch the raindrops, falling like diamonds from the sky. On the good days being the parent of a spirited child is astounding, dumbfounding, wonderful, funny, interesting, and interspersed with moments of brilliance.

The dreadful days are another story. On those days you're not sure you can face another twenty-four hours with him. It's hard to feel good as a parent when you can't even get his socks on, when every word you've said to him has been a reprimand, when the innocent act of serving tuna casserole instead of the expected tacos incites a riot, when you realize you've left more public places in a huff with your child in five years than most parents do in a lifetime.[9]

Kurcinka goes on to say that we probably haven't heard of spirited children before and that's because she coined the term. As she says,

> In 1979 when my son, Joshua, was born there weren't any spirited child classes or books. In fact the only information I could find that described a kid like him used words such as *difficult, strong willed, stubborn, mother killer,* or *Dennis the Menace.* It was the "good" days that made me search for a better word to describe him. On those days I realized that this kid who could drive me crazy possessed personality traits that were actually strengths when they were understood and well guided.
>
> My Webster's dictionary defines *spirited* as: lively, creative, keen, eager, full of energy and courage, and having a strong, assertive personality. *Spirited*—it feels good, sounds good, communicates the exciting potential of these kids, yet honestly captures the challenge faced by their parents. When we choose to see our children as spirited, we give them and ourselves hope. It pulls our focus to their strengths rather than their weaknesses, not as another label but as a tool for understanding.[10]

As Kurcinka points out, all children and adults have a certain temperament. We are born with it; it's our instinctive manner of acting and reacting to people and events—our inherent way of responding to the world around us. Our temperament includes our energy levels, how quickly we adjust to new situations, the intensity of our emotional reactions and the sensitivity of all of our faculties—sight, sound, smell, taste, kinesthetic awareness.

Thus the spirited child, who is temperamentally active, not only likes to move but *needs* to move. When we tell such a child to sit still for long periods and punish him when he doesn't, the child becomes emotionally and physically stressed. His active temperament is a strong inner urge that is very real. When a parent or teacher doesn't understand this and insists upon quiet sitting, a tantrum can be the natural result of the pent-up energy.

Spirited children have an emotional intensity, persistence in activities or ideas they choose, supersensitivity to stimuli, a tendency to be distracted, and difficulty handling change. Thus the road of life is challenging for them, and for their parents.

A Credo for Parents of Spirited Children

Kurcinka has written a credo for parents of spirited children:

1. *You are not alone.* According to the personality research, 10 to 15 percent of all children living in this country fit the description of the spirited child. That means that there are millions of parents who empathize with you and understand the challenges you face. Your child is not an oddity or a freak. You are not the world's worst parent. You are not the only one. You are among friends.

2. *You did not make your child spirited.* You are but one of many influences in your child's life. Other parent(s), relatives, siblings, teachers, neighbors, friends, life experiences, and the world at large all play a part. You make a big difference, but not the only difference.

3. *You are not powerless.* There is information in this book to help you understand your spirited child. You can read it and use it. You can strengthen skills you already have and learn new ones. You can reduce the hassles and live peacefully with your spirited

child—most days. Progress not perfection is your goal.

4. *You have permission to take care of yourself.* Your own need for sleep, quiet, uninterrupted adult conversation, lovemaking, a leisurely bath, a walk around the block, and time to complete your own projects is real and legitimate. It is not a sign of failure to ask a friend for help, to hire a sitter, or to allow relatives the opportunity to build a relationship with your child while you take a break. When you fulfill your needs you generate the energy to meet your child's needs.

5. *You may celebrate and enjoy the delights of your spirited child.* You can concentrate on her strengths, appreciate her tender heart and tickle your fancy with her wild stories and crazy creations. It is appropriate and right to tell her when she is good, instead of when she is bad, to teach her the right way to behave rather than to punish her for innocent errors. Your spirited child possesses personality traits that we value in adults. It is never too early to begin proclaiming her virtues.[11]

If you do not have a child like this, perhaps you have a friend or neighbor who does or maybe you teach a spirited child. These children have tremendous potential. They simply need to learn by careful, loving instruction how to handle the tremendous energy that is flowing through them.

There are many methods of discipline. Most are intended to help the child learn respect for the boundaries of family members, neighbors and the broader community. And the way we manage ourselves in relating to our children speaks louder than our words. Children learn to be kind if we are kind, to be respectful if we are respectful, to be self-disciplined if we are self-disciplined. We set the foundation of character in our children.

As Father Edward J. Flanagan, founder of Boys Town, taught, "The character of a child is like clay—it is pliable and can be moulded very easily. Place it in the hands of powers for good, it is moulded accordingly; placed in [an] environment that is poor, the results are shown in our prison records."[12]

This beloved father to many is also known for his succinct appraisal, "There are no bad boys. There are only bad environments, bad examples, bad thinking."[13]

Every Action Has Its Consequences

One of the most important lessons young people need to learn is that every action they take has consequences. If they do a good deed, they feel good about themselves. If they stay up too late watching TV, they are tired and sleepy the next day. If they are nice to their friends, they feel good and their friends do too. If they study and do their homework, they get good grades. If they don't, they get bad grades.

Children need to learn they can't control other people but that they are in charge of their own behavior. And their behavior affects other people's attitude toward them.

Let's say your son wants to quit losing his cool when his teacher is unreasonable. You might help him by role-playing teacher and student.

Put yourself in the place of teacher, advise your son that you are in charge of the classroom and you expect him to accept your decision. And explain that if he argues or gets mad, you will stiffen your position. However, if he accepts your decision *and* says he'd like to figure out a way to do better next time, you will respond more positively.

Next practice the dialogue with your son (with you play-ing the role of teacher). No matter how effectively or poorly he does his part of the dialogue, praise him for his effort. Then switch roles: you play your son and let him play the role of the teacher.

In a best-case scenario your son will learn how to handle himself when he disagrees with his teacher. In a worst-case scenario—where the teacher doesn't bend and doesn't want to discuss it—your son will know how to handle a difficult situation without losing his cool.

Self-Awareness Exercise

To expand your skills as a parent, try this self-awareness exercise:

- Ask yourself: Is our home environment loving and sup-portive? Is it conducive to our children's well-being? Does it express our values and standards? If our minister or one of the children's teachers stopped by for a visit, would we be comfortable? If not, why not? What can we do about it?

  Write down your answers and thoughts in response to these questions. If you see an area that needs improve-ment, there is no time like the present. Your children not only observe and respond to your behavior, they absorb the vibes in the home.

- Now ask yourself: What kind of an example do I set? Do I keep the standards I expect of my children? When my children copy my behavior, do I feel complimented or am I embarrassed? If I feel embarrassed, what do I need to change?

  Make a note of your answers and thoughts. Be honest with yourself and focus on yourself rather than on your spouse. It's an easy out to find a flaw in one's partner rather than focusing on one's own behavior.

Examine your thinking: Are my thoughts positive and constructive? Are they in keeping with what I say? What thoughts do I have that I wouldn't dare share with my spouse or my kids? What do I want to do about that?

Write down your answers, and give special attention to unruly thoughts that may be running around in your mind, even though you don't express them. These are the kinds of hidden thoughts that tend to pop out at a moment when you lose your cool.

- Practice transforming negative thoughts into positive aspirations. You will experience tremendous satisfaction in gaining self-mastery over the wild horses of the mind.

- Change your behavior in accordance with your aspirations. You will feel good about yourself and find it easier to keep your cool with the kids.

2

The Child Is Father to the Man

The great man is he who does not lose his child's heart.

—MENCIUS
Philosopher

*T*ake a moment to picture yourself as a small child, running from a gang of kids, frightened and anxious. Or perhaps hiding from a neighborhood bully who is waiting for you around the next corner. Or maybe you just fell off your bike and need a big hug. In each case, where do you turn? Home. Children instinctively look to home and family as a refuge in a turbulent world, a haven from harm, a safe place of warmth and love and acceptance.

In every mood children invariably turn toward home. Whatever their need of the moment, they are great homers. Sometimes with a tear on each cheek; sometimes with a secret too good to keep; sometimes with a question that won't wait; sometimes just hungry or tired or guilty—always the child turns toward home. The light in the window is the child's symbol of home, and hope.

The family is the training ground for the child becoming

an adolescent, a young adult and ultimately an adult with a family of his or her own. And what is absorbed and learned in childhood and youth stays with us consciously or subconsciously. What is experienced during family interactions—both good and bad—becomes a guideline for how to interact with friends, spouses and children. Most adults realize this has been true for them. And we need to realize it is also true for our children. As the saying goes, the child is father to the man.

Our children are growing up in a time of complex technology and fast-moving information systems, a period in history that is being called the Information Age. The worldwide knowledge base is expanding exponentially, more quickly than we can fully comprehend. And that explosion of information propels children and youth to internalize and put to use an unparalleled mass of facts, figures and diverse ideas.

Generation Y view the world at the flick of the dial or a tap on the keys of the computer. They join chat rooms and converse with young people all over the world. They have open access to diverse cultures and innovative technologies. This is the up side of the age in which we live.

The down side is the ongoing flood of information that propels children to grow up quickly and rely on automation more than their own creativity. As a result there is a loss of imagination and reverie. Today's young people are at risk of losing contact with their soul and spirit.

Family members also find they have less personal time together. The kids have more homework and projects, not to mention music lessons, ballet, karate, softball, swim practice (add your kids' activities to the list!). And parents have more data to put together to fulfill job responsibilities, which often compels overtime at the office or bringing work home. More outside activities are being scheduled in, even on school nights, and everyone is trying to stay more current with the news. The propelling word is "more!"

Countering Culture Shock

We are bombarded with violent images from around the world, and those distressing images stay with us. Most of us alternately heave a sigh of relief at good news and tense up with the next bad news. We find ourselves mesmerized by scenes of terrorist strikes, fires, floods and power outages, armed soldiers on patrol in cities torn apart by war, civilians injured, and families begging for water and food. And the images and commentary produce a graphic impact upon our children and youth.

How do we cope with this? How do we counter the impact of discouraging, heartrending information on our children? And on ourselves?

I don't know about you, but I frequently find myself turning off the news in favor of *The Cosby Show*, a humorous family drama that puts us back in touch with positive values and the everyday life of a loving family in less hectic times. Or perhaps I'll pick up a classic book I haven't read in a while, like *The Secret Garden* or A. J. Cronin's *The Keys of the Kingdom*.[1]

Sometimes I check the newspaper or the Web for humanitarian stories, which are a comforting respite from the war and mayhem that frequently receives more publicity. When I was doing this recently, I found a story about a remarkable teenager, Makenzie, who has a caring heart beyond her years.

Makenzie thought about how she loved to cuddle a stuffed animal when she was sad or lonely, and she has created her own benevolent project by sending stuffed animals to foster children. She also sends a duffel bag because many of these children have no way to carry their belongings from place to place.

A note from Makenzie accompanies the gift: "I want you to always know that you are loved, especially by me. And always remember to be positive, polite and never give up."

This young girl began her mission when she was seven and over the years has reached some 28,000 children. She says she wants to eventually reach all the 530,000 foster care children in the nation. Her gifts are truly a message of love to children who so often feel unloved.[2]

We all need positive experiences to balance the mayhem we see not only in the news but also in movies and on TV. The majority of the shows graphically reflect the down side of today's culture in story form—and the net effect of this so-called real-life entertainment is culture shock. As a psychologist, I believe this is true for all of us but especially for young people.

The bottom line of what youth and children need today isn't that different from what it has always been: loving family relationships and a sense of safety in the home; an orderly school environment in which they can concentrate; a safe neighborhood where they can try out their ideas and skills; the guidance of adults they admire; the instruction and help of mentors; and the example of older youth and adults who are positive role models.

As they mature, youth are in the process of internalizing basic values and creating lifelong habits of thought and action. For success in life they need to develop a positive work ethic, an appreciation of diversity, and qualities that will serve them well, such as determination, honesty and compassion.

In a few years they will be shaping world opinion in their roles as educators, professionals, business people, humanitarians, men and women in the armed forces, politicians, entertainers, newscasters, sports enthusiasts, and fathers and mothers. We want to prepare them so they are equipped to make an effective contribution to the world and to their own sons and daughters.

Mastering the Lessons of Life

What life lessons do our children and youth need to master in order to set the stage for a successful life and the fulfillment of their destiny? Erik Erikson, psychoanalyst and psychosocial theorist, described the basic lessons of life from infancy through adulthood as developmental stages.[3]

- Infants develop *basic trust* versus a sense of mistrust.

- Toddlers learn *autonomy* or tend to feel doubt and shame.

- Preschoolers develop *initiative* or retreat into a sense of guilt.

- School-age children learn *industry* or develop a sense of inferiority.

- Adolescents achieve a sense of personal *identity* or enter a state of role confusion.

- Young adults develop a capacity for *intimacy*.

- Middle-age people develop *generativity* in work and family life.

- Seniors integrate the lessons of life with the essence of their inner being—culminating in what Erikson called *ego integrity*.

Let's look at these life lessons from a spiritual perspective.

The soul intuitively trusts God and the Higher Self,* yet *trust* needs to be balanced with discernment since over a lifetime we meet many different kinds of people. Some are trustworthy; others are not. And we need to discern who is who!

Autonomy is key to pursuing and achieving our soul's mission on Earth and is meant to be coupled with allegiance to the Higher Self and fulfillment of our divine plan.

Taking *initiative* and being *industrious* is natural to sons and daughters of God even though painful earthly experiences may have left a certain residue, a hesitancy to forge ahead.

Whatever our outer physical appearance, the soul's inner identity is shimmering light—a unique integration of facets of the Father-Mother God—because we are spiritual beings in human bodies. Thus the soul's experience of *intimacy* is oneness with the presence of God. And the soul seeks a special kind of *generativity*, which is the fulfillment of her raison d'être, her mission or purpose in life.

As the soul stirs us to move beyond ego integrity we find ourselves pursuing *soul integrity*, meaning to be true to our inner divinity, our Higher Self. The integrity of the soul reveals itself in a life that exemplifies spiritual precepts and offers inspiration and a helping hand to others.

When young people pursue soul integrity, they strengthen their character and firm up their beliefs. As they develop their positive qualities, they draw closer to the Higher Self. And as they grow in wisdom and identify with their spiritual essence, they are less confounded by karmic circumstances.

---

*Real Self, Christ Self, Buddha Self, Atman, Tiferet.

As parents, mentors and friends of children we are called to acquaint them with the soul, to teach them how to balance karma, and to encourage them to be true to their Higher Self. Otherwise, they will feel somehow unfulfilled even though they may be successful in a worldly sense. Inwardly they are propelled to a higher calling—to fulfill the destiny of their soul.

Navigating the Emotional Ups and Downs

Home and family are meant to be the nest of safety from which young people develop their sense of self, spread their wings and discover their rightful place in the world. And when the going gets tough, young people instinctively turn to family for necessary reassurance, guidance and emotional support.

Some of the best and most down-to-earth advice can be taught at home: "Be true to the best in yourself. Say you're sorry when you do something wrong. Help your brother or sister. Be a good friend. Do a good deed for a neighbor. Cultivate your talents. Learn from every defeat. Make a difference in someone's life!"

Families who share moral principles and a faith in a loving God help children navigate the emotional ups and downs in life. Everyone is strengthened by faith and positive guidelines. So ask your Higher Self to be your best friend. Be compassionate to everyone you meet. Spiritually, as the scriptures instruct, "Do unto others as you would have them do unto you."[4]

I remember as a teenager knowing that it was important to be true to myself—to my best self, my Higher Self. At the same time I realized that some of my thoughts and habits were not so good. I remember thinking, "Okay, I know I'm supposed to be true to my best self, but it's hard to do that all the time."

Fortunately for me, my high school friends were my church friends. We conducted our own youth services with the help of an adult sponsor, and we helped each other spiritually and socially. Around the same time I discovered Charles Sheldon's book *In His Steps*,[5] and I was impressed. For a full year members of the church Sheldon wrote about decided to ask themselves, "What would Jesus do?" before taking any important action.

I decided to try it so I began to ask myself, "What would Jesus do in this situation?" The problem was I knew exactly what Jesus would do, but I didn't necessarily want to do it. I found myself thinking, "Maybe I'll embarrass myself; maybe my friends will think I'm crazy."

I decided to ask Jesus to help me. And as I prayed to him, I began to think, "If the people in this book could make that commitment, I can too!" That decision changed my life and became a baseline from which I make decisions today: "What would Jesus do?"

I have shared this with many people, young and old, and they understand. There is a higher ethic, a moral imperative, imbedded deep in the soul. And when we see or hear stories about people being true to themselves in a higher way, our heart and soul are quickened.

Children and youth are most likely to follow family standards when they see their parents upholding the values that underlie the standards—especially in challenging situations. When parents live their values and are honest and caring in interactions with family, friends and colleagues, children are inspired to do the same. By mobilizing the courage to be true to their best self, especially when it's tough, mothers and fathers inspire young people to develop the qualities of courage, honesty and integrity.

Mother: Our First Love Relationship

Our mother is our first encounter with another person. For nine months we are safely nourished in her womb, interchanging our energy with hers, and then we are expelled from that safe place into a tunnel that seems too small and out into a cold, foreign, brightly lit environment. All of a sudden we are separated from our mother and we are helpless to do anything about it. No wonder we start life with a cry!

As therapist Judith Viorst describes it,

> We are sucking, sobbing, clinging, helpless babies. Our mother interposes herself between us and the world, protecting us from overwhelming anxiety. We shall have no greater need than this need for our mother. . . .
>
> In the early years of life we embark on the process of giving up what we have to give up to be separate human beings. But until we can learn to tolerate our physical and psychological separateness, our need for our mother's presence—our mother's literal, actual presence—is absolute.[6]

The younger the child, the more intently the child is focused on mother. Our mother is our first love relationship, and no matter what kind of a mother she is, separation from her is traumatic. In fact, psychologists talk about it as separation anxiety, which derives from the reality that without a nurturing caregiver, the human infant does not survive.

Of course fathers are also loving caregivers, and an older sister or brother may fill that role some of the time. Yet the soul as the infant developed in the mother's womb and never forgets the initial bond with her. When a child feels that basic safety, he is quick to bond with his father and siblings.

To ease the infant's entrance into the world, some mothers today choose the method of giving birth in a warm water pool. Proponents of this practice say that a water birth is soothing to both mother and baby. Of course, midwives have known about this method of delivery for generations. And there are many legends of Maori, Native Americans, ancient Greeks and Egyptians birthing in water.

Many women who have experienced giving birth in this way say they would never choose any other method. And if the babies were to tell us their thoughts, they would undoubtedly agree—it's a much less drastic change for the baby to move from floating in the womb to being cradled by mother in warm water.[7]

Even with a warm-water birth and a nurturing mother, babies and little children feel abandoned at times—and it's scary. Let's say mother goes to work, to the grocery store, to visit a friend, or perhaps just needs to rest from her maternal duties. She seemingly abandons her children by having a life of her own, and the little ones don't like it. This is normal even if we have a good babysitter; the babysitter isn't mom!

Anna Freud, Sigmund Freud's daughter, described the experience of three-year-old Patrick, who was sent to England's Hampstead Nursery during World War II for safety from the bombings. This frightened little boy kept reassuring himself out loud that his mother would come for him, that she would put on his coat and take him home. And as the days went on and she did not come, he added more items of clothing that she would put on him: "She will put on my overcoat and my leggings, she will zip up the zipper, she will put on my pixie hat."[8]

When the child was asked to stop this ritual, he stopped saying it out loud but kept on moving his lips, silently repeating it to himself, over and over. And he began to make gestures of putting on and zipping up his coat, positioning his pixie hat, and so forth. While other children would be playing with their toys, Patrick would be off by himself silently sounding words and making motions "with an absolutely tragic expression on his face."[9] He could not be comforted.

Patrick's story is extreme, but not unique. Little children whose mothers have to leave them, no matter how good the reasons, may go through this kind of trauma. Since the need for mother is innate and powerful, they may withdraw (as Patrick did) or they may try to handle their feelings by seeking a mother substitute. Inside, however, they long for mother to return.

We might think that when the long-lost mother returns the child would joyously run to jump into her arms, but this isn't necessarily what happens. Quite frequently, the child greets his returning mother with a sense of distance, a kind of blankness.

He handles his terror about his mother having left him and the mistrust he now feels toward her by shutting down his feelings and keeping his distance. One can almost imagine the soul saying, "I'm not going to let that happen ever again. It hurts too much."

A mixture of despair, pain and resentment is hidden under the surface aloofness, and the feelings don't go away easily. One shocking example: A sixteen-year-old boy orphaned as an infant actually filed a lawsuit, "seeking a half million dollars on the grounds that in sixteen years he had been placed in sixteen different foster homes." What was the damage he was suing for? He described it this way, "It's like a scar on your brain."[10]

Parenting the Child, Healing the Soul

We relate to these life stories because all of us have had our own childhood crises. And as we do our best to parent our children wisely, we sometimes come to the realization that we need to re-parent ourselves.

We have difficulty teaching children values and virtues that we haven't internalized. We find it difficult to help a child change a bad attitude or master runaway emotions when our own attitude is questionable or our emotions out of control. And we are unlikely to understand a child's soul-needs if we aren't in touch with our own soul.

When we choose to connect with our own soul and to be guided by higher aspirations, we tune into our Higher Self and are intuitively more responsive to our children's soul and spirit.* And the little ones feel comforted and at peace.

A valuable gift we can give our children is the awareness that "God loves you and we love you. You are a child of the light!" Here is a little song that you can sing or recite to your children to help them remember who they really are:

YOU ARE A CHILD OF THE LIGHT

You are a child of the light
You were created in the image divine
You are a child of infinity
You dwell in the veils of time
You are a Son of the Most High![11]

---

*Whether housed in a male or female body, the soul is the feminine counterpart of Spirit. The spirit (lowercased *s*) is our energetic essence; thus we say a person is joyful, lethargic, "high-wired," and so forth.

If we would heal our own soul and spirit, we need to nurture ourselves in the same loving way, fostering our spiritual nature by claiming our identity as souls of light, sons and daughters of God. And we can pursue the fulfillment of our destiny, which includes helping the next generation to discover and fulfill theirs.

Nurturing our soul and spirit means to listen to the prompting of our intuition, to adopt a positive mind-set, to follow our heart and to behave in accordance with our highest principles.

When we live our higher values, our soul is at peace and our spirit uplifted. The same is true for the children and youth entrusted to our care; when their soul and spirit are nurtured they have the best opportunity to fulfill their destiny. And that sense of peace is nurtured, first of all, in the relationship with mother.

Although each parent has a role to fulfill in the family, the mother is like the center of a maypole. From her heart the ribbons of light go forth to nourish and sustain the family. She upholds her special role through sensitivity to the emotional needs of the family. As she attunes to the still small voice of God within her heart, she is blessed with the state of listening grace. As she identifies with the Divine Mother as her inner source, she becomes a fount of nurturing love, wisdom and inner strength. Her daughters will cherish her and share their secrets with her, and her sons will love and admire her and seek a partner who has similar qualities.

As a daughter prepares to leave the nest she looks to her mother for comfort and guidance about womanhood and about how to relate to men. A son looks to his mother for emotional support and how to relate to women. Our mother is our first love-relationship and the lifelong champion of our soul and spirit.

Father: The Guiding Hand of the Family

The role of father is equally important to the development of the child and the soul. The father is the guiding hand of the family.

A son looks to his father to teach him how to be a man. He will emulate the qualities and behavior of father in his attempt to put on his manhood. A daughter looks to her father to teach her how men think and act. She forms her ideas and opinions about men from her relationship with father.

Father typically spends less time taking care of the children and more time playing with them. He tends to provide excitement and activities outside of the everyday routine. Children, especially little boys, enjoy roughhousing with their father, although they may turn to mother when they are hurt or in need of comfort. The connection with father enables them to move away from too close a connection with mother. Father becomes the friend, the ally, the protector.

Judith Viorst describes the essence of the child's relationship with father in these words:

> Our father presents an optional set of rhythms and responses for us to connect to. As a second home base, he makes it safer to roam. . . . Our father is someone to turn to when we need to resist the lure of re-merger with mother—and when we need to mourn that paradise lost.[12]

Many fathers deeply invest in their relationship with their children and spend quality time with them. And this is just as necessary as nurturing time with mother. When children have father as guide and mentor, they feel safer to explore the world.

I remember my father's loving guidance and how he played with us children and taught me to ride my bike. I remember him teaching me how to do math in my head. And I remember him patiently teaching me how to drive a car on long stretches of the road in the desert where it was safe for a novice driver.

When I was in high school my dad hired me part-time in his installment financing office. I learned how to handle the front desk and interact with customers, how to record payments and do basic bookkeeping. Best of all, I learned how to hold a job. These skills have benefited me all my life.

Since the fatherhood of God is deeply embedded in cultures worldwide and father is the masculine representative of God, it is not surprising that children often see God in the image of their father. Thus, a boy or girl will look to their father to understand manhood, and to understand God.

As a child I remember watching in wonderment as my father prayed. And I would sense the presence of God when he pointed out the constellations, which, to me, seemed really close to heaven. My father's faith in God was a major factor in my adult spirituality.

The Journey of the Soul

Each soul enters life on Earth bathed in innocence, bearing the purity of God's light. That is why everyone smiles at a baby, and the baby smiles back. This little one has a relationship with God, and so do we. As parents it is vital that we give the best of ourselves to the infant so that the soul has the necessary foundation and support to move forward in life.

Our role as parents is to assist the soul, a spiritual being who has lived many lifetimes on Earth, in making the adjustment to her four lower bodies—the physical, emotional, mental and memory bodies—in this lifetime. And our children look to us to take care of them the way God would take care of them.

Perhaps the greatest blessing we can bestow upon our offspring is to introduce them to God as the Divine Father and the Divine Mother and to help them develop a personal relationship with their guardian angel. It is a great security to children to know that they have loving parents here on Earth, a guardian angel to guide them and divine parents in the heaven-world.

We need to realize that each child is a special soul who comes into our particular family for a divine purpose. That soul desires to love and to be loved—and mutual love and respect within the family sets the tone for that child's self-esteem.

Loving parental behavior encourages loving obedience and teaches children to be compassionate to others. And father and mother each have a special role to play in the spiritual drama of child raising.

Spiritually, the husband and father is the head of the household—a high and holy office, earned by behavior that teaches the family that he is, in spiritual terms, the rock of the Christ. This is a special calling, one to which all fathers can aspire.

By word and example he teaches the children the value of work and self-sufficiency. When he is the exemplar of the Higher Self, his sons will identify with him and strive to be like him; his daughters will love and appreciate him and seek a partner who has these higher qualities.

The wife and mother holds the equally important office of representative of the Divine Mother, nurturing the family, praying for each one, teaching them to exercise self-control over their lower nature. Even though she may be a working mother, she is the one the family relies on to tend hearth and home and to give the loving hug and gentle comfort that makes everything better.

In a single parent household, mom or dad fills both roles, which can be challenging indeed. In other families the roles are switched. The husband may be staying home and have a larger role in raising the children because the wife can earn more money. Or the wife may need to have her husband share household duties because she also has a demanding job. And in large families, the oldest girl or boy may also become a caregiver for the younger siblings.

When mother and father show love and respect for each other, the children learn to love and respect one another. When the parents' spirituality is expressed in wise and caring behavior, the children are encouraged to develop their own spiritual nature. In such a bonded family, each son and daughter receives a strong foundation for a successful life.

As we seek to assist our youngsters maximize their talents and virtues, we benefit by asking for spiritual help, for example, asking the angels to help us nurture our infant and guide our children. We may also teach the children to ask the angels to guide them. We may ask our Higher Self to help us mentor our adolescents so they will safely navigate the rites of passage to adulthood. And we may pray to Archangel Michael and saints we revere to keep our loved ones out of harm's way.

Outwitting the Impact of the World

Many times people say to me, "We know we need to have quality time together as a family. But how do we create family time when everyone wants to watch TV or surf the Net or catch up with the news? There are only so many hours in the day. And it's important for all of us to keep up with what is going on in the world, isn't it?"

These are legitimate questions, and the answers are complex. Families today face a dilemma that has been brought about by the rapid advances in technology, communication systems and the demands of the modern workplace. While such advances have resulted in a variety of career choices and a wealth of information, facts and figures at our fingertips, they can also produce information overload.

When we get overloaded we become confused, irritable and edgy. This affects our decision making and interactions with other people. It's like what happens when our computer jams. Trying to process too much information at once creates a logjam in the mind. And it can have a negative impact on family life, even families with the best of intentions.

Children and youth tend to sit in front of the TV once they finish their homework—or instead of doing homework. This is particularly true in homes where no adult is there to welcome them when they come home from school. Such latchkey children are all too common when parents and children do not have easy access to the extended family—cousins, aunts, uncles and grandparents.

In today's society not only do relatives rarely live in the same house or neighborhood, they may live across the country or overseas. Yet the extended family, particularly grandparents, are important to the well-being of children.

Dr. Jack C. Westman, Department of Psychiatry, University of Wisconsin, states:

> As grandparents we have important symbolic and practical functions in our cultures. We are important

simply for what we mean as the oldest living representatives of our families.... Without grandparents, there is
no tangible family line. Children who have no contact
with grandparents miss knowledge of their ancestry.
They may not be able to muster a confident sense of the
future as concretely represented by the fact that older
people have seen their futures become the present and
the past.

As grandparents we are the links to the past in our
families. We can recall when the parents of our grandchildren were young, not always to their liking! We are
the repositories of information about our genealo-
gies.... That information often becomes useful material
for themes that our grandchildren write in school, and
sometimes it flowers into full-fledged writing about our
family trees.

As grandparents we can provide advice to our children that is hopefully appreciated. That is best done
tactfully and when asked for!... We can play healing
roles in assuaging the challenges, hurts, and disappointments in our families.... We are the conveyors of traditions in our families and in our cultures.[13]

Disengaging from the Problems of the Day

When parents come home they are often still engaged
mentally and emotionally with problems on the job. It takes
skill and determination to switch off the job concerns and
focus on family life. However, that is exactly what is
needed—for the parents and for the family.

You are likely thinking, "That's a lot easier said than
done," and you are right. With the thoughts of the day running around in our heads, there is always one more business
decision to contemplate, one more e-mail to answer, one

more analysis to complete, one more phone call to make—the list goes on. In order to switch it off, we need to consciously choose to do so. And some kind of physical exercise can help us shift gears.

After work, moms and dads might go for a walk or a jog, a bike ride, a swim, or play with the dog. And this can include the children, especially if they have been sitting at a desk, writing answers to a problem, chalking a diagram on the blackboard, doing mostly mental activity all day long and still have homework waiting for them. Everybody needs a break from the mental gymnastics of the business or school day.

Families also benefit from sharing the evening meal together. It's a good time to catch up with one another, to share thoughts and feelings, to talk about triumphs or disappointments, and to support one another. Of course, in busy families this doesn't happen every evening. If this is the case for you, you might choose one evening a week when you and your family have the evening meal together.

No matter the howls of protest, turn off the TV, the computer and the phone. Make it a practice for everyone, parents and kids, to share the high points of their day. Give each other verbal praise and encouragement; make it a happy time. Once the family gets into the habit of having a fun dinner at least once a week, everyone will look forward to it.

A suggestion: Make that family dinner inviolable except for emergencies. You will be sending a positive message to your children and teens: "Our family is important to us!"

Resilience in the Face of Stress

Perhaps one of the most important qualities all of us need to develop is resilience—the ability to bounce back from daily stress. And that means working on our confidence, planning skills and ability to stretch when life throws us a curve ball.

No matter how positive our motives or how excellent our plan of action, we may not succeed. When the inevitable setbacks occur or we are confronted with an accident, serious illness, loss of a family member or close friend, we need resilience. How do we develop it? One important aspect is the determination to keep going, no matter what. Another is to practice keeping a cool head, thinking quickly and bouncing back in low-stress situations.

When a youngster rehearses how to handle himself under stress he trains himself to be successful even when life gets tough. That's a basic principle in sports or in developing skills of any kind. As young people practice in low-stress situations they cultivate a habit of resilience that serves them well in more stressful circumstances. Here is an approach that many families have found useful in developing the quality of resilience.

- Choose to believe in yourself, in your talents and in your capability.

- Write down your positive beliefs about yourself. List your talents and capabilities.

- Frame the document and look at it daily as a reminder of who you really are. Post the list over your desk or wherever you will notice it on a daily basis.

- Practice taking charge of your own behavior and being nonreactive to other people's behavior.

- Set specific goals that will impel you to exercise talent, capability and resilience. Write them down and create an action plan to achieve them.

- Rehearse the action plan until you are comfortable doing it. Then do it for real.

- Enjoy the up side and problem-solve the down side of any difficulties you encounter.

- Ask for help from a mentor when you need it.

Strategies for Problematic Situations

We also need to formulate strategies to handle problematic situations. Adults need strategies to deal with overwhelming amounts of information and those never-ending "to do" lists. Children and youth need strategies to deal with day-to-day worries like school bullies and mountains of homework. All of us benefit by figuring out ahead of time how we want to handle perplexing situations.

Think about improving your own ability to strategize at the same time that you teach young people how to do it. When young people get in the habit of analyzing difficult situations, they develop problem-solving skills and have more confidence when they do take action.

Strategizing Exercise

1. Spell out the difficult situation in writing.

2. What is your goal in this situation?

3. Come up with three possible strategies.

4. Make a list of "Benefits" and "Risks" for each strategy.

5. Choose what you believe to be the best strategy.

6. Write out a specific plan of action.

7. Take action.

8. Assess the results.

9. Learn from mistakes.

10. Celebrate the victories!

The Inspiring Story of Rudy Ruettiger

I watched a movie the other night that heartened me and I trust it will do the same for you. The movie *Rudy*[14] is based on the life of Rudy Ruettiger, who after a tough time as a teenager is now a motivational speaker who spreads the message, "Yes, I can!"

Rudy was the third of fourteen children. He was a young fellow with average grades in high school and not a gifted athlete. Nevertheless, Rudy had a dream—to play football for Notre Dame. He faced seemingly insurmountable challenges since his family opposed the idea, he had no money for such a venture, and nobody thought he could make the grade.

Rudy set out on his own to pursue his dream. Even when priests at Notre Dame tried to dissuade him, he was firm in his resolve. Some lines from the movie capture Rudy's intensity of desire: "Ever since I was a kid, I wanted to go to school here, and ever since I was a kid everyone said it couldn't be done. My whole life people have been telling me what I could do and couldn't do, I've always listened to them, believed in what they said. I don't want to do that anymore."

Living on a shoestring, Rudy worked hard on academics at a junior college that hopefully would pave the way into Notre Dame. And he spent every spare moment keeping his body fit to play football. He was in his mid-twenties when after many disappointments and setbacks he was at long last accepted as a transfer student.

With diligence and hard work he earned a spot as a practice player on Notre Dame's "scout team," the team that varsity players run plays against to prepare for their games. After two years on the scout team, Rudy was finally allowed to suit up for the final home game of his college career.

With only twenty-seven seconds left to play against Georgia Tech, Ruettiger was put into the game, and amid shouts of "Ru-dy, Ru-dy," started by his teammates and picked up by the crowd, he sacked the Georgia Tech quarterback. And the crowd, including his family, went wild.

When the game was over, Rudy's teammates carried him from the field on their shoulders. And, even today, Rudy Ruettiger remains the only player in Notre Dame's history to be carried off the field by his teammates. And yes, Notre Dame won the game!

This young man exemplified the courage, dedication and persistence it takes to fulfill the difficult tasks of life. Whether it is on a football field or on the broader field of life, the "I will never give up! I will never turn back! I will win my victory!" motivation is one that propels us forward to fulfill our life goals.

In addition to his work as a motivational speaker, Rudy Ruettiger has co-authored several books—*Rudy's Insights for Winning in Life; Rudy's Lessons for Young Champions: Choices and Challenges;* and *Rudy and Friends*.[15] He certainly knows whereof he writes. Our youth today need the grit, determination and resilience of a Rudy to fulfill their hopes and dreams.

3

The Family's Initiations: The Cosmic Clock and the Karmic Clock

A traveler am I and a navigator,
and every day I discover a new region within my soul.

—KAHLIL GIBRAN
Sand and Foam

All of us move through the cycles of life: birth, infancy, childhood, adolescence, adulthood, middle age and the senior years. And we meet the tests of life in our own unique way. Yet for every individual the journey from infancy to adulthood and beyond is enriched when we receive encouragement and guidance.

Each cycle of life not only includes lessons we are meant to master but also spiritual initiations our soul is intended to pass. When we greet life's lessons with a positive attitude and strive to pass our tests with excellence, we make a worthy contribution to our families, friends and community. When we do so in partnership with our Higher Self, we maximize our soul's opportunity to win a victory—and we help to shape a better world.

Classical theorists and researchers have offered a variety of ways to understand and chart the cycles of children's physical, emotional, mental and social development. Specific developmental stages have been described in the works of Sigmund Freud, Alfred Adler, Jean Piaget, Erik Erikson, Glenn Doman, Maria Montessori and others.

Many families also want to know how these life stages relate to their children's spiritual development. As one parent put it, "How do the developmental stages connect with the journey of the soul and the lessons the soul needs to learn?" And another parent, who had just had her children's astrology charts done, commented, "My children love to look at the stars. Do you think the soul is somehow connected to the stars in the heavens?"

Four Cycles of Development

Elizabeth Clare Prophet has developed a systematic approach to understanding the development of the four lower bodies (etheric,* mental, emotional and physical) that house the soul. And she describes the soul's journey through life in terms of what she calls the "cosmic clock."

The Four Quadrants

_____

*or spiritual.

Mrs. Prophet discusses this journey in terms of our development, beginning with birth. She teaches that during the first seven years of life, we anchor the etheric blueprint, the divine matrix of who we are. In these years, children are rapidly developing and anchoring the blueprint physically.

From the age of seven to fourteen, the potential of the child's mind is being tapped continuously as he or she moves through grade school and masters the fundamentals of reading, writing, history, geography and mathematics. In today's culture, many children are also mastering the computer during these formative years.

From fourteen to twenty-one, the adolescent is primarily focused on mastering his or her emotions and desires. During this period, the adolescent learns through experience with family and peers to be more sensitive to others. He or she also experiences emotional ups and downs related to hormonal changes. In addition, the young person begins to receive the karma (good and bad) he has made during this lifetime and previous lifetimes.

From twenty-one to twenty-eight, a young adult is establishing the patterns of adult life. By the time young people reach the age of twenty-one, they are typically in college or in the work world. Some have already married and started a family. Regardless of whether it's been a rocky road or smooth sailing, the young person's success in higher education, job or family depends a great deal on his or her mastery of the earlier cycles of life.

The Unfolding Higher Identity

Mrs. Prophet has given tremendous teaching on the stages of development and how they are a step-by-step preparation for the soul to achieve an integrated personality in God. She describes how this is a process of separation, or detachment, where the soul is gradually freed from the bindings of karma and the unreal associations of the outer personality. At the same time, the soul is integrating step by step with the Real Self.

As the mother of five children, spiritual teacher, director of The Summit Lighthouse for twenty-five years, cofounder of Montessori International private school, and worldwide lecturer on the initiations and karmic factors of the spiritual path, her insights are invaluable.

She explains that in the early years father and mother need to be sensitive to the inner reality of their children. They need to realize that their love holds the balance for their children as each child begins to express his or her own individuality. As children move along in life, parents do best to continue guiding them but also to gradually step back from a protective role and allow children to make choices and develop more on their own. By doing this in the formative years, they lay the foundation for the child's separate and higher identity to naturally unfold in the later stages of development.

Mrs. Prophet teaches:*

> It is through the mother and the father that the child discovers his own Higher Self, and from the moment of birth the child sees the father and mother as his own Higher Self.... And gradually through the love of the physical manifestation, there has to be translated to the child that allegiance and loyalty and integration with the inner Christ Self.

---

*Unless otherwise noted, the excerpts from Elizabeth Clare Prophet in this chapter are taken from her lecture "The Freedom of the Child," given July 4, 1983.

But one cannot abruptly say, "I must withdraw so the child can be alone and find God." This is a mistaken notion. We have to realize that in a very literal sense we as parents are God to our children. We are God incarnate physically to them.

Mother and father are the guardians of this process of individualization. The child does not know that he has a synthetic self and a Real Self. What the child is, is. . . . The totality of his integrated being, even the light in the flow in the body, is the total manifestation of self. By the correct training, by the correct attitudes, by upliftment, by emphasizing the positive, the child will internalize the Christ [the Real Self,] without having to be shown this analysis of identity, of the Real and the unreal. . . .

In actuality, when you occupy the office of guru to your children, it is through your attainment of Christhood [putting on the Christ consciousness; oneness with the Higher Self] that the child discovers his own. What he sees in you he will find in himself and he will connect to his own previous attainment and to his own Godhood at inner levels.

So there is a selflessness on the part of the parent when manifesting the beauty of God and all the wisdom of God and yet gently bringing it back to the point of the *child's* discovery, the child's awareness.

Then there are parents who allow the child freedom but do not take precautionary measures as to where the child will reattach his allegiance, his devotions and his loyalty.

This typifies the unconcerned parent who allows the child to run wild or just "grow like Topsy" with no parental direction. . . . This laissez-faire attitude toward children almost always results in the child's seeking the grosser, lower vibrations of himself, the astral aspect of his being,* and in the attachments that the child makes when he operates mainly from the position of his emotional body, which is generally the place where the ego goes when it is undisciplined. We will see in these attachments the unwholesome side of friendship, where the friendship is not based in the understanding of the Sun behind the sun, the God relationship.

So the parents have a great, great influence on the direction of the flow of consciousness, the raising of energy of the child. In fact, the parents set limits on how far the child may rise. And they temper his individualization of the God flame and his attainment by their own limiting concepts of themselves, sometimes their jealousy or their envy.

Many parents are in competition with their children from the day they are born. . . . They do not understand the roles of teacher and pupil. The teacher that is benevolent always wants the pupil to excel and exceed his level of attainment.

We want our children to be everything we are and more. We want to give them [elements of] our Christhood through discipleship, through love, through teaching. We want to give them the tools so they can multiply their own Christhood. And when they are as old as we are, we trust they will be many times more integrated and the master of life.

---

*The astral plane is a frequency of time and space beyond the physical, corresponding with the emotional body. It is the repository of mankind's collective thought and feeling patterns, both conscious and unconscious. The pristine purpose of this frequency is for the amplification of the pure thoughts and feelings of God in man. However, it has been polluted with impure records (vibrations) of the race memory multiplied ad infinitum by an evolution caught in the riptides and repetitive cycles of its own negativity.

But those who are in competition with their children do not want their children to exceed them, to do better than they do. And therefore, they put proscriptions on them through the whole childhood, psychological proscriptions—"You may not do this. . . . You cannot do that."... And so, the child grows up thinking, "Well, only my parents are able to do this. I cannot do it."

Correlating with Our Real Self

Each cycle of life with its inherent lessons is an opportunity to review our life performance. How well are we correlating with our Real Self? How are we doing at the physical, emotional and mental levels and at the level of our soul? How are we doing in raising our children? What is our cosmic report card?

As parents, teachers and friends of children we are intended to nurture and instruct the next generation, to help them discover their special talents and to encourage excellence in whatever they do. Throughout their formative years we are meant to help young people integrate their spiritual nature with the material plane. They are meant to master a body of information and develop skills that will maximize their inherent gifts—the gifts of the soul.

Cycles of Development: The Cosmic Clock

Mrs. Prophet has charted the cycles of psychological and spiritual development on what she has named the "cosmic clock." This is a way of mapping our spiritual initiations from birth to our present age and into future years. As you will see in the diagram on page 90, each initiation correlates with age and relates to a specific chakra, astrological sign and the God-quality the soul is meant to strengthen at that age.

Infancy: The Judge

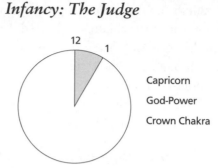

The twelve o'clock line of the cosmic clock correlates with birth and infancy and relates to the crown chakra, the astrological sign of Capricorn and the spiritual quality of God-power.

This period of development, beginning with birth, is what psychoanalysts call the oral stage—the stage where the mother is the source of life and power for the infant. And that little one relates to mother by being cradled by her and through suckling at the mother's breast. We understand an infant's task during the oral stage as the mastery of taking in nourishment. And the infant also begins to discover himself* as a person separate from mother.

Mrs. Prophet explains:

> The child needs to discover—psychically [at a soul level], psychologically and emotionally—the mother as a separate identity. The soul may know this, but the consciousness of the outer self must understand it and experience it. The taking-in process requires that the child see the mother as a separate identity from himself—a person whom he unconsciously or consciously knows he is dependent upon for his survival.

---

*The teaching on the stages of development applies to both boys and girls.

Now this is the line of God-power. The child recognizes that the mother is the power source. The mother is all power. The child in the soul level is actually dealing with the universal Mother in the relationship of son [or daughter]. It's a one-on-one relationship with mother that sets the stage for all successive close relationships that will occur in life. . . .

For the child to master this stage, he needs the assistance of the mother, who must gradually teach him that the milk comes from her and that it is her freewill choice to feed him. This sets the example for the child to learn that it is only by the grace of God that we are fed and taught. It is not a right; it is something that is a gift of God. . . .

The mother demonstrates her love to the child and demonstrates that she is making a freewill choice to nurse him and to provide the proper nourishment and care: "I don't have to do this; I do it because I love you.". . . The relationship is based on love.

Psychologically, in the relationship of mother and child, the child is learning to give as well as receive. A short delay before nursing the baby gives the mother a breathing space, and then the child receives the nourishment he needs. He begins to realize his cry is a signal, and mother will respond as quickly as she can. This sets the stage in a physical way for the child to understand that life is give and take.

The infant is also learning by his mother's example to give by free will instead of allowing someone to simply take without his consent. All of us need to develop both capacities: to give and to receive—and to do so lovingly.

Mrs. Prophet continues:

At this age, the child must also learn to develop his own will and to be able to reject food when he has had enough. This means that the parent must be willing to accept that rejection and understand it as healthy. Accept the child's indication, "No, I have had enough. I do not want any more." The process of eating at this age is the process of assimilation. The child is learning to take in only that which he needs and no more than he can assimilate. . . .

So the initiation of the twelve o'clock line of Capricorn is the initiation of being without power and with power, the energies of life. The separation from the parent can be mastered if the experience is not too overwhelming to the child by either too much or too little parental attention or inconsistent responses and behavior, all of which can cause physical or emotional trauma.

Now we have one word on each of the lines of the clock that Mother Mary gave to me,[1] words she gave me in the very wee hours of this morning—a very wonderful experience. The one word for the office of the child on the line of Capricorn is the *Judge*.

You say, "What, how can a child zero to one year old be a judge?" Well, here are the first judgments that are made in the life of the child. The child says, "I eat, I sleep, I move, I grow, I think, I feel, I am aware.". . .

The child is making decisions. Allow him to make them. They center around his food, his intake, but they also center around a lot of other things. . . . If this separation or the definitions* are not mastered, the child may begin a path of manipulating the outside power (the mother or the mother substitute) rather than receiving from it. The child's relationship to the world is then based on his perspective that he is making his mother give to him rather than experiencing the mother as a

---

*i.e., the *Judge* and the other stages of development.

separate, giving person. This can result in the belief that the world owes him a living. . . .

If the mother identifies with the child as being there to meet *her* dependent needs, the child will not be able to form a separate identity apart from the mother. The guru-chela relationship,* the twin-flame relationship, the husband-wife relationship, friend relationships, are all based on needs. But the needs are based on "You are who you are; I am who I am. We need each other. We have something to give each other for the larger considerations of life." Not that "You are a part of me and I use you" or "I am inside of you and I fulfill your personality." . . .

If a child believes he exists to fulfill the emotional needs of a parent, he will open himself to fulfill the emotional needs of others. This can create a spatially undefined aura [unclear boundaries], which causes confusion in his own identity. He readily confuses himself with the consciousness of others, thinking their thoughts are his own. . . .

Psychologists have often observed that even at birth children have different tolerance levels to separation from the mother. So the soul comes in with different levels of attainment and different levels of mastery, perhaps based on the etheric memories. The child at this stage is given the choice to control and manipulate versus the choice to accept his dependency and helplessness and then to move on in the most exciting adventure of the first year of his life, integration of power.

The child is continually moving, stretching his limbs. He has little bars to raise himself in his crib. He sees the power of the mother, loves the mother, wants to be like her, and busies himself in the exercises (mental, physical) to develop that body. And he's working hard to eat and

---

*i.e., the master-disciple or teacher-student relationship.

increase his size and to grow into that position where he now can have at least some of the power that has come to him from the mother.

So the yin and the yang* are starting to be in an interchange. This is perfect love. This is admiring a quality in someone, loving that person for that quality and saying, "I'm going to be like her. I'm going to be like him. I'm going to develop my capacity to be the same." And that's what we want to give our children—the hope to do and to be.

One-Year-Old: The Alchemist

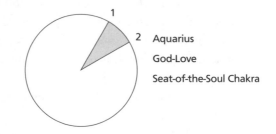

1
2   Aquarius
    God-Love
    Seat-of-the-Soul Chakra

The one o'clock line of the cosmic clock correlates with the one-year-old child and relates to the seat-of-the-soul chakra, the astrological sign of Aquarius and the spiritual quality of God-love. During this period of the infant's development, the mother continues to be the primary influence in the life of the child. However, as Mrs. Prophet teaches, father and mother become the Alpha-Omega circle of authority, the two-in-one that the child looks to for care and comfort.

Since the child develops in the mother's womb and emerges from her body, it is through her that the child is

*In Chinese philosophy, yang is the active, positive, masculine force or principle and yin is the passive, negative, feminine force or principle in the universe.

introduced to the universal Mother; the soul intuitively looks to mother as the representative of Mother God.

Since the father represents the fatherhood of God, the soul in embodiment looks to father as to Father God. And the mother, by her instruction and the way she relates to her husband, helps the child respect and revere the father. When she appreciates the father's higher qualities and seeks his spiritual wisdom, the child is quick to do likewise.

The father does his part in the way he relates to mother. When he values his wife's higher qualities and relates to her as a representative of the Divine Mother, the child is comforted. When it is obvious that mother and father respect and love each other, the child is at peace. And the child has her own pre-birth experiences with father from the moment of conception on.

As an infant in the womb, the child has known both mother and father—the little one knows the father's voice, the mother's voice and is sensitive to the kinds of interchanges they have with each other.

If, instead of loving and respecting one another, the interaction between husband and wife is packed with tension, discord and rivalry, the child experiences devastating emotional distress. And the child's relationship to both parents, as well as to Father-Mother God, is compromised. Infants and one-year-olds are definitely aware of tensions between father and mother, more than most parents realize.

Mrs. Prophet continues:

> Now on the one o'clock line, centered in the soul, the child is the *Alchemist*. The path of love of Aquarius is the path of bhakti yoga, the devotional path. In order to follow this path, we must have an object of love. . . . The child must know himself and define himself

as separate and choosing to love mother and mother choosing to love him. . . .

From birth on, the child learns to trust that the mother is going to be there, recognizes both parents, has a sense of joy, a sense of being comforted, protected and cared for.

This is the age of the development of absolute trust. If you cannot trust your parents and parents do not establish the trust relationship, dependability, the child will always be in doubt about the trustworthiness of God or the ascended masters or the guru. . . .

The problem of absence of trust, and of doubt and fear, is an internal problem of the soul or the individual with the authority figure, the parent relationship, and previous incarnations of not having had trust in Almighty God, either through psychological problems or because the person himself is not trustworthy and therefore has not been worthy of God vesting his trust in the person. So there's not a cohesive, integrated relationship with cosmos.

And you will find that such an individual trusts no one and cannot . . . give and cannot receive and cannot stand in any way to be let down. . . . We can trust friends and have wonderful friends, but once in a while they might let us down, and that's human nature. But we don't throw away the friendship. We pick up and we go on; we realize people make mistakes, people have their weaker moments. And basically, the friendship, the marriage, the association of business partners, remains intact because people have more to give than just a brittle attitude toward the relationship. So here [at age one] the trustworthiness must be developed. . . .

The mother becomes the object of the child's fulfillment and his object of adoration and delight. He delights in being like her. Alchemically, he is becoming her, made in her image by choice. The soul reflects her smiling face or her frowning face. Your child at age one is the great alchemist creating himself in your image and likeness.

The helpless surrender of a child is a very delicate trust. As Mrs. Prophet says, "It is the little bird held in the hand.... You can hear its beating heart; you can feel its helplessness. You do not let that one down. This mutual trust is outpictured in the radiant love that appears in the face of the mother and child, unmatched except in the love between the guru and the chela."

We also understand that early in life there can be internalized within a child's psyche both a "good mother" and a "bad mother." The child trusts the good mother, the one who nurtures, teaches and protects the child from dangerous situations. The so-called bad mother is formed from abuse or neglect, which leaves the little one in pain or unprotected from danger.

When a child is abused, deserted or separated from mother or if the mother is overly possessive, the child may have difficulty emotionally. As we saw in the story of Patrick during his World War II separation from his mother, trust may give way to withdrawal, unresponsiveness and anxiety. And these feelings may become anger or hatred later in life. The seeds of this sad dilemma can be planted in the child's subconscious as early as age one.

If the bad mother becomes foremost in the child's eyes, the child may find it difficult to accept a healthy, giving relationship as an adult. He or she may avoid close relationships and those that are unfamiliar or even unintentionally seek out an abusive partner. Or as the result of the internalized bad mother, the adult may actually become the abuser.

Of course, the same is true in the child's internalization of the father. Although much of the psychological literature has focused on the mother-child relationship, the child may also internalize a "good father" and "bad father," particularly if the major caregiver has been the father. And this dynamic comes into full play in the teens and young adulthood.

In the '60s we saw a version of this where young people rejected whatever they didn't like in their parents, in religion, in the "establishment." And in that state of rebellion they were magnetized to sex, drugs, rock and roll, alcohol, free love and acting-out behavior. This produced a major change in our culture, which has become even more problematic today. Thus we understand how influential parents can be in setting the stage for the behavior their children express in their teens and early adulthood.

It is worthy of note that this drama has happened in other generations throughout history. There was even a generation gap in Shakespeare's play about Henry IV, where his son, Prince Henry, did his acting-out in the taverns with Falstaff before settling down in the last two years of King Henry's reign.

Karma is the other major player in the drama of family life. Teachings on karma and reincarnation tell us that we come into a lifetime in a particular family for karmic reasons. We have lessons to learn, gifts to give and karma to balance with our parents and siblings. And although we may not understand all of the ins and outs of the karmic equation, we enter life through our parents because that situation has the best potential of teaching us the karmic lessons we need to learn.

We are wise to contemplate the equation and ask ourselves: "If I came in to my parents to learn a lesson, what is the lesson? They have given me physical life, a physical body, an opportunity to evolve on Earth. And that itself is worthy of my gratitude—that they cared enough to bring me into embodiment. What specifically does my soul need to understand and learn from this family?"

We can pray for an understanding of our lessons and opportunities. We can ponder: "What if my parents did do things that were wrong? What is that lesson all about?" And we can gradually gain a higher understanding: "Even though they did some things wrong, I can follow their best example. I will love God, separate out from my parents lovingly and express the best of me in my behavior. I will give compassion to others. And I will not demand that life pay me back for the difficulties I had as a child."

If we have thought ill of our parents, we may tend to have a chip on our shoulder with our spouse or in relations with authority figures. We may not accept that other person as an individual who has a right to be the way he or she chooses to be.

When we do accept other people for who they are, including their virtues and flaws, we can rid ourselves of irritability, anger, vengeance and the sense of betrayal and mistrust. We can be wiser in what we expect from that person. When you get right down to it, we can't expect people to be someone other than who they choose to be. We may prefer that they be more kind or giving, but they do not exist solely as instruments for our self-growth or self-gain. Even as we have free will, so do they.

We might ponder whether this is one of the reasons the divorce rate is so high—that people expect other people to be someone they are not.

Two-Year-Old: The Adept ("All by Myself!")

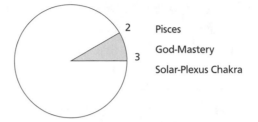

2   Pisces
     God-Mastery
3   Solar-Plexus Chakra

The two o'clock line of the cosmic clock correlates with the two-year-old child and the toddler stage. It relates to the solar-plexus chakra, the astrological sign of Pisces and the spiritual quality of God-mastery. This is a stage of active exploration in which the child has an almost unlimited sense of what he can do. He begins to experience his own creativity, to sort out what he likes and what he doesn't like. As the child begins to master his basic needs and the environment around him, he begins to depend upon himself instead of always looking to mother or father.

Mrs. Prophet says:

> This is the "all by myself" stage of independent action when the child takes delight in his own talents, skills, his own body, his own physical movement.
>
> If there is too much parental interference in this process—by either not allowing the child to struggle (and thereby taking his initiations for him) or by pushing and forcing the child to do more than he is able—the child can collapse into a passivity, a nonaction and a dependency.... When the child collapses into helplessness, he can become clinging, doubtful of his own abilities, ... filled with fear.

To correct passivity, the mother must step down the initiations until the enthusiasm and mastery of the child can be engaged. . . . If the child can be motivated, desiring to overcome a sense of limitation, he will surrender passivity and strive for continued self-transcendence. This self-transcendence requires the letting-go of the energies of life—people, objects, ideas—that have served their purpose. . . .

A child is very malleable, and mothers can stop the creative, expanding, evolving energy either by too much praise or too great an expectation. . . . Parents can actually thwart the child's good momentums of mastery contained in the etheric body, but they can also correct poor momentums. It is the interplay of forces between the parents' momentums and the etheric records that forms the yin-yang influence upon a child's lifestream. . . .

This is the age of the *Adept*, and the adept does over and over again what he needs to do. In the Montessori method, the child is allowed to handle and do as many things for himself as he is capable of doing. The point of greatest creativity occurs at the edge of his maximum capacity and effort, when all of his energy comes together and he pushes beyond yesterday's attainment.

If you watch two-year-olds, they love to explore, to see how everything works. In fact, they enjoy getting into anything and everything that is within their reach. As they become adept at any task, they beam with joy and run to mom or dad to show what they can do. And they will do a task over and over, which is helping them to gain mastery of that task.

Two-year-olds are also in the period of being toilet-trained, and when this task is accomplished with love and encouragement, the child takes pride in the mastery of his own body. This is important because it sets the stage for the development of physical skills in the future. And, as always, the encouragement and support of mom and dad are vital in the process.

At the age of two, a child is developing a sense of self-mastery or lack of it, which can become a part of his make-up for life. The child who is held back by a fearful parent or who does not gain a sense of mastery may very well develop doubts or fears that he can't do new tasks. He may hold back from new experiences, which can limit his learning capabilities. This stage of development is important in the life of the child—he is taking the early steps of exploring and mastering his physical world.

As the child gains in mastery and skills, the mother experiences a greater degree of freedom, a gradual lessening of 100 percent attention on the child at all times. This is a blessing to the mother as well as to the child's independent development.

Three-Year-Old: The Orderer

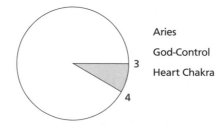

own body. This is important because it sets the stage for the development of physical skills in the future. And, as always, the encouragement and support of mom and dad are vital in the process.

The three o'clock line of the cosmic clock correlates with the three-year-old child and relates to the heart chakra, the astrological sign of Aries and the spiritual quality of God-control. At this stage of life, the child is experimenting with order: "I organize, I speak, I create." This is the inner voice of the emerging self, either as the confident self or as a sense of self that is unfulfilled or falsely enhanced. An unfulfilled sense of self typically culminates in an inflated or deflated ego instead of a genuine sense of selfhood.

When all is going well, a child at this age experiences a budding self-confidence, a pride in making choices, and an emerging sense of orderliness in daily routines.

Mrs. Prophet explains:

> When the joy of achievement and mastery becomes sufficient, choices emerge with their own order and ritual. It is a time when the child comes into a beginning awareness of his own independent cycles, especially his body cycles.
>
> He can take all day to arrange his toys or arrange his room and needs to be encouraged to do so.... Everything needs to be in order and at his scale in the home. And chaos should be turned into order by the *Orderer*, by the individual child, so that he knows that he can tackle chaos and be a co-creator.
>
> This is the consciousness of "I am who I am," which will come around the next round of the clock at age fifteen.* A new sense of identity has dawned upon the child. The child is speaking abundantly at age three, and because he has the power of speech, he senses his authority to create, to command. There is an inner sense that the child has enough tools and skills to get whatever he wants to control himself and his environment.
>
> He can even make himself a sandwich; he can do very simple tasks around the house. And the more you let him do, the more he is becoming that integrated personality in God [that is to manifest] at age thirty-three,

---
*See pp. 102–4.

which is clocked on the opposite line, the nine o'clock line of the clock.

There is a tenacity and a determination in the three-year-old child. If he cannot get what he wants directly by taking it or doing it, he can become very vocal—reasoning, rationalizing, coming up with every possible excuse, or if all that doesn't work, he may manipulate, fuss or whine. He generally has enough skills that something will work.

If the mother and the father are too weak, a three-year-old child can actually end up in control—he can rule the roost. There can be a switch in the yin and yang relationship [i.e., parent-child relationship] and the child can actually take on the power position in the household. . . . If the parents are overindulgent or overstimulating, the child can become omnipotent, full of pride and ego, wanting to receive all the time—physically, emotionally and mentally. Instead of "I order," it becomes "I want.". . .

At this age, the child's awareness of himself as boy or girl, unless emphasized by parents or by playmates, is not enormous. As the boy attains control, he comes into a sense of his own importance. This may result in a direct confrontation with his father, and in the case of a girl, with the mother.

The child cannot maintain his omnipotent position unless the parents allow it. . . . He can, however, get locked-in very early to forms of control, always attempting to gain parental approval. If the child does not need to resort to controlling his parents, he can become very creative, an energy which eventually polarizes to bring in the flow of the Holy Spirit on the nine o'clock line.

Four-Year-Old: The Hierarch

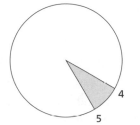

Taurus
God-Obedience
Third-Eye Chakra

The four o'clock line of the cosmic clock correlates with the four-year-old child and relates to the third-eye chakra, the astrological sign of Taurus, and the spiritual quality of God-obedience. At this age the child is quickened to be obedient to the Higher Self. This is a time when children need to learn to be obedient to their parents and to follow teachers' instructions for projects in preschool or behavior on the playground. Inwardly, the four-year-old is in the process of building character.

Mrs. Prophet says:

> It is during this age that the child must give up his omnipotence and come to a resolution of the question of where the authority will reside—in the parent or in the child. The child needs to recognize all those who are ahead of him on the Path, and it really becomes a testing of who's going to be the guru and who's going to be the chela*—who is going to obey whom and who is going to own the house. . . .
>
> Discipline is very necessary at this stage, but if you *start* at this stage you are too late. . . . If you coddle,

---

*In the family, the parent is in the role of guru, or teacher; the child is in the role of chela, or student.

cuddle, and never cease handling your children up to this age and all of a sudden start giving them orders, it does not work at all....

Hierarchy now is being established very much on the physical level. It will be tested, even if you have disciplined before this. If the child does not experience humility [through accepting correction] at age zero to one, one to two, two to three ... and bend the knee before the parent, ... he may become stubborn, defiant and rebellious.

The time that you lose your sixteen-year-old is age four. Go around the clock another twelve lines and you'll be at the four o'clock line of Taurus and your son or daughter is sixteen. If you can't control them at sixteen, it's because you didn't do it at four.

The task of disciplining the child is a quality of the middle way. Generally, the overanxious mother or father gives the child no leeway—no time to pass the initiation. If the child doesn't respond immediately, it's an immediate discipline. And it's the mother's or father's anxiety of the moment, conveyed from the solar plexus, and the desire to control.

On the other hand, the overrelaxed, passive parent gives the instruction to the child, waits too long for the child to take the initiation, loses momentum, never follows through, and thereby gives all the power and authority to the child....

The middle way of disciplining the child takes effort and mastery for the mother and father because they should direct the discipline from a point of harmony and compassion rather than from positions of pride and anger. But compassion has a sternness and a fire that the child must respect, or fear. The fear of God is the beginning of wisdom. Fear is not negative when it is a profound respect.... You are communicating to the child:

"You will have to take control over these forces that are controlling you."

Through loving discipline, the child learns that father and mother are the authority figures, that they have that position in the hierarchy of the family. The child will have respect for that authority when it is reasonable authority, and when the parents back each other up. It is confusing for the child to learn to be obedient when the parents disagree about the rules or how they are to be enforced. And that in itself can lead to disobedience in the child.

When the parents remain in the proper roles, they become the true teachers of the child, and the process of internalizing the good parent takes place within the child. In a healthy way, the child takes on the patterns of father and mother. When you observe a four-year-old playing with a teddy bear or doll, you begin to see what the child has internalized.

As a child learns to be obedient to the parents, he or she is learning obedience to the inner father and mother, who are meant to be the best simulation possible of the Father-Mother God. And as the soul incorporates the lessons being learned, the soul comes under the dominion of the inner teacher, the Higher Self.

Five-Year-Old: The Sage

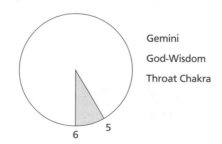

Gemini
God-Wisdom
Throat Chakra

The five o'clock line of the cosmic clock correlates with the five-year-old child and relates to the throat chakra, the astrological sign of Gemini and the spiritual quality of God-wisdom. At this age, the child has developed speech, can communicate her needs, and is beginning to learn to read and write. Children at this age are ready to expand on what they have already learned. They delight in imitating people they admire and in learning new skills.

The child realizes she doesn't know everything, and she has a deep desire to learn about what she doesn't know. She is striving for a sense of wholeness, the balance of yin and yang energies in her world. The sign of Gemini is also known as the Gemini twins.

Mrs. Prophet explains:

> The Gemini twins are Alpha-Omega. The child is a very yang figure, very concentrated in energy, extending the yang out to discover the Omega universe, bringing the Omega into himself as the knowledge of all of his environment.
>
> When the child cannot learn, he begins to manipulate and attempts to please by giving the parents (or teacher) what they want. That is the case when a child is not placed in a maximum learning situation.
>
> An example of this would be a child who has not yet learned to read but notices several other boys in his class reading, who then goes to his mother and asks her to show him what he has to do to learn to read.
>
> He wants particularly to know if he needs to wiggle his nose or raise his eyebrows or do some such thing to make it possible for him to read without really learning—there must be something magical that he can do. . . .

Learning itself is a magical process which the child enjoys.... Thus we must encourage our children at the age of five and be aware that they can learn almost infinitely... from birth through age seven. They have a far greater capacity to take in than we realize....

So the child is contemplative, meditative, prayerful, finding the Inner Self, discovering the Real Self—very active and eager to learn because the learning process enables the child to bring out this Inner Self. These are the years when maximum learning potential exists, when the intellectual powers are at their peak.

Sexual energy is almost nonexistent in the focalized sense because the child is using all of his sacred energies in the developing of his mind. He is preparing the channels of the chakras, of the spine, of the nervous system for the raising of the kundalini fires* later in life. The light of the base chakra is actually diffused and distributed evenly through the child's body, not by a raised kundalini but by the nature of the circuit of wholeness of Alpha and Omega—from the heart, the crown, through his entire body.

Maximum energy, maximum taking-in—the child learns with his whole body. The mind of the child is throughout his cells, his genes, the coursing of his blood; the whole body is engaged in assimilating the mind of God. It is a time when the energies of mother and father are drawn together for the realization and focalization of the Real Self within the heart.

When education is the education of the heart, as in the Montessori environment, we find that the child is focusing development in the heart rather than merely through the

---

*The kundalini fire is a cosmic or divine energy in human beings located at the base of the spine and released upward by means of yogic techniques or spiritual attainment.

intellect, or merely through the lower mental body.

It is the age of innocence that should last until the karma begins to descend at the age of twelve. The protection of that innocence and that absorption in the mind of God in those years is the responsibility of teachers and parents.

Let us let our children be children. It is so wonderful to be five and not told you should be acting as if you're seven or eight. It's so wonderful to be able to enjoy life at twelve and do everything a twelve-year-old loves to do and not feel that you have to look like a teenager and be a fifteen- or sixteen-year-old.

Six-Year-Old: The Harmonizer

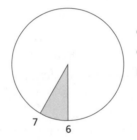

Cancer
God-Harmony
Base-of-the-Spine Chakra

The six o'clock line of the cosmic clock correlates with the six-year-old child and relates to the base-of-the-spine chakra, the astrological sign of Cancer and the spiritual quality of God-harmony. The child is learning to care for his possessions and to experience a sense of well-being that originates in his inner world. He begins to separate out from mom and dad and to explore his own resources.

Mrs. Prophet continues:

The more a child learns, the more numerous his choices become and the more options he has available.

He begins to experience the freedom and flexibility of his own use of free will and develops a great patience that comes from increased flexibility—all creating greater inner harmony.

He can begin to occupy himself and to play alone. If there is not enough going on in his outside world, he has alternatives and can go inside of himself. His fantasy world emerges and he busily creates an internal life that has an individuality all its own.

This is entering now the quadrant of the desire body, a very important time for the imagination. Much of what we say for each line is like the bud and the little shoot that has already been growing since day one. But now is when it is most noticeable. Now is when it is coming into physical focus.

A certain detachment from desires can be observed in the child at this stage, and there is a definite separation from the mother's world. . . . Little boys at this age love frogs, but their mothers and their teachers don't.

Now, if this process does not occur and the child's energy is still attached to outside objects and persons, he may be dominated by his feelings of dependency and acquire the characteristics needed for manipulation and control.

These include sympathy, self-pity, defensiveness, indecision and the use of attention-getting techniques—silliness, forbidden behavior, sexual remarks. It is as if there were not enough energy for life from inside the child's own world and the energy needed to be constantly supplied from the outside. . . .

If the parents have demonstrated harmony for the first six years of a child's life, he will flow right through this line and derive immense energy from the white fire of it and come into a sense of dominion and a certain inner power—inner resources, the resources of the depths of the Mother flame in that base chakra, being able to rely on one's inner resources for entertainment, for amusing oneself.

If you've propped him up in front of the TV set or always had entertainment, always had noise around him, he's already going to be disoriented when he is alone or in silence. . . .

Seven-Year-Old: The Lover

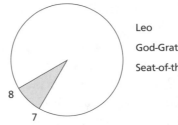

Leo
God-Gratitude
Seat-of-the-Soul Chakra

The seven o'clock line of the cosmic clock correlates with the seven-year-old child and relates to the seat-of-the-soul chakra. The astrological sign is Leo and the spiritual quality is God-gratitude. This is an age when the child is learning to give love. He is meant to be the lover of his own soul, of his parents and of God.

Mrs. Prophet says:

> As the child develops a deeper and harmonious, flexible inner world, the separation from the mother becomes much more complete. With the greater independence that the child now has, he relinquishes not only control of the mother but expectation that the mother be a certain way.
>
> His demands change to requests. Concern and

thoughtfulness begin to emerge, and he is actually able to think of the mother and the mother's reality as different from his own. The child's caring for the mother now becomes more conscious with the awareness that mother does not have to give him what he wants but gives out of love.

The child is appreciating . . . the mother and father, sensitive to them and their needs. . . . The child is desiring to give back to the parents what they have given, . . . loving to do chores and serving. This understanding is necessary in order for feelings of gratitude to emerge.

If the child has not successfully made the separation from the mother by this age, he may become ungrateful, bitter, blaming, and angry.

Eight-Year-Old: The Moralizer

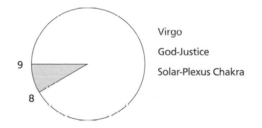

The eight o'clock line of the cosmic clock correlates with the eight-year-old child and relates to the solar-plexus chakra, the astrological sign of Virgo and the quality of God-justice. By this time the child is internalizing the morals of parents, teachers, older siblings, friends, whoever she looks to as role models.

Sometimes the child gets into "It's not fair!" as she is try- ing to figure out why rules do not apply equally to every- body. And this sense of injustice can generalize to all kinds of situations as the child experiments with rules within the family, school, and with friends and tries to project the laws of her inner being upon life and others.

Mrs. Prophet explains:

> He must deal with the discrepancies and relinquish his black-and-white perceptions of the world. It is a time when the child has to deal with the disaster that mother or father could possibly be wrong or that what his teacher is saying is not the same as what his parents are saying.
>
> Life seems to go beyond the simple set of rules that he has encountered in his childhood, and frustration and anxiety can come when potential solutions become more complex and allow for more possibilities.
>
> If a child cannot be flexible or cannot contain these frustrations, he then lapses into a sense of injustice—which may later be channeled into negative social actions, causes, or attitudes, e.g., vengeance, control, emotional tyranny.

The eight-year-old can take on a mentality that we see with many adults these days, where a person gets into a great sense of injustice about someone else's beliefs or decisions. Such individuals may very well consider it their duty to vehemently put down anyone whose sense of morality or way of accomplishing a task is not theirs.

At this stage the child is compelled inwardly and outwardly to recognize the right of the freewill choices of others, even though he or she may not agree with them. And this is a challenge. In a best-case scenario, the child begins to understand and appreciate the necessary balance of justice and mercy.

Before we continue, here are diagrams illustrating the cycles of the cosmic clock going through age thirty-three.

Diagrams of the Cosmic Clock

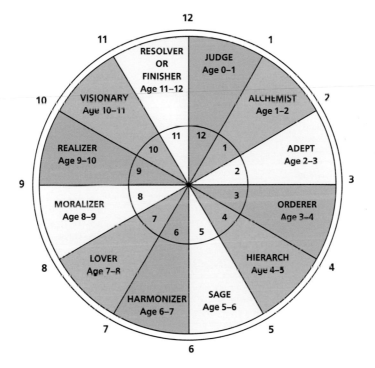

Figure 1
First Twelve-Year Cycle
Age 0–12

12 / CAPRICORN
GOD–POWER
Crown Chakra
Age 0–1, Judge
"I am aware"

Integration of God-power with helplessness
Taking-in, receiving
Begins separation from mother
Judgments, definitions of self
Develops will

1 / AQUARIUS
GOD–LOVE
Soul Chakra
Age 1–2, Alchemist
"I trust"

Understands mother principle as life-giver
Returns love to mother
Awareness of father as lawgiver
Creating self in image of mother

2 / PISCES
GOD–MASTERY
Solar Plexus
Age 2–3, Adept
"I can do"

Independent action
Creativity—sorting process
Begins mastery of needs
Dependency transferred to self
Decision-making begins
Delights in talents, skills

3 / ARIES
GOD–CONTROL
Heart Chakra
Age 3–4, Orderer
"I order my life, I create"

Real self emerging
Organizer of life
Self-confidence/co-creator
Power to speak/to command
Independent cycles
Tenacity and determination
Recognition of masculine and feminine ray

4 / TAURUS
GOD–OBEDIENCE
Third Eye
Age 4–5, Hierarch
"I will and I work"—the builder

Correct order of hierarchy established
Resolution of authority—he is hierarch only insofar as he is master of himself
Internalization of parents

5 / GEMINI
GOD–WISDOM
Throat Chakra
Age 5–6, Sage
"I learn"

Speech and communication
Striving for wholeness in Alpha and Omega
Intellectual powers at a peak
Learning and absorption in the mind of God
Discovering Real Self and development of mind of Christ

6 / CANCER
GOD–HARMONY
Base Chakra
Age 6–7, Harmonizer
"I am responsible, I care"

Inner harmony and ownership of self
Shares yet can play alone
Uses free will
Develops patience, imagination, individuality
Dominion from inner resources

7 / LEO
GOD–GRATITUDE
Soul Chakra
Age 7–8, Lover
"I love"

Develops love, gives love
Independence and inner world
Relinquishes control of mother
Thoughtfulness and service
Gratitude toward parents

8 / VIRGO
GOD–JUSTICE
Solar Plexus
Age 8–9, Moralizer
"I deliberate"

Moral integration
Learns concept of justice and selective judgment
Recognizes freewill choice of others
Confronts crisis that parents might be wrong

9 / LIBRA
GOD–REALITY
Heart Chakra
Age 9–10, Realizer
"I bring forth"

Realizes fruits of previous 8 years
Stands on own merits
Differentiation process
Abstract thinking
Values others' opinions
Aware of authority higher than parents
Community responsibility

10 / SCORPIO
GOD–VISION
Third Eye
Age 10–11, Visionary
"I see"

Learns to raise and sublimate energy
Creative endeavors—time of completion
Vision beyond self to community, nation
What he will be, skills he will develop
Ability to see visions come true

11 / SAGITTARIUS
GOD–VICTORY
Throat Chakra
Age 11–12, Resolver or Finisher
"I am resolute"

Resolution of first 12 years
Victorious, responsible
Author and finisher of his life—he *must* finish what he starts
Senses the whole and larger goal

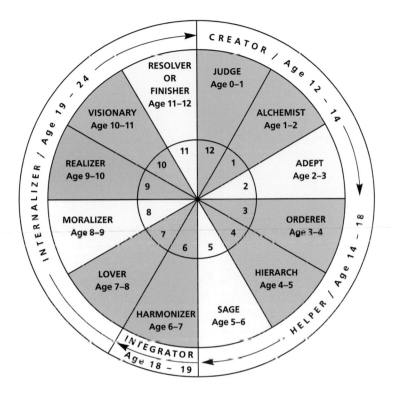

Age 12–14, Creator
"I face life"

Karma descends

Designing life for the next 12 years and what he will be for life

Search for identity outside the family

Hero worship, personality, popularity

Mastery of self within a larger group

Age 18–19, Integrator
"I am centered"

Completing and integrating identity for mission, adulthood

Master finances, right livelihood, dharma

Internal balance of father and mother

Consider chelaship and the masters

Age 14–18, Helper
"I increase"

Identity coalesces

Helper transmutes the indulger

Correct expression of love through community service, group projects

Vertical relationships with God, the masters and role models must be firmly established

Career options, apprenticeship

Age 19–24, Internalizer
"I go within"

Secret rays—building inner identity

Rounding out identity with a sacred labor

Internalization and absorption of mission, education, profession

**Figure 2
Second Twelve-Year Cycle
Age 12–24**

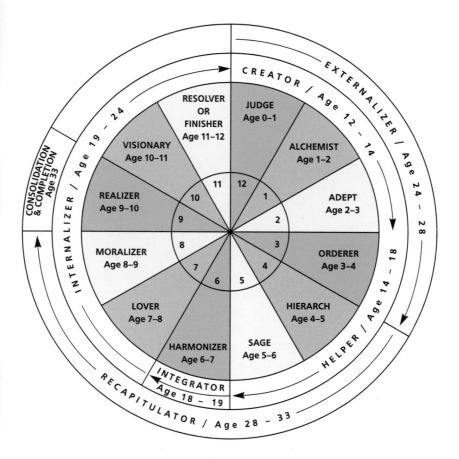

Age 24–28, Externalizer
"I emerge"

New thrust

Identity and personality developed and sealed

Ideal time for marriage

Child has accepted adulthood

Age 28–33, Recapitulator
"I reflect"

Recapitulation of accomplishments

Reevaluating values, ideas, directions

More serious commitment to life

Sense of destiny

Careful planning

Age 33, Consolidation and Completion
"I am who I am"

Integrated personality in God, the Christed One

Self-made man or woman, mastery of life

Moving toward height of career

All qualifications are set

Service to family, community

Approaching midpoint where anything you have must be returned to God

Figure 3
Third Twelve-Year Cycle
Age 24–33

Nine-Year-Old: The Realizer

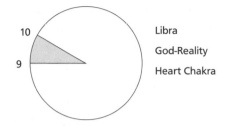

The nine o'clock line of the cosmic clock correlates with the nine-year-old child and relates to the heart chakra, the astrological sign of Libra and the quality of God-reality. At this age the child is bringing into physical manifestation everything he has been building for the previous eight years. And he realizes that what others perceive and think may not be the same as what he sees or believes.

Mrs. Prophet elaborates:

> Now, we need to get through this at age nine so all our lifetime we are not naïve, thinking that everybody else views the world as we do ... or that everybody else wants truth when they really don't want the truth because the truth will make them change their lifestyle.
>
> So, if at nine years old we become realists, realizing these factors, we will have a healthy outlook, not become cynical, not become disappointed, not be shocked by discovering what is in people, but take it as a course of action that this is the world we live in, this is how people are, and have a healthy attitude toward it.
>
> The child gives up the illusion that mother or father can read his thoughts and realizes that people think in many different ways. This process is known as differentiation.

The child becomes aware of the uniqueness of all individuals. Concrete thinking is moving toward the development of abstract thinking, and the nature of illusion becomes a fascination for the child. He's interested in mysteries and perhaps science fiction.

It is at this age that the child begins to become aware of other's impressions of him. If what someone else thinks of him seems more important than his own perceptions of himself, a child may lie, be deceitful, allow half-truths, and choose not to correct false impressions. . . .

If a child prefers this idealized image of himself rather than reality and he falls into dishonesty, phoniness and secretiveness, it brings the creative process to a stagnant point, since praise from another has become more important than the internal process of growth and evolution. . . .

The child has to understand that he is entitled to reality when he can say, "I realize this reality. I've internalized it. I've become it. It belongs to me, I've earned it."

This is a time for parents to be on the alert. If a child is rewarded or praised for something he didn't earn, he needs to learn to be honest about it—with himself and the other person. He also needs to follow through and make any necessary restitution. He will be better able to do this if his parents set the example and give him proper guidance.

If the parents help the child to learn this lesson in a positive way, he or she will understand the need to respect others and to follow the inner guidance of the Higher Self instead of the wanting and wishing of the lower self.

Parents can explain to the child why a particular family or school rule exists, that such rules are for a purpose. And the child will gradually come to accept reality rather than phoniness or dishonesty. He will internalize reality instead of unreality.

Ten-Year-Old: The Visionary

The ten o'clock line of the cosmic clock correlates with the ten-year-old child and relates to the third-eye chakra, the astrological sign of Scorpio and the quality of God-vision. This is a time when the child can learn how to sublimate his inordinate impulses and raise his or her energies. It is an opportunity for the child to develop a higher vision for himself and choose the highest creative endeavors that he is capable of at this age.

Mrs. Prophet tells us:

As the child's identity becomes more complete and separated from his parents, his vision also expands beyond the parents. He has a sense of himself beyond childhood. He's looking to the future. He becomes concerned with what he will be when he grows up, what skills he will develop.

The nearest image that he respects, he'll want to become. He wants to become a policeman. He wants to become a fireman. He wants to become somebody that he sees that has a real neat job and some position of authority.

You can learn a lot about your children by who they want to be like or who they want to become. It's very healthy. Don't tell them, "Oh no, you're not going to become a fireman when you grow up." Say, "That's a great idea. Let's go down and visit the fire station.... Let's talk to the fire chief. Let's go and visit a situation where firemen are in action."

He has a sense of an existence or lifestyle beyond his own domain and can begin to see himself as part of a greater whole—the school, the community, the nation.

God-vision is perverted through self-centeredness and the sense that the world revolves around one's self.... This can manifest in the child as the desire to make things come to him. Here the child is more concerned with popularity, academic achievement, getting his own way, and anything that draws attention to himself.

How about getting him an ornery pet that he can't control—a little dog or a little duck or a goose or something else?... Let him understand that now he has to train this little one and it may or may not obey him, and he may or may not be in control.

Now when the child can begin to see a larger vision, he can begin to postpone his immediate gratification in exchange for the delayed gratification necessary for more complicated tasks or projects, including working in a group....

At the age of ten the child can become the visionary with a practical ability to make those visions happen *now*.... The child has visions. Help him make his dreams come true right then and there in his ten o'clock year. Help him see that a vision can become physical by channeling intelligently and constructively his creative energy.

It's a good time to build a tree house. It's a good time

to help dad finish an extra room or help mother do something that's creative, like sewing.... You know, in the six weeks...before a birthday, it's a time for recapitulation: What have we accomplished in this year? What will I bring to the doorstep of the new year as my harvest of attainment that will now become the foundation of my building for the next year and the cumulative harvest of my life?

So, we look at unfinished things, things that have been begun. The child has begun a scrapbook, but he hasn't finished it. So you say, "Let's finish up the scrapbook. Let's make this complete so we can send it to Grandma or so we can enjoy it and we can put it on the library shelf."

So it's the completion of each year—understanding what the child should take with him, filling in where you feel the child is weak. If he doesn't have any imagination, then this is the time to help him build it.

Eleven-Year-Old: The Resolver or Finisher

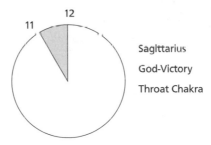

The eleven o'clock line of the cosmic clock correlates with the eleven-year-old and relates to the throat chakra, the astrological sign of Sagittarius and the spiritual quality of God-victory. The completion of this year is the culmination of the twelve-year cycle, the conclusion of childhood in the formal sense. And the child is coming to the place where he needs to have that kind of awareness of himself.

He is entering a new age of responsibility and will benefit greatly if he completes the first twelve-year cycle with a sense of victory. To develop that feeling of accomplishment, the young person needs to complete the tasks he starts and undertake projects that enhance his sense of achievement and accountability, for example, organizing parties, doing projects with friends, helping plan the family vacation.

Young people need to practice finishing their cycles, completing their school assignments and carrying projects through to completion so they are well prepared for the next twelve-year cycle. When they succeed in completing cycles, they establish a momentum that carries them through junior high, high school, college and on through the rest of their life.

As Mrs. Prophet describes it:

> During the whole circle of the twelve, beginning at the twelve o'clock line, the child is the author of his life. And coming back to the twelve o'clock line, he is the finisher. God in us is the author and the finisher of our faith in ourselves, our faith, our hope and our charity.
>
> So above all things, at age eleven, a child must be taught to finish what he starts and not start anything that he is not going to finish. . . . And stick with it—help your children learn to complete projects, help them with the enjoyment, the enthusiasm and the desire of getting that victory. . . .
>
> Children at this age who can master taking responsibility have a good foundation for receiving their karma, which will come on that twelfth birthday. Those who have failed to accept responsibility are likely to become

embittered and vengeful by the return of their karma. They may rebel against their karma and go out and dissipate life, ignore their studies, rebel against the established order by way of rebelling against their karma, have a good time, not get involved in school, blow their opportunities for college and a bright future....

So the love of the return of one's karma—that is conditioned by the parents' attitude to the vicissitudes of life. If they welcome every challenge and don't absolutely destroy themselves because of the failure in business or a personal failure in life, then their children will also have a healthy attitude toward the same diverse conditions that do arise.[2]

Karma's Impact and Resolution

Let's take a brief look at the role of karma in the development of the child and how we can understand our lives in terms of the impact and resolution of karmic conditions. Karma is the Eastern concept of the law of cause and effect, also called the law of the circle, which decrees that whatever we do comes full circle to our doorstep for resolution.

So we understand that karmic return is the result of our physical actions, our emotional responses, our ideas and intentions as well as the impact we make on other people's lives. As Saint Paul said, "Whatsoever a man soweth, that shall he also reap."[3]

Eastern religions believe that karma is a determining factor in each stage of life as well as in the soul's next lifetime. The law of karma necessitates the soul's reincarnation so that she can pay the debt for her misuses of God's light and energy, learn her lessons and move on. And good karma brings opportunity and blessings to the individual. Thus, from lifetime to lifetime we determine our fate by our choices in thoughts, feelings, words and deeds.

The ascended masters teach that karma can be balanced by good deeds and by invoking the violet flame, an action of the Holy Spirit, a sacred fire energy that transmutes the cause, effect, record and memory of sin, or negative karma. The violet flame is also known as the flame of transmutation, mercy, forgiveness and freedom, for it frees the soul from her karmic burden.

We can invoke the violet flame by reciting mantras such as "I AM a being of violet fire. I AM the purity God desires." And as we give this mantra, the "I AM" means "the light of God in me is." So we are saying, "The light of God in me is transforming and forgiving all that is not right. And I AM the pure son or daughter that God desires."

The next step is to determine to be true to our Higher Self and to take the kind of action God would have us take. We can ask ourselves, "What would Jesus do? What would Buddha do? What would my favorite saint do?" And do it!

Let's take a quick look at Mrs. Prophet's teaching about another clock, which she calls the "karmic clock," a way to map our progress in balancing karma.[4]

The Karmic Clock

Imagine a large clock face and see it divided into four equal sections as we did with the cosmic clock. Our karma is distributed over the etheric, mental, emotional and physical dimensions of being.

Mrs. Prophet discussed how karma is distributed over the karmic clock and that when we balance 51 percent of our karma, we have reached a major milestone on the homeward path to God.* She reminded her students that all of us, including children and teenagers, are meant to rectify our misdeeds through prayer, self-discipline and right action. Parents are key, through instruction and example, to their children's understanding of spirituality and self-mastery.

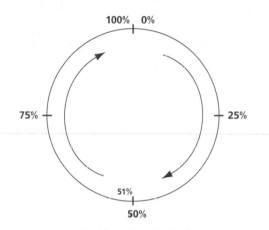

Clocking Karmic Cycles

We cannot overstate the benefits children receive from their parents' loving oversight and discipline. As children internalize what their parents teach them, they prepare themselves for higher learning. As young people transform parental guidance into healthy exploration, and parental discipline into self-discipline, they add to their body of knowledge and forge necessary life skills.

Parents are a gift to their children, even as parents consider their children to be God's gift to them. All of us owe a debt of gratitude to our parents for creating the foundation from which the soul is able to explore new vistas and reach for the stars.

---

*Spiritually, the culmination of the homeward path to God is known as the "ascension." The ascension is the return of the soul to the heaven-world, reuniting with God after accomplishing her mission on Earth.

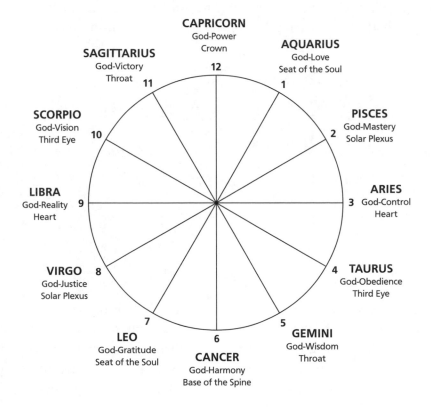

**The Astrological Signs,
the God-Qualities and the Chakras**

4

A Rapid Cycle of Self-Transformation

You have brains in your head. You have feet in your shoes.
You can steer yourself any direction you choose.

—DR. SEUSS
Oh, the Places You'll Go!

At the age of twelve young people initiate a rapid cycle of development and learning. From the ages of twelve through fourteen they repeat the spiritual initiations of the *Judge*, the *Alchemist* and the *Adept*. If the foundations have been well set from birth to age twelve, this early adolescent period can be rewarding.

Teenagers are completing elementary school, middle school or junior high and preparing themselves for high school. During this period, their physical bodies are maturing and social skills are developing. At the same time, emotions tend to be extreme, and young people may be irritable, particularly when they are teased or if they aren't getting along with friends.

The emotional ups and downs of early adolescence are

typically fueled by hormonal activity, and a son or daughter may appear to be making major personality changes. Home can be either a place of comfort and reassurance or a situation of agitation, depending on how parents handle the challenges.

The son may be upset because he is determined to grow taller and more muscular, but his body doesn't seem to be cooperating. As a result he may be down on himself and quick to anger. And he may try to prove his masculinity by strutting around or dominating his sister.

The daughter may be in despair because her figure isn't maturing as quickly as she sees happening with her friends. And she may be embarrassed and withdraw from friends and family. She is also likely to burst into tears at the slightest provocation and to fly into a fury over her brother's teasing.

If positive self-esteem has been developed over the first twelve years, the young person usually navigates the turbulent teens without serious problems. However, if the young person has a momentum of failure, this period of physical change can be difficult. Parental support and encouragement are a comfort, even if the teen doesn't say so.

The Role of Siblings and Birth Order

Another important dynamic is the role of siblings, unless the teen happens to be an only child. Sibling relationships tend to be complicated, sometimes ambivalent, always powerful, and usually enduring. Although we do not consciously choose our siblings, our souls have karmic reasons for coming into embodiment in the same family. It may be good karma or not-so-good karma. If it's the latter, we may find ourselves at odds with each other for no seemingly good reason.

In a best-case scenario, siblings support each other, with the older siblings helping the younger ones and the younger ones looking to the older sisters or brothers as role models. However, the situation may become problematic if any of them are mischievous or rebellious or the siblings are rivals for family attention. Parents can counteract this by positive one-on-one time with each young person plus enjoyable times together as a family.

Sometimes a sibling relationship is ambivalent because the young people have different or opposing needs and desires. While siblings may enjoy some togetherness, they also want to be recognized individually and have their own friends. This can result in vying with one another for special favors or in hurt feelings when one of them feels left out.

Teenagers often need reassurance that they are loved and appreciated for who they are. When parents relate to each one as a special person with his or her own talents and gifts, they are comforted and encouraged.

One of the reasons a sibling relationship is powerful is that it is irreplaceable. We can lose a friend or divorce a spouse, but a sibling is a sibling all of our life. Whether or not sisters and brothers remain close or even friends in their adult life, their memories of growing up together create an inner connection. It is an invisible bond for life. And for many people, the sibling bond is the basis of mutual love and support. It's nice to know that someone knows all about you and loves you anyway!

Why are sibling relationships typically lasting, even in the absence of frequent contact as adults? Each generation reacts to its formative years, even if unintentionally and unknowingly. And our siblings are the people we have known our entire life. They are the ones who shared our family experiences and can confirm our earliest memories. This is a comfort to the heart and soul.

Dreams and Visions of Youth

Young people have their dreams and visions of who they are and who they may become. Every hero or heroine has had a vision and the fortitude to pursue it that has resulted in its realization. Young people are inspired by people such as Mahatma Gandhi, Mother Teresa, Martin Luther King, Jr., Michael Jordan and Charlotte Church (the teenage Welsh soprano who made such a worldwide splash). Teens enjoy the opportunity to investigate the lives of such people when they realize that they can apply to their own lives the keys that led to their hero's or heroine's success.

As I reflect on these outstanding individuals, I realize one thing they all have in common is a specific goal they desired to accomplish. There are also plenty of unknown people from all walks of life who are heroic in everyday life as they pursue their hopes and dreams by helping others to do the same.

Maria Montessori, my favorite educator, dedicated her life to children and youth. And she understood that the best education is about creating an environment that allows the "inner teacher" of the child to emerge. In Montessori's Erd-kinder program, teenagers learn by using their talents and skills to make a worthwhile contribution to society. They further their development by learning various trades and making their own projects or businesses happen.*

Teenagers like to be active and to gain hands-on experience instead of sitting around as passive receivers. What sparks the spirit of teens are activities such as accelerated learning; music, sports, art or drama; writing stories or

*If you are interested in learning more about Montessori's work with older children and teens, I suggest *From Childhood to Adolescence Including 'Erdkinder' and the Functions of the University*, by Maria Montessori.

poems; traveling, a canoe trip down a river or on a lake; helping build a boat or a house; interacting with teens in other countries or helping needy children. The list could go on and on.

The trick is to find that special something that sparks each young person—it's different strokes for different folks. And teens appreciate adults who offer inspiration, friendly support, positive suggestions, helpful guidance and recognition for a job well done.

Teens are also very aware of and somewhat enthralled by the media. They can be inspired in a positive direction by movies such as *The Miracle Worker*, the life story of deaf and blind Helen Keller and her devoted teacher and companion, Anne Sullivan. Or *Forrest Gump*, starring Tom Hanks, a fictional story about a boy with an IQ of 75 who has a uniquely positive perspective on life and becomes wildly successful at everything he does—playing football, fighting in Vietnam, investing in stocks, even starting his own business.

Some of the oldies, classics at this point, uplift us with their humor and nostalgic reminder of basic values. Especially inspiring are movies such as *It's a Wonderful Life*, with Jimmy Stewart, Donna Reed, and Henry Travers as Clarence, the lovable bumbling angel; and the heartwarming production, *The Bells of St. Mary's*, with Bing Crosby as Father O'Malley and Ingrid Bergman as Sister Benedict.

There is a lot out there about angels, soul and spirit. These are no longer terms that are foreign to anyone, including teens. In the upside-down world we live in, it's important for teens to explore the spiritual side of life, to realize that they are here for a special purpose. And they need to hear these kinds of messages: "God loves you. You are a special person. You are a gift to your family and friends, and your job is to develop the gift of you!" What are your hopes and dreams? How will you make them happen?

Twelve through Fourteen: The Creator

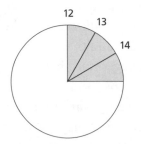

When the first cycle of the cosmic clock concludes at the stroke of the twelfth birthday, the young person begins the second cycle with the residue of life experiences from the first round. The adolescent also faces the initiations of puberty and a thrust of God-power surging through the spiritual, mental, emotional and physical bodies.

Unless a child is an advanced soul, an initiate, or has requested that karma be returned earlier, the spiritual overseers[1] allow the first twelve years (birth to age twelve) for the child to synthesize the blueprint of life, the mastery of the mind, the standards of culture, and the teachings of religion. As children, even if we are old souls, we need to internalize the legacy of thousands of years of culture before we encounter more advanced initiations.

On that twelfth birthday, as the birth clock and the cosmic clock strike 12:00, the lessons the young person didn't master during the first twelve years will come again. For example, the twelve-year-old who had screaming tantrums as a baby when he didn't receive immediate attention will experience similar frustrating situations. Perhaps this time around he will learn to exercise some patience and understand that mom isn't always immediately available to answer his beck and call.

Now the twelve-year-old has additional lessons to master—not only those from the first cycle of this life but also karmic lessons from past lives that weren't mastered at that time. The youth is also designing life for the next twelve years as he searches for his identity outside the family. This begins the time of personality development, identifying with heroic figures, striving for popularity and learning to master oneself in a larger group. Turning twelve usually coincides with entrance into junior high, another milestone for the young person.

In addition to karmic factors, those of the family, school and social experiences have a strong impact on the budding teenager's sense of self-esteem. And supportive and loving parents and siblings go a long way toward helping a young person weather the emotional ups and downs of the teen years.

When the youth turns thirteen, he or she celebrates the entrance into the teenage culture. Many young teens consider themselves quite grown up at that point. Young people at this age look for peer support and tend to form buddy relationships or cliques of similar-age teens.

The thirteen-year-old is also experiencing the onset of hormonal changes, unless puberty has already begun at the age of eleven or twelve, which is not infrequent these days. And with the onset of puberty comes an interest in the opposite sex. Out of shyness, young people at this age tend to eye one another from a distance and to have fantasies about relationships.

At the end of the school day, boys tend to put their energies into competing in sports, investigating technology and surfing the Web. Girls are also into sports and the Web, and they spend many nonschool hours sharing with one another and shopping at their favorite stores. All the teens are fascinated by the advances in space travel, including the *Viking* spacecraft that first landed on Mars in 1976 and the Mars rovers, Spirit and Opportunity, launched in 2003, that have been exploring and sending back data from that planet.

Even though young teenagers tend to hang out with friends of the same sex, this does not stop them from developing a crush on someone of the opposite sex. And some precocious teens begin dating as soon as their parents allow it. Many parents find it more palatable to allow teens to spend time together in a group or in an activity such as biking, skating, skiing, horseback riding, and so forth.

Teens at this age enjoy hanging out at the local mall— girls experimenting with makeup, jewelry and dress styles; boys browsing the gadgets, pinball machines and sports equipment. And when they happen to encounter the opposite sex, it's usually jokes on the surface and shyness underneath.

Parents typically have their own challenges, especially coping with teenagers' fads. Most parents try to respect their teens' choice of friends and appearance, even if they aren't thrilled with the hairstyles, the earrings or other adornments. They can compliment their son and daughter when they apply themselves to their studies and show responsibility at home. And most of all, they can love them simply for who they are. A quick hug of support, a high five for a victory or an affectionate pat on the back can mean a lot to a frustrated teenager.

The preteen and teen years are crucial in determining the direction a young person's life will take. At this age young people are meant to move forward in emotional mastery, social skills and academic achievement. When they do so, they build self-esteem.

Young and Depressed

If instead of moving forward, teenagers get confused, depressed or rebellious, they can get stuck. And they are more apt to fall prey to alcohol, drugs or promiscuous behavior. These activities not only affect the physical body for the worse but also undermine the young person's sense of identity and self-worth.

Fourteen-year-old Cecilia was depressed when she came for her first therapy session. She had all the comforts of a middle-class family, loving parents and an older brother she admired. Yet she had gotten into alcohol and drugs and her life was falling apart. As a part of her recovery program, she entered therapy. As she said, "I can't figure out how I let all this happen, and I'm actually glad my parents caught me. But I'm scared I'll get into it again. Part of me wants to and part of me doesn't."

"Why don't you tell me about these two parts of you?" I suggested.

She responded, "Well, my friends are still into all of the stuff that got me in trouble, and I miss them. That's a big part of me. The other part of me doesn't want to let my parents down again. So I'm stuck."

"It sounds like you think you have to choose between your friends and your parents," I commented.

"Yeah," Cecelia said, "and I shouldn't have to do that!"

"What would you do if it were entirely up to you?" I asked.

Cecelia looked a bit taken aback. She thought for a few minutes, sighed and threw up her hands. "Oh, I suppose they're right. I know I don't want to be an alcoholic or a drug addict."

"Do you know anyone who isn't into drugs and alcohol?" I asked.

Reluctantly Cecelia replied, "Yes, but nobody I'm really close to."

"What could you do about that?" I asked.

Cecelia pondered the question. "I really hadn't thought about it. I suppose I could go skiing with Julie. She's in the program I'm in, too. But I don't know her very well."

"That might be a good way to get to know each other better," I commented. "And you wouldn't feel awkward because you're both in a recovery program."

"That's true," Cecelia admitted. "Maybe I could give it a try. But what if she doesn't want to do it with me?"

"Let's cross that bridge when we come to it," I replied.

To make a long story short, Cecilia and Julie went skiing together and had a good time. They met some other skiers and made some new friends. From then on the sessions with Cecelia were entirely different in tone.

We talked about how important it was to Cecelia that she have friends. And she admitted, "I'm kind of glad to be out of the drug-alcohol scene. My mind is a lot clearer and I'm not feeling depressed. I guess I'll just keep taking it a step at a time."

Cecelia is now in college, doing well, and she and Julie are still friends. As Cecelia said, "Well, one good thing came out of that mess—Julie! Actually, three good things because I'm feeling good about myself and I don't want to do drugs and alcohol. I like me better without them."

Trying on Different Identities

The teenage years are a time that young people try on different identities as they begin to set their sail for adult life. And this occurs particularly in relation to clothes, hairstyles and demeanor in social situations.

Mrs. Prophet comments:*

> It is the beginning of a search for one's identity outside of the family—a "new birth," a time of discovery. We need to encourage it, give a certain amount of freedom, but supply also a certain amount of . . . discipline or direction. . . .
>
> It is a time of observing others—of hero worship, of idols, of awareness of personality and popularity patterns. The young teen begins to identify as part of a group, and cliques come into being. At fourteen, the child emerges as a grown-up "teenage toddler." He's at the two o'clock stage of when he was two years old. . . .
>
> And so, many decisions that the fourteen-year-old makes are made on the basis of what you allowed him to decide at age two and what example you set. You are teaching the two-year-old to be the master at fourteen, and now is your harvest of good sowing as a parent and a teacher. He has evolved from the learning of the mastery of his own being to learning the mastery of himself as part of the larger group. He begins to experiment with many identities.
>
> You can see the many identities of teenagers in the clothes they wear, the punk rock, all the different styles, the different language. It's all trying to put oneself into an identity.

---

*Unless otherwise noted, the excerpts in this chapter are taken from Elizabeth Clare Prophet's lecture "The Freedom of the Child," given July 4, 1983.

It's a good time for drama, good time for acting through plays and coming to a realization of doing these things, putting on costumes, putting on makeup, seeing oneself in different modes, and doing it with a legitimate sense of learning.

Classic dramas such as the Shakespearean plays offer young people a benign opportunity to try on different identities. By acting the parts youth get to try out what it's like to be a betrayer, a hero, a thief, a king or queen, a beggar. The role the person plays can provide the experience rather than the young person having to experiment on the streets and getting into drugs or other shady activities.

Fourteen to Eighteen: The Helper

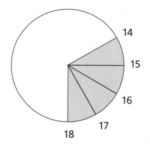

During the high school years the identity of the teenager coalesces as the young person meets the more advanced initiations of the *Orderer*, the *Hierarch* and the *Sage*. Mrs. Prophet called this stage of development the *Helper*. On the cosmic clock, young people once again experience the challenges of control, obedience and wisdom, this time with sexual energy as a major part of the equation.

If these energies are not channeled into constructive activities, the young person may feel physically burdened and try to solve the situation with drugs, alcohol and rock music, all of which propel the energies downward, leading to premature sexual activity or acting out in negative ways.

The teenager needs guidance to develop the emotional maturity and physical control to handle the kundalini energy[2] in a wholesome and creative way. And he needs to discover healthy ways to help himself. Otherwise, he or she may enter into a premature sexual relationship and set an entirely different course in life.

Young people need this time to expand their knowledge and to relate to their peers through sports, drama or group projects. It is a time to develop solid friendships where they can share and pursue their dreams with the support and encouragement of friends and family. This is also a time for community service, concern for the underprivileged and appreciation of culture and family. Many young people make lifelong friendships during these years.

Mrs. Prophet continues:

> These are the senior high school years when the identity of the individual coalesces, and he once again works through the initiations of control, obedience and wisdom—this time with the overlay of having to master the life-force, the sexual energies that are soon going to be upon him or her with the responsibility of marriage and procreation.
>
> These energies, if they become activated, reinforce the horizontal relationships before the vertical relationships are anchored.* In other words, intense involvements with members of the opposite sex rather than the intense involvement with the personality of God, the masters, or

---

*Horizontal relationships are between people. Vertical relationships are with God.

merely the enjoyment of friendships, solid friendships experienced, love in a wholesome and a creative way, sharing of dreams. These need to be made concrete....

Love must be expressed at this age, and the correct expression of love fulfilling the needs of this age is one of the most important examples that we can give our youth. They benefit from a continuation of community service and awareness, concern for the underprivileged, appreciation of culture. Life needs to be full, stimulating and busy at this age. Career options may be considered by apprenticing oneself under or assisting professionals, experiencing the world.

This is the age of the *Helper*. And the helper transmutes the indulger, who can turn this into the age of supreme dissipation and indulgence. The experience of love in friends of the same and the opposite sex needs to be worked out and realized so that it is acceptable to the person who is in that age, so that he does not feel overwhelming guilt for his feelings, a sense of self-condemnation, a sense of having lost or failed. Instead, he or she feels an ability to channel energy, to experience deeply his feelings and yet have these as an ongoing, onlooking force that is shared for the preparation of the responsibilities that are soon to come.

Eighteen: The Integrator

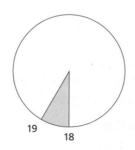

19   18

When the young person reaches the age of eighteen, he or she meets the tests on the six o'clock line of the *Harmonizer* once again, this time harmonizing all that has been learned from birth onward. In particular, the eighteen-year-old is called to maintain harmony within at the same time that he or she is learning to be responsible and harmonious as a young adult.

Mrs. Prophet says:

> The age of eighteen, on the six o'clock line, should mark the beginning of the completion of the self. One is not finished internalizing God as Father and Mother. By the age of eighteen, one has not finished sorting out one's parents. . . .
>
> The age of eighteen is the age of the *Integrator*. I think that the internalization of parents is a lifelong experience, especially if one has had difficulty with one's parents or sharp, traumatic problems. It goes on for a lifetime. One takes the best; one becomes the parent that one internalizes.
>
> In college at age eighteen one studies psychology* and philosophy, analyzes world outlooks, economic policies and systems, and is constantly selecting where he positions himself politically, economically, how he thinks things should be done, many revisions coming back full circle, learning lessons. . . .
>
> It is that point of the *Integrator*—Who am I? What do I want to retain of my entire childhood experience? What will I take with me? What is the greatest I have received from my parents and teachers? How will I integrate this

---

*Psychology as referenced here means the modern study of psychological dynamics. However, spiritually and in the original Greek meaning of the word, psychology also means "the study of the soul" (*psych* = soul; *ology* = study of).

for my own mission and adulthood and in my own responsibilities?

At eighteen years old, the person may believe he does not need his parents, but this is also a stage. His internal self-awareness of father and mother needs to be in some state of balance in order for him to be able to comfortably leave home.

It is unfortunate when a person of eighteen has to leave home in desperation to escape the abuses of parents. . . . The comfortable leaving of home is the best way to leave. The best way is to have . . . the parents' blessing and understanding that the child can tackle the world and that they have done their best.

The integrated eighteen-year-old can determinedly and actively prepare himself for his right livelihood and dharma [his duty or reason for being] without floundering in states of indecision and the perversions of the six o'clock line.*

Since the age of twelve he has been learning to master his finances, becoming economically independent from his parents, beginning to properly care for his needs—his food, his clothing and his lodging. Usually he's going off to college, having to do all these things for himself yet still having a certain dependency of financial support.

It's a good time for apprenticeships to a teacher other than the parents, or for testing one's independence—perhaps only to find out that parents really know more than they are given credit for.

It's a time of consideration of the path of chelaship that one may contemplate taking on between age eighteen and thirty-three, getting ready for the understanding of what it means to have a lifelong relationship to a master.

*i.e., inharmony, self-pity, defensiveness, indecision, feelings of dependency, being grasping, using attention-getting techniques.

Nineteen to Twenty-Four: The Internalizer

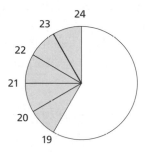

In the second cycle of the seven to twelve o'clock lines of the cosmic clock, the young person incorporates the initiations of the *Lover*, the *Moralizer*, the *Realizer*, the *Visionary* and the *Resolver* or *Finisher*—as the *Internalizer*.

This period of life, age nineteen to twenty-four, is a time when the young adult is meant to round out his or her identity with the tools of a sacred labor, meaning one's livelihood, profession or special service to life integrated with one's spirituality. This time period also relates spiritually to the secret rays, five spheres of light in the inner dimensions of being that have subtle effects on our consciousness.

Mrs. Prophet continues her instruction:

> The building of the inner identity—the search for the identity—is not really concluded until the return to the twelve o'clock line, age twenty-four, when the second full cycle of twelve is completed and once again one begins the Alpha thrust.*
>
> This is the period of absorption, of internalization.

---

*The Alpha thrust is the thrust of Spirit, the going out from God or the descent of the soul by the light of Father. It is charted from the 12:00 to 6:00 lines of the cosmic clock. The Omega return is the coming in to God or the ascent of the soul by the light of Mother. It is charted from the 6:00 to 12:00 lines. (See diagram on p. 109).

Many people spend this entire period in school or learning their trade, learning their work. If one did not learn to "take in" from birth to age one, then that one o'clock line is not going to be the fulcrum for age nineteen, on the seven o'clock line, for the absorption now of one's mission, one's education, one's profession.

Twenty-Four to Twenty-Eight: The Externalizer

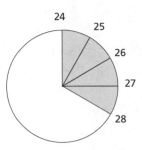

We come back to the twelve o'clock line at Capricorn, at age twenty-four, beginning the third set of twelve years.... This is the age of the *Externalizer*. By twenty-four there has been sufficient opportunity for the young adult to experience all the roles that will be necessary for the fulfillment of his divine plan, including interaction with others in other roles—infant, child, son, daughter, brother, sister, friend, mother, father. And at this particular age it's a very good time to be married and experience that relationship.

It is time for a new thrust. The reason it is ideal for a marriage is because one is finishing up two cycles of the clock before age twenty-four. One needs to know who one is and what one is in order to enter into a lifelong contract with another.

In earlier marriages, both individuals are going through the identity search and may emerge entirely different from what they were before their marriage. They must develop their identity before they can surrender it to the greater love of the whole in a marriage union.

So the sealing of the development of the identity and personality at twenty-four—this is a certain stage of Christhood whereby one can give oneself, then, to the greater union. . . .

If the child did not get through this process, if he didn't enter those twelve gates twice—you can think of the whole first cycle as the Alpha thrust, the whole second cycle as Omega return—coming through the door of initiation on those twelve doors to the Holy City, if you have not helped your child through that by age twenty-four, he is not ready, not ready for marriage, not ready for life, and he can be the perpetual child.

It is as if a conscious choice were made to refuse to grow up, evolve and accept responsibility. I've had parents complain to me that their children will not leave home. Their adult children in the twenties and beyond are staying at home. They're still cooking for them, still doing their wash, still paying their bills, and they cannot get them to move out of the house.

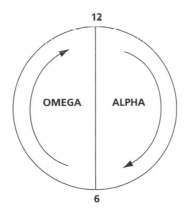

The Alpha Thrust and the Omega Return

Twenty-Eight to Thirty-Three: The Recapitulator

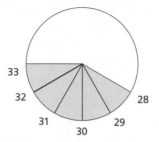

At age twenty-eight we are meant to reflect on what we have accomplished in life, in education, in career, in marriage since our age of maturation, age twenty-one. We can think of this as the age of the *Recapitulator*. When we look back at the seven-year cycle from age twenty-one to twenty-eight, we get a picture of our adult principles and achievements, whether they are in keeping with our life goals. If they are not, this is the time to self-correct.

Age twenty-eight is also a time when people who find themselves off track may decide to end a marriage that isn't working, change employment in order to correct their course, or renew their commitment to higher values.

Mrs. Prophet comments:

> It's undoing what one can see, at an age of maturity, that one should not have done and looking toward that initiation of age thirty-three. The twenty-eight-year-old realizes he's not going to be in his twenties much longer, he is getting on to his thirties, and there's an inner sense of approaching the line of the thirty-three.
>
> A sense of destiny and careful planning is in order. A sense that life is not forever, and even human resources do run out. There is a certain small amount of slowing

down from the age of being a teenager, when there was no end to the boundless energies of life.

So between twenty-eight and thirty-three, it's reaching for that Christ,... moving toward that integrated personality in God, which is the Christ. It's on the nine o'clock line of absolute God-reality.

One should know one's self. One should have dealt with one's psychology, parental associations, rejections. One should have gone through the lines of the clock and corrected these aspects of childhood. Even if you have no remembrance of those years, you do prayer work on them; you name the conditions and the problems that could have existed. Search your own personality, seek professional help if you like, seek counseling.

Thirty-Three: The Springboard of Life Consolidation and Completion

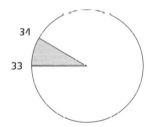

By the age of thirty-three we are meant to have a real sense of "I am who I am" and to be in charge of our adult life. We are likely established in a career and married and raising a family. And this is a time when service to God and the community comes more into focus. We are meant to have integrated our personality with our Higher Self and to be living our spiritual values.

Mrs. Prophet teaches:

Thirty-three is an age of consolidation and completion. It's the time of the self-made man and the self-
made woman. You should be at the height of your career
or moving toward that height, which peak should be at
the age of forty. One should be able to carry on the mastery of one's life from thirty-three or earlier, if one has
gotten it together earlier, all the way through the years of
retirement and beyond....

This is the time of the real springboard of life, where
all of your qualifications are set, you've learned what
you need to do. You can be a professional at what you're
going to be. You do it well, and you get in a spiral of
service to your family, to your community.... You're constantly engaged in giving of yourself, you're approaching
the midpoint where everything you have must be returned
to God.

Let's say forty is middle age. The first half of your
life up to age forty is the going forth; the second half is
the return. On the return you pick up the dropped
stitches, you balance the karma, and you give, give, give
and give to life because you are whole, you are complete,
you are confident, you are settled down. You know who
you are, and now is that moment of election...to give
one's Christhood in service to the world.

The thirties generally mark an acceptance of the role
of being an adult, even in this time in history of the denial
of chronological age and the search for eternal youthful-
ness in outer appearance, which is equated with eternal
abandonment, eternal freedom and nonresponsibility.

The person who fully integrates his personality can
express any of the personages on the cosmic clock whenever
he is called to do so. On an ongoing basis we are called to be

the *Judge*, the *Alchemist*, the *Adept*, the *Orderer*, the *Hierarch*, the *Sage*, the *Harmonizer*, the *Lover*, the *Moralizer*, the *Realizer*, the *Visionary* and the *Resolver*.

We are also called to be the *Creator*, the *Helper*, the *Integrator*, the *Internalizer*, the *Externalizer*, the *Recapitulator*, and ultimately at age thirty-three, to have *Consolidation and Completion* of our development as an integrated personality in God.* When we are on track we become one with our Real Self.

As we move on through the life cycles and chart our progress on the cosmic clock, we continue to refine our character and behavior, and we may find it helpful to keep track of our progress.

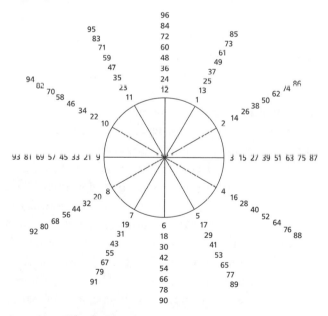

The Years of Life on the Cosmic Clock

---

* See figures 1–3, following page 80.

The Real Self and the Dweller Self

As we examine ourselves we often discover parts of ourselves that keep getting in our way. Some people develop neuroses, which can be personally detrimental and harmful to family life. Here is a snapshot of what happens energetically and psychologically.

Mrs. Prophet says:

> Energy which moves unhampered from one age to another forms an upward coil for the healthy, so-called normal maturing child. Trapped or blocked energies form the neurotic personalities.
>
> Now what is a neurotic personality? What is a psychoneurosis? It's an organized, crystallized complex of emotional defenses used by the ego to protect itself against the early damage from parent and parent substitutes. These neurotic defenses are usually maladaptive and create problems in adjustment to life.
>
> Neurotic defenses are often unconscious and are usually like homogenized milk in the ego. They're islands of substance in suspension which the individual is not necessarily aware of but affect his behavior....
>
> Blocked, stored energy may result in creating its own magnetic forcefield, having a pull of its own. These pulls between evolving healthy drives and neurotic drives set up the drama of life, the ambivalences within the psyche, and the two opposing forces Freud originally referred to as the life force and the death instinct.*...
>
> We sometimes talk about the Real Self and the unreal self, or the Real Self and the synthetic self. We speak about the dweller-on-the-threshold as the conglomerate

---

*Freud later referred to these forces as the aggressive instinct and the sexual desires.

of the carnal mind, which would be the whole combination of unresolved encounters at the subconscious level.

The earlier the energy is perverted, the more difficult it is to correct. In fact, psychiatry has found some of the damage done at the oral stage, birth to one year old, almost untreatable, especially conditions of addiction, narcissism, sociopathic behavior and other character disorders, which can all be the result of a disturbance in the very early relationship with the mother.

Often in order to correct the cycles, the person must undo the original perversion and then cycle around the clock rebuilding each step until he has sufficient mastery in the God-qualities that he can use freewill choice to choose to identify with the God-qualities rather than with the perversions.

The situation here is that the person is subconsciously harboring ill feelings toward authority figures. In order to move on, the individual needs to consciously resolve the negative feelings and surrender the desire to resent, blame and retaliate.

Spiritually, the totality of these negative aspects produces what has been called the dweller-on-the-threshold, a distorted or false personality that perverts the true personality as outlined on the cosmic clock. This dweller of distortion lives inside of one's self and can pop up as instantaneous hatred or a vengeful reaction.

When we get to the core of the false personality we have created, we need to love God and ourselves enough to do the spiritual work of transforming that dweller into the reality of who we are meant to be. We can do this by establishing the forcefield of light known as the "tube of light," giving prayers to Archangel Michael for spiritual protection, and calling to the angels to bind and remove that vindictive dweller.*

We can determine to transform that not-self into the pure qualities of our Christ consciousness, our Real Self. When we let go of the dweller self, we can express our true identity as sons and daughters of God.

Cycles of Life:
Chart the Cycles for Yourself and Your Family

In order to maximize the expression of who they really are and want to be, many of my clients find it helpful to chart their personal cycles, as well as those of family members. Once parents understand their own cycles and those of each family member, they are better able to make the most of each cycle in a positive way and help their family to do so too. Parents can also better appreciate their child's development at each age and not get exasperated because they are expecting more mature behavior.

Teenagers are often intrigued by looking at their cycles in relation to their hopes and wishes. They can chart events and opportunities in their life, pinpointing their areas of strength and those needing further development. And families can have a fun time discussing the ins and outs of the various challenges and opportunities. Somehow it seems a lot easier to use a chart to discuss the kind of difficulties that everyone in the family has likely met at one time or another.

---

*For an explanation of how to invoke your "tube of light" and Archangel Michael's protection and for instruction on dispelling the dweller-on-the-threshold, see pp. 123–30.

Birth: God-Power

If you would like to make a spiritual chart for yourself or your family, draw a circle like the face of a clock. On the twelve o'clock line place the day, month and year of your birth. At the hour you were born you began your first initiation, of God-power, under the spiritual hierarchy of Capricorn. As Mrs. Prophet tells us, "The initial thrust of power was your first breath and your first cry, and the initiation you passed was to seize the flame of life and claim it as your own."[3] So put a victory mark on that line!

Age One: God-Love

On your first birthday you began the initiation of God-love under the hierarchy of Aquarius. Your soul was infused with an increment of love. The initiation was to identify with love, to love yourself and to increase your love for mother and father, sisters and brothers, and caregivers you may have had. Perhaps your parents or scrapbooks can give you an idea of how you did with that initiation. Were you smiling or frowning in the pictures?

Age Two: God-Mastery

With your second birthday you entered the initiations of the hierarchy of Pisces. The test was to develop God-mastery, including mastering your emotions. Have you ever watched a two-year-old have a tantrum? It's a sight to see! When you were a baby, your parents comforted you and tried to please you when you cried. Now they wanted you to *stop* crying.

You were also turning into a master explorer, examining everything you could put your hands on or put in your mouth. This was likely both amusing and trying for your parents. Most two-year-olds push, pull or squeeze everything in sight as they toddle around happily investigating their small universe. And yet they can get upset and cry at the drop of a hat. How did you do as a two-year-old explorer?

Age Three: God-Control

When you reached your third birthday, you had a budding awareness of your own identity, "I am who I am," under the hierarchy of Aries, and you were confronted with the initiation of God-control. By now you knew your name and had the posture of "I want to do it all by myself!" Your ego was developing, and your parents would have been wise to encourage you to do things by yourself. They might have made the mistake of doing it for you, which would have been frustrating to you. In this year you were establishing a sense of identity that would accompany you through life. How did age three work out for you?

Age Four: God-Obedience

Your fourth birthday brought you the tests of God-obedience under the hierarchy of Taurus. You were gaining increased mastery of your body and the physical environment. And you might have exhibited stubbornness from your parents' point of view, but this was actually stubbornness for good reason. That tenacity was your will to be, to have a separate identity, to master the physical aspects of your life. And this was important for your development. What kinds of activities did you like at the age of four?

Age 5: God-Wisdom

When you had your fifth birthday, you came to the tests of God-wisdom under the hierarchy of Gemini. You were tested on the wisdom of the mind—would it be your human mind or the mind of your Higher Self? Your mental development was increasing, and you may have been rather precocious. You wanted to learn! You did this through games and playing. The genius of Maria Montessori is that she knew this, and many children have benefited from her work. What do you remember learning when you were five?

Age 6: God-Harmony

When your sixth birthday arrived, you came under the hierarchy of Cancer and the flow of God-harmony. And you learned about the flow of energy-in-motion. You were tested through your emotional reactions and how you handled the energy moving through you. Your parents may have been tested if you got sulky or had tantrums. What feelings or emotional reactions did you have as a six-year-old? And how did you handle them?

Age 7: God-Gratitude

Now let's examine your seventh birthday, when you were working on mastering the energies of love, this time under the hierarchy of Leo. Your test was to learn about one kind of practical love, God-gratitude. This would have been a good time for you to learn to behave lovingly, develop manners, learn how to be polite and say "thank you." You would also have been gaining an increased awareness of how to respond positively in the family setting and in the classroom. How did you handle the tests of love when you were seven?

Age 8: God-Justice

When you came to your eighth birthday under the hierarchy of Virgo, you explored God-justice in a practical sense. You likely had encounters with siblings or friends or your teacher where you felt "It's not fair!" And when you experimented with sharing, that may or may not have felt good. You learned what "fair" meant in interactions with other people. You developed standards of justice and injustice. What do you remember about your sense of fairness when you were eight years old?

Age 9: God-Reality

As you celebrated your ninth birthday, you came under the hierarchy of Libra and received a new awareness, an awakening to the Holy Spirit and God-reality. You likely began to gain a greater measure of independence. And your test was how you would define reality. Probably when you were growing up, the media presented all kinds of cartoons and stories and fantasies. You might have identified with some of the characters, but most likely your teachers and parents tried to keep you anchored in a more objective reality.

On a spiritual level, one of the saddest dramas is when parents or teachers tell children that "angels aren't real" or "there isn't any God," and children believe them. How necessary is the role of the parent who can reaffirm the higher realities and teach the child the importance of faith and honor and integrity! What was your sense of reality when you were nine years old?

Age 10: God-Vision

Coming to your tenth birthday, your test was vision, God-vision, under the hierarchy of Scorpio. And it likely involved what is known spiritually as "the test of the ten," the lesson of learning to give selflessly. You might have had difficulties in sharing with friends. Or perhaps you had a great year because you enjoyed sharing. And you may have developed your own vision of what life is all about. You might have started to recognize the rhythm of ups and downs in life and begun to think about what you would do when you grew up. What was your vision of yourself and of life when you were ten?

Age 11: God-Victory

Arriving at your eleventh birthday, your tests would have been given by the hierarchy of Sagittarius in the spiritual flame of illumination. Your goal was to claim God-victory, not only for that year but also for the twelve-year cycle. If life didn't seem to be unfolding the way you envisioned it, you might have become resentful. If your friends weren't being friendly or treating you fairly, you may have wanted to quit or get even with them.

The positive way of handling these situations would have been to try to do your best no matter what—and if you had a problem with your friends or teacher or parents, to talk it out. In other words, you would have needed to persevere with a positive attitude. Think back about that year and ask yourself, How did I do? What did I learn? Write down your answers.

I suggest you look over the first twelve years of your life, and ask yourself, What in myself do I need to master that goes all the way back to my first twelve years? And decide to do it now. It's never too late to self-correct.

Age 12 to 24: Second Time Around

You might continue to examine your self-mastery according to cosmic clock cycles by charting your major life wins and losses over the next twelve years, beginning with your twelfth birthday (twelve o'clock line).

Keep on Clocking: Adult Cycles

The third round begins at age twenty-four, the fourth at thirty-six, then forty-eight, sixty, seventy-two, eighty-four, and upward.

When I analyzed five rounds as I approached my sixtieth birthday, I realized a few old habits were stubbornly hanging on. I made a promise to myself to trade each one for a specific higher quality or positive approach. I asked God to help me, and I set new goals for myself and made them happen. This has become a rewarding, ongoing process. And I continue to remind myself, "If old habits try to surface, I'm not going there!" I suggest that everyone say "goodbye" to outworn habits and "hello" to a higher aspect of self.

Spiritual Formulas for Family Harmony and Soul Liberation

The inner power that can liberate our soul and promote family harmony is the blue fire of God, which we release through the throat chakra. Archangel Michael releases that fire when we call to him for protection and for the will of God to manifest in our life.

You can prepare yourself for the action of the blue fire by invoking the light of God to cleanse and uplift your consciousness. First, take several deep breaths, exhaling slowly, as you focus your attention on your heart. Then envision a shower of brilliant white light enfolding you, descending from your I AM Presence* into your aura, consciousness, being and world as you give the following mantra:[1]

---

*For a pictorial representation of your I AM Presence, Christ Self and soul, see the Chart of Your Divine Self, p. 330.

TUBE OF LIGHT

Beloved I AM Presence bright,
Round me seal your tube of light
From ascended master flame
Called forth now in God's own name.
Let it keep my temple free
From all discord sent to me.

I AM calling forth violet fire
To blaze and transmute all desire,
Keeping on in freedom's name
Till I AM one with the violet flame.*

Now invoke Archangel Michael's blue-fire power and protection:

TRAVELING PROTECTION

Lord Michael before,
Lord Michael behind,
Lord Michael to the right,
Lord Michael to the left,
Lord Michael above,
Lord Michael below,
Lord Michael, Lord Michael
    wherever I go!

I AM his love protecting here!
I AM his love protecting here!
I AM his love protecting here!

---

*Recite the "Tube of Light" and "Traveling Protection" decrees one time, three times, or as many times as you wish, in multiples of three.

Once you have invoked the "Tube of Light" and Archangel Michael's protection, you are ready to give the fiery decree for the angels to bind the dweller-on-the-threshold. This is an alchemical formula for casting out the conglomerate of the carnal mind.

The dweller decree is a dynamic prayer that liberates us from layers of unreality—the scar tissue of bygone traumas that needs to be cleared for our soul's resurrection. When we give this decree, we champion our soul and defend our right to be who we are as our Real Self.

Center in your heart and envision the angels binding and casting out the dweller-on-the-threshold and freeing your soul as you give the decree:

I CAST OUT
THE DWELLER-ON-THE-THRESHOLD!

In the name of my beloved mighty I AM Presence and Holy Christ Self, Archangel Michael and the hosts of the LORD, in the name Jesus Christ, I challenge the personal and planetary dweller-on the threshold, and I say:

You have no power over me! *You* may not threaten or mar the face of my God within my soul. *You* may not taunt or tempt me with past or present or future, for I AM hid with Christ in God. I AM his bride. I AM accepted by the LORD.

You have no power to destroy me!

Therefore, be *bound!* by the LORD himself.

Your day is *done!* You may no longer inhabit this temple.

In the name I AM THAT I AM, be *bound!* you tempter of my soul. Be *bound!* you point of pride of the original fall of the fallen ones! You have no power, no reality, no worth. You occupy no time or space of my being.

You have no power in my temple. You may no longer steal the light of my chakras. You may not steal the light of my heart flame or my I AM Presence.

Be *bound!* then, O Serpent and his seed and all implants of the sinister force, for *I AM THAT I AM!*

I AM the Son of God this day, and I occupy this temple fully and wholly until the coming of the LORD, until the New Day, until all be fulfilled, and until this generation of the seed of Serpent pass away.

Burn through, O living Word of God!

By the power of Brahma, Vishnu and Shiva, in the name Brahman: I AM THAT I AM and I stand and I cast out the dweller.

Let him be bound by the power of the LORD's host! Let him be consigned to the flame of the sacred fire of Alpha and Omega, that that one may not go out to tempt the innocent and the babes in Christ.

Blaze the power of Elohim!

Elohim of God—Elohim of God—Elohim of God

Descend now in answer to my call. As the mandate of the LORD—as Above, so below—occupy now.

Bind the fallen self! *Bind* the synthetic self! Be *out* then!

Bind the fallen one! For there is no more remnant or residue in my life of any, or any part of that one.

Lo, I AM, in Jesus' name, the victor over death and hell! (repeat sentence two times)

Lo, *I AM THAT I AM* in me—in the name of Jesus Christ—is *here and now* the victor over death and hell!

Lo! it is done.

After giving the dweller call, invoke the violet flame to transmute any residual debris or sense of burden:

VIOLET FLAME FROM THE HEART OF GOD

Violet flame from the heart of God, (3x)*
  Expand thy mercy through me today! (3x)
Violet flame from the heart of God, (3x)
  Transmute all wrong by forgiveness ray! (3x)
Violet flame from the heart of God, (3x)
  Blaze into action through all to stay! (3x)
Violet flame from the heart of God, (3x)
  O mercy's flame, fore'er hold sway! (3x)
Violet flame from the heart of God, (3x)
  Sweep all the earth by Christ-command! (3x)
Violet flame from the heart of God, (3x)
  Thy freeing power I now demand! (3x)

Take dominion now,
To thy light I bow;
I AM thy radiant light,
Violet flame so bright.
Grateful for thy ray
Sent to me today,
Fill me through and through
Until there's only you!

I live, move, and have my being within a gigantic fiery focus of the victorious violet flame of cosmic freedom from the heart of God in the Great Central Sun and our dearly beloved Saint Germain, which forgives, transmutes, and frees me forever by the power of the three-times-three from all errors I have ever made.

_____

*Repeat each line three times when the notation "(3x)" appears.

Seal the alchemical action of your mantras and decrees by accepting and amplifying the light you have called forth:

And in full faith I consciously accept this manifest, manifest, manifest! (repeat three times) right here and now with full power, eternally sustained, all-powerfully active, ever expanding, and world enfolding until all are wholly ascended in the light and free! Beloved I AM! Beloved I AM! Beloved I AM!

Complete the transformational process by invoking the presence of your Holy Christ Self and by affirming your higher qualities and the victory of your soul's mission:

INTROIT TO THE HOLY CHRIST SELF

1.   Holy Christ Self above me,
Thou balance of my soul,
Let thy blessed radiance
Descend and make me whole.

Refrain:*

Thy flame within me ever blazes,
Thy peace about me ever raises,
Thy love protects and holds me,
Thy dazzling light enfolds me.
I AM thy threefold radiance,
I AM thy living presence
Expanding, expanding, expanding now.

---

*Recite the refrain after each verse.

2. Holy Christ Flame within me,
   Come, expand thy triune light;
   Flood my being with the essence
   Of the pink, blue, gold, and white.

3. Holy lifeline to my Presence,
   Friend and brother ever dear,
   Let me keep thy holy vigil,
   Be thyself in action here.

And in full faith I consciously accept this manifest, manifest, manifest! (repeat three times) right here and now with full power, eternally sustained, all-powerfully active, ever expanding, and world enfolding until all are wholly ascended in the light and free! Beloved I AM! Beloved I AM! Beloved I AM!

Complete the transformational process by affirming your higher qualities and the victory of your soul's mission:

I AM AFFIRMATIONS

I AM a soul of light.
I AM walking the path home to God.
I AM the will of God manifesting in my life.
I AM the wisdom of the Christ and the Buddha.
I AM the compassion of the Divine Mother.
I AM the purity of my Higher Self.
I AM one with the flame of Truth.
I AM the servant of the Christ in all.
I AM joyfully balancing my karma.
I AM lovingly obedient to my Real Self.
I AM passing my soul initiations.
I AM winning my ascension.

THE PRAYER OF
SAINT FRANCIS OF ASSISI

Lord,
Make me an instrument of thy peace.
Where there is hatred let me sow love;
Where there is injury, pardon;
Where there is doubt, faith;
Where there is despair, hope;
Where there is darkness, light; and
Where there is sadness, joy.

O Divine Master,
Grant that I may not so much
Seek to be consoled as to console;
To be understood as to understand;
To be loved as to love.
For it is in giving that we receive,
It is in pardoning that we are pardoned, and
It is in dying that we are born to eternal life.

SEALING BENEDICTION

May the words of my mouth and the meditations of
my heart be acceptable in thy sight, O LORD, my strength
and my redeemer.

PART TWO

Karmic Factors in Family Psychology

5

The Psychology of the Soul

We sow our thoughts, and we reap our actions.
We sow our actions, and we reap our habits.
We sow our habits, and we reap our characters.
We sow our characters, and we reap our destiny.

—AUTHOR UNKNOWN

When we think about our basic values, ideas and motivations, we realize that they reflect the family we grew up in. Whatever we sensed, saw, heard and felt as children continues to live within us and to mold our posture toward life.

Why is this true? Because everything is energy—we are energy. From conception on we absorb energy patterns: values, thoughts, feelings and even complex interactions with our parents, siblings and others who live in the home or are close to the family. Unconsciously, subconsciously and consciously we adopt the energies of the people around us. All of this becomes a part of us unless we make a specific effort to modify our consciousness.

Our Origin: Human or Divine?

Our soul has been born many times and has seen many things on Earth and in heaven. And each lifetime the soul is born into a particular family for the mastery of her karmic lessons. Consequently, a major dynamic in our growing-up drama comes through our genetic inheritance and family interactions, which prompt us to react in certain ways. Our attitudes, thoughts, feelings and behavior relate to family and individual karma coming down the ancestral lineage.

Thus, in order to understand our psychological predisposition, we need to examine the impact of ancestral as well as family patterns. For example, let's say great-grandfather had a temper, grandfather had a temper, father had a temper, and we have a temper! Or great-grandmother played helpless, grandmother played helpless, mother played helpless, and so do we! Of course, some of our positive qualities, gifts and talents also relate to the family line.

Some of these negative patterns exist just below the surface of awareness in the subconscious—what we mean when we say, "It's just on the tip of my tongue." Other patterns reside deep in the unconscious where they are relatively inaccessible except when they surface as a result of similar experiences later in life or in our dreams.

The core spiritual problem is the acceptance of our origin solely in human parents instead of realizing that we are also sons and daughters of Father-Mother God. When we accept our origin as human, we identify with the human self. However, when we accept a divine origin, we also identify with our Higher Self and the patterns of our "causal body."

The causal body consists of the seven concentric spheres of light and consciousness that surround our I AM Presence,*

*See the Chart of Your Divine Self on p. 330.

our God Presence, in the planes of Spirit. It contains our spiritual resources and the energy records of our virtuous acts throughout all of our incarnations.

This higher energy body is the storehouse of the talents, graces, gifts and genius we have garnered by exemplary service on the "seven rays." These rainbow rays that originate in our God Presence and emerge through the prism of the Christ consciousness are a source of inner power, wisdom, love, purity, sense of truth, quality of peace, and ability to forgive. When we identify with these higher qualities and follow the footprints of Christ, Buddha, Lao Tzu and advanced adepts, we transcend our human ancestry and access our soul's divine nature.

Our soul was originally formed as a divine being, created in the image of the Father-Mother God. Yet as a result of lifetimes of experience on Earth, the soul no longer radiates her pure divine essence. Instead, the soul carries an overlay created by her misuse of God's energy as well as what we take on from other people. That misqualified energy distorts the original nature of the soul and is often the source of psychological problems.

When we reflect on the psychology of the soul, we realize that the soul is uplifted when she is congruent with her original nature and is in a state of unrest when she is at odds with it. So when we find ourselves anxious, distressed, and we can't quite pin it down, we need to look at what might be upsetting our soul. We may be carrying energy of other people that the soul has taken on in moments of conflict. Our soul may be angry with people who have hurt us even though we consciously attempt to be gracious. Or the soul may be carrying unfinished business from another lifetime.

These disturbing energy patterns are often alive and well

in what is known as the "electronic belt." This belt sits in the aura around the lower position of the physical form. It is the repository of negative energy that we have created or taken on in unpleasant interactions with other people.

The soul desires to be freed of this burden (and we do too!), but we don't know how to release it. So we hold onto the negative energy unintentionally. That accounts for the occasional temper tantrum, the quick retort, the uncomfortable feeling in the pit of the stomach when we have an argument with someone or are confronted with disapproval of our actions. The solution is to understand the psychology of the soul and to help heal the wounds of the soul even as we would try to help anyone who is hurting.

How do we contact our soul? We touch our soul in moments of bliss and moments of pain. Nearly always, when we are in bliss our soul is uplifted, and when we are in pain our soul is despondent.

Ana's Story

I remember Ana, a client of mine, who came for therapy because she had an uneasy feeling that she couldn't put her finger on. Supposedly her life was moving along okay, and she hadn't had any major accident or other upheaval. Yet she found herself bursting into tears for "no particular reason," as she put it. And she would wake up in the morning feeling depressed.

Ana was an accomplished single woman, who had a good job. She had a few close friends but her family lived in Spain. She had immigrated to the United States and didn't feel like she fit in at first. She said that was getting better and her bigger problem was a feeling of despondency that she couldn't figure out.

At the beginning of the therapy session, she asked me, "Is it possible that my soul could be depressed?" And I said, "Yes." She told me that she had this uncomfortable feeling deep in her belly and that she would wake up at night with bad dreams. They were usually about her running away from someone and being scared that he would catch up with her and hurt her. Yet she hadn't had that kind of experience in this life.

I asked Ana to close her eyes and try to contact her soul. She was quiet and unmoving for several moments, and then she said, "I think my soul is angry with me."

I replied, "Ask her why she is angry."

Ana did so and reported that her soul was angry because she wasn't protected. She asked her soul what that meant, and her soul said, "He was chasing me, trying to hurt me, and I froze."

"Ask her when this happened," I responded.

After a few minutes, Ana suddenly opened her eyes in surprise. "I can't believe this," she said, "but she says it was when I was my great-grandmother married to my great-grandfather. And he was chasing her to beat her because she had defied him."

"How did she defy him?" I asked.

Ana closed her eyes again. Several minutes later she spoke. She had tears in her eyes as she told me that her soul had been very angry and rude to her husband and then took off running.

"Ask your soul, 'What can I do for you right now?'" I replied.

Ana was quiet for a time and then opened her eyes and smiled. "My soul says he wasn't a bad man. He was actually a good man. All he wanted was some respect." She added, "He told her, 'I'm not chasing you to hurt you. But I want you to stop being rude. I need you to respect me.'"

She closed her eyes again and whispered, "I know you are right, and I do love and respect you. Please forgive me."

Several moments later Ana stretched and sighed with relief. "Do you want to know what happened?" she asked somewhat mischievously.

"Certainly, if you want to tell me," I responded.

"Well, he put his arms around me and gave me a big hug. I feel at peace with him now."

"Is there anything more you need to do right now?" I responded.

She closed her eyes again. After a lengthy period of time, she opened them and smiled. "My soul wanted me to know that he really was a good man, that he just wanted me to love and honor him. I feel at peace now. Isn't that amazing?"

As we discussed what had happened, Ana realized that her soul had been burdened for lifetimes because she had not apologized, and her marriage in that life had been miserable from then on. But now she felt her soul's relief that she had inwardly taken the step she hadn't taken in that life.

"I can't believe how much better I feel," she said. "I guess helping my soul come to peace with herself is what it was all about. I hope his soul has had some healing since then."

We talked about how Ana could continue the healing process by having regular "soul talks." She came in for a few more sessions to work on other issues, but the dialogue with her soul had been a major turnaround. On a recent Christmas card from Ana, she wrote, "Love from me and my soul—we're together, and doing just fine!"

Reclaiming Our T'ai Chi Wholeness

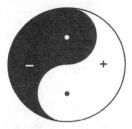

The T'ai Chi
The Polarity of Wholeness Showing the Flow of Energy
from Spirit to Matter, Matter to Spirit

Elizabeth Clare Prophet has described the kind of soul distress that Ana had felt as a distortion of our original T'ai Chi wholeness. She has taught her students spiritual methods for handling soul pain, including clearing the electronic belt so that the soul has the best opportunity to fulfill her mission.

Mrs. Prophet described the electronic belt:

> Extending from the waist to beneath the feet, the electronic belt is similar in shape to a large kettledrum. It contains the aggregate records of an individual's negative karma. That kettledrum is sealed. And what is accessible to us is determined . . . before each embodiment.
>
> On certain days of the year under certain cycles, . . . certain things open to us where we can see them; we can have an incisive view of ourselves and our [karmic] records. And if we are alert . . . and do our Astreas* and do our calls to the violet flame,† we can clear those records.

---

*Astrea is the Elohim of the fourth ray of purity; "Astreas" are decrees, rhythmic spoken prayers, given to direct God's light into individual and world conditions.

†The violet flame, a high-speed spiritual energy, transforms negativity into light, thus giving us a sense of freedom from inner burdens. For more information, see pp. 88, 127.

But if we bob along in life without studying our-selves, studying our moods, our emotions, the workings of our mind, what thoughts lodge there, what memories come to the surface, if we are not students of ourselves and observers—and objective observers, because that is what we need to be—then we can go along having all kinds of mishaps and unexpected experiences.

We can have all kinds of tensions, depressions, hap-piness, joys alternating with the sunshine and the shad-ows and the storms—and yet not see that there is a plan, there is a map, there is a puzzle that can be dealt with.[1]

The soul is originally created by the Father-Mother God as a fiery ovoid, a concentration of divine light, energy and consciousness. By the mysterious hand of God an individu-alized being is formed as a trinity of sacred fire: the I AM Presence, the Higher Self and the soul.

The shining I AM Presence is a reservoir of God's light and consciousness. And the Higher Self (Christ Self, Buddha Self) is the mediator between the God Presence and who we are as souls in embodiment. Spiritually, our soul looks to the Higher Self, the I AM Presence and the Father-Mother God for guidance.

Even as our Father-Mother God comforts and enlight-ens us through our Higher Self, we are intended to love, nourish and teach our children. And we are called to heal our personal psychology and to eliminate the barriers we may have erected between our soul and God. Through self-study, getting help when we need it and invoking the violet transmuting flame, we help our soul heal old wounds and progress on the spiritual path.

"*Mackerels*" *in the Subconscious*

Mrs. Prophet instructed her students on the kinds of issues people have at a subconscious level. She gave this information in a humorous discourse about "mackerels," yes, fish! I'll give you a few highlights from her lecture because it's an interesting way to describe the negative aspects of our psychology that typically shock us when they suddenly erupt like a big fish jumping out of the water.

These shadowy elements lurking in the subconscious are an important and tricky aspect in our world. They lie just below the surface of awareness and come up at the most inconvenient times. We typically wish we could reverse what we end up saying or doing, but it's usually too late.

The subconscious is the focal point for the negative aspects of father and mother, generation to generation, all the way back through the family lineage. For those of you who may have seen it, the movie *My Big Fat Greek Wedding* is an example of family lineage. In this hilarious and poignant movie, the main character tries to free herself to have a life beyond the expectations and limitations of her Greek family.

The mackerels are a representation of the negative energy that is passed down from our parents, grandparents, great-grandparents and all of our progenitors. We carry that energy around with us until we replace it with positive aspirations, ideas, emotions and actions. In order to do this we build on our positive attributes and transform the negative aspects. This means recognizing and redeeming all that is contrary to who we are as God's progeny.

The worldwide culture is suffering from unconscionable happenings—terrorism, war, crime, vandalism,

kidnapping, child abuse, prostitution, drug trafficking—
the list is endless. And there is an inordinate focus on
murder and mayhem in the entertainment field. Our West-
ern culture, in particular, seems bent on producing explicit
TV and horror movies and anticipating negative thrills
with a kind of shuddery delight. It's as though our conscience is asleep while the culture promotes excitement—
the gorier the better.

For the most part children are attracted to horrifying
images only because the culture promotes it. And teenagers,
especially through the influence of the pop culture, get a
certain thrill out of the danger aspect. In a way it's like
extreme sports—the adrenaline surge is enlivening. But
sports are a much more healthy way to get a boost.

Sometimes people subconsciously try to neutralize horrifying experiences of their own by watching horror films.
There is a certain comfort in the old "If you can't beat 'em,
join 'em" kind of thinking. But it's risky. The more we take
in ugly or horrifying images, the more we sully our consciousness.

We can reach the point where we don't see any harm in
it, and then we wonder why we have difficulty synchroniz-
ing with the Christ consciousness. It's similar to what happened to Adam and Eve in the Garden of Eden. They bought
the Serpent's lie: "Ye shall not *surely* die," and they forfeited
the innocence of their souls.

The Amazing Process of Re-Creation

If we would outwit the cultural decline, we need to wrestle with our own psychology. And spiritually, we can benefit
by following the example of the biblical Melchizedek,[2] who
overcame the concept of a human lineage and a human

ancestry. He had the consciousness of being without human father and mother. He had resolved his human-consciousness psychology. He saw himself as an independent emissary of God, walking the earth as the priest of the Most High God.

We too can walk the earth as emissaries of our Maker. As parents and teachers, aunts and uncles, grandfathers and grandmothers, we can be influential in a positive way. We can help our children and youth perfect their talents. If young people are athletically inclined, we can encourage them to excel in the sport they choose. When they get excited about reading books or writing poetry, we can be interested and supportive. If their interest is in art or sculpture or music or dance, we can arrange for lessons. By our response to their interests, we encourage youth to express their talents and broaden their horizons.

And in order to do this, we need to wrestle with our psychology. We can have the best of motives and yet walk into the kitchen and start an argument with somebody because that person has hurt our feelings. We need to pull the reins on the human consciousness and say, "Whoa. I'm not going there. I'm going to resolve my hurt feelings and relate in a positive way."

We are more than our mind, our feelings and our reactions to other people. We are living souls, sons and daughters of God. And every time we win a wrestling match with ourselves, we feel relief that we have outwitted the dweller. We defeat discouragement every time we win a victory within ourselves.

We can choose to rebuild the entire structure of our self. And the way we rebuild it is brick by brick. If we were to knock down the whole building of self all at once, we would have no identity. Our identity is based upon our self-definition—we need to accent the positive and refine the negative aspects of our selfhood.

As Mrs. Prophet taught her students, "When you first become really profoundly aware of your own imperfection, your own sense of sin, your own sense of limitation, and you are a chela [a student or disciple] on the Path, you run to your guru and say, 'I want to be rid of this human creation. And I want to be rid of it all at once. Take it from me.' I was such a chela. I ran to Lanello* and I ran to El Morya. And they said, 'We can't do it. If we would take it from you, we would take away the whole ball of wax of your human identity.'"[3]

All of us benefit when we replace an element of whatever isn't our true self. And the violet flame is a great way to do it. This action of the Holy Spirit transforms whatever we are ready to release and put into the sacred fire. What is necessary is a determination to change for the better. Once we surrender that negative attitude or behavior or reaction, we claim a virtue to take its place. We practice that virtue until it becomes our natural response. And that's the wonderful process of re-creating one's self.

Access the Gifts of Your Causal Body

Our parents may have had a spiritual realization of themselves as representatives of the Father-Mother God and passed higher qualities on to us as virtue. Yet we may or may not have an awareness of the divine qualities that reside in our causal body.

---

*The ascended master Lanello was embodied as Mark L. Prophet, Mrs. Prophet's husband. They served as messengers for the ascended masters.

The Causal Body

This magnificent spiritual treasure-house contains the good works manifested by our soul in past lives as well as the good works we achieve in this life. And this virtue and awareness is accessible today, moment by moment, as we need it. We can access the spiritual resources and creativity stored in our causal body by invocation to the God Self, our I AM Presence, in the name of the Christ Self, our Higher Self.

We may also have received tremendous good from our parents as they offered us love, taught us obedience and endowed us with wisdom. They may have blessed us with compassion and inner strength and wise guidance as they raised us. They may have taught us good habits and positive morals. We may have experienced their devotion to God, their sense of honor and integrity.

Now back to those mackerels—the perverted or false images of father and mother lodged in our electronic belt. There they sit—our mackerels and ancestral lineage—all in the subconscious and unconscious, all awaiting transmutation.

Until the ancestral mackerel consciousness is transmuted, our true identity, our T'ai Chi in Matter (the Father-Mother God within) is obscured.[4]

Mrs. Prophet describes the action of transmutation:

> In the process of transmutation—the action of the violet flame—all of the atoms and molecules of energy have been [spiraling] for repolarization to our own great central sun, the individual I AM Presence, the center of that Presence, the white-fire core.*
>
> So each time you invoke the violet flame, the energy—its misuses, its particles—is broken down... cycling back to your great central sun. These particles rise over the fiery coil, moving in a clockwise direction, going to the center of Being, and you are attaining greater light in your causal body.... This doesn't happen all at once, but it happens each time you use the violet-flame mantras and decrees.[5]

Through the process of transmutation, we move to the center of our own higher consciousness, forged and won in the earth plane. This spiritual consciousness can carry us all the way home to the Father-Mother God. We do this by generating the fruits of good works for our God, our families and ourselves.

As Mrs. Prophet says: "What a great gift it is from Mother Mary and the Holy Spirit that we would know how to tackle the mackerels, how to tackle the ancestral tree to get to this place of this glorious higher consciousness. Higher consciousness is not just a mist; it is a very specific outlining of God. This [Tree of Life] is the real family tree.... It is our real family of the mystical body of God on Earth and in heaven."[6]

*See the Chart of Your Divine Self, p. 330.

All of this relates to the scriptural description of the "twelve manner of fruits of the Tree of Life"[7] stored in the spheres of our causal body. So we undertake the alchemy of transmuting the mackerel consciousness of our human lineage and claiming the fruits of our good works.

Going through this process of identifying ancestral substance and replacing it is challenging. It has been likened to cosmic surgery. It is difficult to detach ourselves from family and family attitudes and reactions because of the sympathetic ties we have with our family. But once we do so, we can have the consciousness of a Melchizedek, without the human sense of heredity but made like unto the Son of God.

To Be or Not to Be Who You Really Are

All of us share certain karmic lessons with our ancestors and with our birth family, and this is a major reason that one after another in a family line may live out the same or similar patterns.

A quick temper, a rebellious nature, a passive approach to life, a predisposition to alcoholism or drug addiction, may run in families where parents, grandparents and great-grandparents have had the same or similar problem. Such families are drawn together by the magnet of mutual karmic lessons they need to learn. It takes great determination and often some type of professional assistance to break out of these family patterns.

As we move along in life, we may find ourselves unwittingly re-creating with our spouse and children the hurtful experiences we had in our family during our formative years. We may have said to ourselves, "I'll never do that when I grow up and have my kids!" And yet we find ourselves doing the very same thing we said we would never do.

How many of us have had the experience of going home to visit our parents and as we walk in the door of that old family home, we suddenly find ourselves thinking, feeling, even reacting just as we did as children? It is a very disconcerting experience to find our five-year-old coming out in the thirty-five-year-old we are today.

All it takes is a trigger: some way our mother or father behaves that annoyed us as a child or youth, and all of a sudden there we are again, annoyed and reactive! It isn't so easy to stop it because it's an automatic, unconscious reaction until we make it conscious. Once that reaction is conscious we have a choice—to be annoyed and irritable or to be nonreactive and pleasant.

This is one of the reasons we need to observe our reactions and perhaps seek counseling in order to catch ourselves and change reactive habits. We can benefit from the help of a compassionate therapist as we strive to transform negative attitudes, feelings or behaviors that sabotage our lives and hurt those we love.

People who remember past lives often come to realize that certain intellectual or emotional patterns have been around for thousands of years. For example, I have had clients who remember the fall of Atlantis and how they contributed to it. These people entered therapy because the aftermath of the emotional trauma on Atlantis was affecting their attitudes, emotions and behavior in this life. Others born and raised in the United States this time around, and never having traveled beyond its borders, have talked about European and Asian embodiments, including details about their family life and the customs of the village or tribe.*

---

*Past lives and energy therapy will be a major focus in my next book, the seventh in my Sacred Psychology series, coming in 2005.

For these individuals, the karmic predicament of having unresolved past-life patterns has drawn a birth family in this life that was bound to bring the past-life drama to their attention. Many of us, adults and children, have a similar situation. The good news is that thoughtful people can recognize their own reflection in the magnifying mirror of the family and decide it's time to change!

Of course, ultimate change comes through partnering with our Higher Self. When we have a higher vision, we can mobilize the will and determination to transform outmoded patterns of behavior. So we offer our prayers for God's mercy and intervention. We invoke the action of the violet flame to transmute the cause, effect, record and memory of our pack of negative karma. We determine to conduct ourselves honorably in whatever provoking situations we encounter. As we do this, we free ourselves to express who we really are as souls of light with a special mission to fulfill.

When we assimilate who we really are as sons and daughters of God, we can transfer this understanding to our children and youth and those we meet along life's way. We can build on the good we have gleaned from our parents and teachers and develop more inner strength, wisdom, compassion and sense of honor. When we identify with our higher qualities, we find it easier to deal with the push-and-pull of karmic substance that shows itself in resentment, dislike, irritation, a sense of injustice, rebellious behavior, and human egos vying with one another.

We can also benefit from understanding our personal astrology, the impact on our lives of planetary cycles as they relate to our astrological birth chart from a spiritual perspective. And this doesn't mean the catchy write-ups we see in the newspapers! Our birth chart defines our karmic challenges in this life, and we benefit from being aware of them. Thus, it's a good idea to be aware of our astrology and to keep it updated by an astrologer who takes into account the spiritual dimension of who we are.[8]

One more point: We need to give up whatever it is that keeps us from letting go of past hurts or thinking we have to be compensated for every injustice.

Now you might be thinking, "This person owes me. He's hurt me for thirty years, and you expect me to walk away and forget it?" The answer is "Yes!" When we find ourselves revolving a hurt or injustice, we need to ask ourselves, "Who is hurting me right now?" Once we realize we hurt ourselves by dwelling on the past, we are more ready to forgive and let it go. And who benefits from that? We do!

Every day we have the opportunity to re-create ourselves, to become a new man, a new woman, to go beyond any sense of limitation or karmic bondage. As the days' victories add up, we increase our spiritual attainment and synchronize more and more with our Real Self. And that is the highest benefit we can achieve.

A Twinkle of Mirth

One of the most important results of that synchronization with our Real Self is a feeling of joy and happiness. Yet sometimes people who get overly serious on their spiritual path sacrifice the sense of joy. Which is a big mistake. We need to fill our cup of joy to the brim and let it run over. Joy and happiness are contagious and the world is in need of it. To be spiritual doesn't mean to be somber. It means to celebrate the gifts of God, to offer them to others. And a gift that is appreciated by everyone is joy and laughter.

Joy uplifts our spirits. Laughter helps us relax, boosts our immune system, stimulates the endorphins (our body's natural painkillers) and lightens us up. When we find something humorous in a crisis, we feel more of a sense of control of ourselves. And joking about the problem actually helps us rise above it. Laughter is also a great way to release pent-up anger or frustration. Just make sure you laugh at yourself and not someone else. Best of all, laughter is free and good for all of us.

Mary Ann O'Roark, executive editor of *Guideposts*, writes about an experience she had in church during a time of troubles in her life. She focused so intently that she developed a bad headache. Then the minister came to the verses in the Gospel of Luke about Jesus wrapped in swaddling clothes and announced that the baby was "strapped in waddling clothes." Even though Mary Ann buried her face in her hands to stifle her laughter, it was to no avail. But guess what? When the giggles stopped, the headache was gone.[9]

No matter what the circumstances, we always have spiritual recourse. And that includes the uplifting joy of laughter. As the ascended master El Morya tells his students, "A twinkle of mirth is needed on Earth."

6

The Karmic Equation of Marriage and Family

Kindness in words creates confidence.
Kindness in thinking creates profoundness.
Kindness in feeling creates love.

—LAO TZU

Marriage and family in the context of the culture in which we live today is for many of us quite different from the milieu of our formative years. We face somewhat different challenges today, and of course we bring with us our karmic momentum. We continue to play out our karmic drama until we learn our lessons.

Our children are born into our family, loving and needing to be loved, their souls knowing they have a destiny to fulfill. As they move through life, they explore who they are and who they may become. They exercise their talents and skills and learn from their mistakes. They experience their inner world even as they relate to family and friends. They study and play and learn. And along the way they come face to face with their karma—in the person of family members, friends and teachers.

Good karma with other people fosters strong friend-ships, positive interactions, feelings of love and caring, and a sense of mutual support and seeing eye to eye in problem-atic situations. Not-so-good karma tends to create blocks in relationships, feelings of wariness or open dislike of someone even if one hasn't had a lot of interaction with that person. Such negative karma often instigates difficult interactions and prickly relationships.

When we set ourselves to learn our karmic lessons, we are more at peace with ourselves and more real in our relation-ships. We are better able to exercise our talents and skills, to learn from our mistakes, and to empathize with our loved ones. And this sets the tone for more loving relationships.

The Role of Karma in Marriage

Let's look at a young couple, Alan and Grace, who had been married for two years and were experiencing marital difficulties. In the glow of love before marriage, their rela-tionship had seemed wonderful and the future bright. Together they could conquer the world! Yet when they came in two years later for marriage counseling, they were very much on edge with each other.

Alan was drawing back from Grace because he felt she was "too possessive and needy." He went on to explain that his business required him to be more than full time, and since he was the provider in the family he expected Grace to understand that. Grace was upset with Alan because they didn't have the loving relationship they had when they were first married. She tearfully explained that he had "shut down" to her. She was hurt by his lack of emotional support and companionship and angry at the way he ordered her around.

They came in for counseling when they realized that their married life was on a downhill slide unless they could resolve these problems. As Alan put it, "I love Grace, but I wish she would get her own life together!" And Grace replied, "Why did we get married if we are going to live separate lives! We're supposed to be a team," to which Alan retorted, "A team, but not Siamese twins!" Grace promptly burst into tears. Alan apologized but kept his distance.

Once they both calmed down a bit, I asked them to give me a thumbnail sketch of their birth families. As they did so it became clear that their marital problems were directly related to unresolved problems Alan and Susan had with their own parents.

To put it in a nutshell, Alan had felt smothered by and rebellious toward his loving but engulfing mother and was now determined to be his own person. Grace had been dominated by and angry with her overprotective and "father knows best" father, yet she had relied upon his advice and support so much that she didn't trust herself.

What happened when the proverbial honeymoon was over and Alan and Grace began to have major rows? Grace wanted Alan to love her but not to overpower her, yet she relied on him whenever she encountered household or personal challenges. Alan withdrew emotionally because he felt engulfed by his wife's neediness, yet he insisted on setting the rules of the house. Grace was hurt by his emotional withdrawal and angry at his bossiness. They ran headlong into major clashes and wounded feelings on both sides.

These sharp disagreements were painful and heralded lessons each one needed to learn. Alan needed to realize inwardly that Grace was not his engulfing mother but his loving wife. And on a practical level he needed to recognize that household rules could be a partnership instead of Alan being in command. Grace needed to learn to stand on her own two feet as a person and in the daily routine of the home instead of expecting Alan to take charge while resenting him for being overbearing like her father. And they both needed to take time together to reignite their love for each other.

Since they were both spiritually oriented, I asked them what they thought their karmic lessons were. As we explored this topic Grace began to realize that she was too dependent and what she really resented was her own dependency. She said she thought her karmic lesson was to learn to take charge of her own life and at the same time to love her husband unconditionally. She determined to do just that. However, she added, "I need to know that Alan loves me."

This was a wake-up call for Alan. He was startled because he did love Grace and believed she understood that. However, as they discussed it, Alan began to realize how much Grace needed him to say the words "I love you" and to show it in loving behavior.

As Alan examined himself, he realized he had been seeing his wife through a lens of annoyance with his mother. And that while he did need to claim his own space, he didn't have to withdraw love or order his wife around. He decided that his karmic lesson was to be true to himself—particularly in relation to women—but to do so lovingly. He began to make an effort to behave more lovingly toward Grace and respectfully toward his women co-workers.

Both Grace and Alan recognized their issues were karmic lessons, which helped them a great deal in turning their behavior around. They understood that although they might have the best intentions, until the karma was balanced and the lessons learned, they would likely play out the same drama in raising their children. Neither one of them wanted that to happen. Alan and Grace committed to marriage counseling and spiritual work to resolve these issues. As they did so, their relationship improved dramatically.

The Challenge of Changing Times

Couples today are caught up in an accelerated pace of life due to changing times. John Gray, Ph.D., in his book *What Your Mother Couldn't Tell You and Your Father Didn't Know,* describes the dilemma this has caused. He reminds us that we have had major social and economic changes in the past forty years that have revolutionized our traditional roles as man and woman.

He writes:

> In a sense, we could say that all men are out of work. They no longer have the job they held for countless centuries. They are no longer valued and appreciated as providers and protectors. Although they continue to do what they have always done, it suddenly isn't enough to make their partners happy. . . .
>
> In the same way that men are out of work, women are overworked. Not only are they mothers, nurturers, and homemakers, but now they are also providers and protectors. . . . How can a wife be expected to be relaxed, sensitive, and pleasing to her husband when an hour before she's had to fight a man for a cab?[1]

Obviously we require new relationship skills, or perhaps we might say "updated" relationship skills. I believe the basic skill remains the same—to relate to one another, heart to heart. When we come from the heart, we interact from a position of compassion, understanding and a will to negotiate differences.

From my perspective as a psychologist and minister, I see most people interested in creating a loving and satisfying marriage relationship. However, as Dr. Gray points out, the traditional ways of doing this are changing. For today's typical working man, the increasing complexity of his job or profession requires full-time attention—and more. Men work overtime and come home hoping for sanctuary from the world, yet they are still husbands and fathers. When the father retreats from the family scene, the working mother is even more overloaded and the marriage relationship definitely suffers.

Julie's Dilemma

As Julie, in a fit of exasperation, told me, "I don't have enough energy or hours in the day to do all I'm trying to do! My husband has a demanding job and I never know when he's going to get home. So I'm the one trying to take care of the children and the household. After they take off for school, I race to work. And then I need to be sharp because I'm the administrative assistant to our corporate manager.

"After work there's ferrying the kids to activities and making sure they get their homework done—not to mention making dinner, doing the laundry, the vacuuming and the dishes. The kids try to help, and Ben does the best he can, but I'm doing a double job. I stay up late at night to catch up, and it's hard to be as professional as I'd like to be on the job. It's too much!"

Julie and I talked about shortcuts and how she could lighten her workload. She had a talk with Ben and the children, and they took it to heart. They began doing as much as they could to help, and the situation is getting better. However, Julie is still stressed-out a good bit of the time. She told me ruefully one day, "I really love my family, but sometimes I wish they would disappear for a week or two so I could catch my breath!"

Julie's dilemma is not unique. Many a mother is accomplishing the household tasks at the end of the day that her mother could take the whole day to do—and consequently many women find themselves exhausted. When both husband and wife are tired and stressed-out at the end of the day, the wife often feels emotionally unfulfilled, and the husband, unappreciated.

Modern Women Feel like Imitation Men

Women often tell me they feel like imitation men, partly because the work world is still mostly a man's world. In their jobs women have few female role models, and the ones they have do not necessarily guarantee success.

As Billie, a woman in the insurance business, told me with a sigh of frustration, "My supervisor is a woman and you might think that is a good thing. I'll tell you differently. She's basically what we used to call 'a tough broad.' She tries to copy the managing style of the men in the office, and it isn't working. And yet I understand. How does a woman act professionally, strong, assertive and feminine at the same time? That's quite an art to master—not to mention coming home from work, waving a magic wand and becoming the sweet little wife!"

I could understand her frustration. And yet, as we talked about it, we both realized this is true for many women today. It's a major challenge that necessitates a woman's juggling her masculine and feminine natures so she can be (1) businesslike at work while retaining her femininity, (2) nurturing at home while doing a fair amount of the physical work, and

(3) still remain a balanced person.

John Gray's solution:

> A woman can most successfully cope with the stress
> of experiencing non-nurturing relationships in the goal-
> oriented work world by coming home and experiencing a
> loving, caring, and cooperative relationship.... Through
> "talking" in a non-goal-oriented way, without having to
> get to the bottom line, without having to solve the prob-
> lem, a woman is gradually released from the domination
> of her masculine side.... The art of listening to a woman
> does not entail solving problems or offering advice....
> A male listener's goal should be helping his partner
> regain her feminine/masculine balance.[2]

A woman might add that she would appreciate a warm
hug and loving, focused attention as she shares her day. And
it's not necessary for her husband to agree with everything
she says, only to listen with an understanding heart.

Modern Men Feel Unappreciated

In turn, the husband may feel powerless to make his
wife happy. His job is demanding, and he realizes that she is
working too. But in most cases he is still the major bread-
winner. So he feels his job takes precedence. If he dares to say
something like that, it's like gasoline and a match! His wife
gets upset; he feels misunderstood. And he may withdraw
from her, even though he still loves her, because he can't handle the drama.

John Gray describes these dynamics succinctly:

> When a man loves a woman, his primary goal is to
> make her happy. Through history, men have endured
> the competitive and hostile world of work because, at

the end of the day, their struggles and efforts were justi-
fied by a woman's appreciation. . . .

If a man is not appreciated, he feels his work is
meaningless; his wife's unhappiness confirms his defeat.
To him, her unhappiness signals that he is a failure.
"Why should I bother to do more?" he asks himself.
"I'm unappreciated for what I do already."[3]

What does a husband really want from his wife? A
woman's happiness lets her mate know that he is loved and
relieves his own stress from a hard day on the job. As Gray
describes it, "Her warm responses are like a mirror reflecting back to him a shining image. . . . Her happiness is like a
shower that washes away the stressful grime of his day."[4]

When the husband catches on to the fact that his wife
feels nurtured when he communicates with her, he can rekin-
dle the sparks of affection. And when the wife realizes that
her husband is thirsty for her appreciation and offers it honestly, he feels nurtured. Mutual understanding and respect
generate love and appreciation—and foster loving relationships.

The Story of a Modern Job

I remember a couple I counseled some years ago where
the husband was so burdened that he compared himself to a
"modern Job." You may remember that Job was the biblical
character who lost his family, his possessions and his health,
and whose three "friends" commiserated with him in a most
obnoxious way.

Figuratively speaking, any long-suffering person can be
said to be "as patient as Job."[5] And Jake wasn't trying to
be humorous—he was quite serious in equating his troubles
with Job's.

Jake couldn't seem to please his wife, and his friends weren't much help because their marriages weren't in very good shape either. Jake had challenges at work that his wife didn't seem to understand. They had little to no intimacy anymore. And he felt he was losing his sense of spirituality. It seemed that everything he touched turned to ashes. He actually believed he had failed his family—and God.

His wife, Susan, explained that she received little or no appreciation for her contribution to the family—making the meals, doing the household chores, taking the children back and forth to activities, trying to cheer her husband up, and doing all of this in the absence of affection from Jake.

As she put it, "When we were first married, we were really happy. We loved each other. We spent time together. We enjoyed each other's company. But now it seems like we can't connect. Sometimes I feel like I'm living with a stranger. I don't even know what he's thinking these days. And that makes it difficult for me to talk to him, much less be affectionate."

I asked each of them in turn, "Do you love your husband (wife)?" And the answer was the same: "I don't know." So we began rebuilding a relationship that had gone awry even though both partners had tried what they considered to be their best.

Fortunately, these two people were spiritually aware and understood the role of karma in marriage. They wanted to understand their karmic lessons, but they were so discouraged that they didn't know whether that would make a difference. As they put it, "Maybe we have too much karma to be together." And I replied, "Let's work on your relationship with each other, and in the process you will likely recognize your karmic lessons. Then it will be your choice whether or not you stay together."

To kindle the process I had each of them, separately, write down their deepest hopes and dreams, including what they hoped for from their marriage. I was struck by a certain similarity in their lists, even though they hadn't communicated with each other.

They both wanted to be loved and appreciated. And each one blamed the other for not being sufficiently loving and appreciative. Jake said that anything he said to Susan was wrong in her eyes; Susan said Jake never took what she said seriously. They both wanted affection, but they had different modes of expression that they valued.

Susan valued kind words from Jake, his listening to her when she was describing her day, and nonsexual affection. Jake valued Susan's listening to him unwind from the workday, the way she would do little thoughtful things for him, and her giving him space.

Jake and Susan had very different styles of showing affection. Susan felt that everything she did for Jake was an expression of her affection. Jake didn't see it that way. He wanted more of a sexual relationship, but a sexual approach minus real affection turned Susan off. They were at an impasse with each other, and yet there was an underlying desire to resolve the dilemma.

I gave them relationship homework. I asked them to spend a private hour with each other, once a day, before coming to their next session. They both looked shocked. Jake said, "I can't do that! My work schedule is too crowded as it is." Susan said, "How can we be alone when the children are there?"

Now their "children" were in their early teens and had plenty of activities to keep them busy. But, in fact, that brought up another problem because it was usually Susan who ferried them around. The only time this couple was getting together was at dinner, when and if Jake could get home in time. And dinnertime was really more of a family time, listening to the kids, talking about vacation plans and settling family disputes. It was hardly an intimate moment for Jake and Susan.

I suggested they choose one evening a week when Jake and Susan would go out to dinner without the children and focus on appreciating each other. This met with various levels of resistance. Jake, an accountant, wasn't sure he could do that because he was expected to stay at work until the job was done. I asked him if he was really going to lose his job if he took his wife out for dinner one evening a week. He rather sheepishly said, "I guess not." When I pointed out that this might be a subconscious way of avoiding intimacy, he relented.

Susan said she didn't want to leave the children home alone because she was afraid they would get into fights with each other. I asked her if it might not be a good thing for them to have to work it out with one another instead of having her intercede. After a few minutes of thoughtful pondering she said, "Maybe so. I guess what I'm really afraid of is that Jake and I don't have much to talk about when it isn't about the children."

That gave me another inroad. I asked both of them to make it a point in their private time to share themselves with each other instead of discussing the children. They were a bit uneasy but agreed to try it. I set up another session for a week later and told them I was looking forward to their progress. At that point they laughed and I could see they were beginning to relax and trust the process.

When they came back in, I asked, "Well, how did it go?" They both seemed reticent to talk about it. I kept probing and finally Susan said, "Well, I don't think we're very good at this. We didn't really share our feelings with each other." Jake said, "I agree we're not very good at this. Susan kept telling me to share my feelings—and I got tired of listening to that. So I shut up."

"So, basically, you both cooperated to keep your distance from each other," I commented. "What was the point of that?"

Long silence. Then Jake said, "Well, when I try to share my feelings, she says I'm not." And Susan said, "It doesn't feel like sharing your feelings to me!"

I could see we were getting nowhere fast. So I asked them to talk to each other during our session, and I would coach them so that they would feel more comfortable with the process. They both, rather hesitantly, agreed. And I was thinking to myself, "What have we gotten into here? Do they really have any love left for each other?"

So we began. I asked Susan to tell Jake something she really appreciated about him. She thought for a few minutes and then said, "Jake, I appreciate the way you work so hard for the family." I commented that this was not about Jake as a person, it was about what he was doing for the family.

Susan: "Jake, I appreciate the way you used to bring me flowers before we had the kids." ("Oh boy," I thought to myself, "here we go." And sure enough, there we went.)

Jake: "So you can't think of anything that you like about me today, huh?"

Susan: "I was just trying to follow Dr. Barrick's instructions. Maybe this whole thing is a waste of time."

Jake looked impassive, but I could feel his inner alarm.

So I interrupted, "Jake, would you please tell Susan something you really appreciate about her?"

To all of our amazement Jake teared up a little and said, "It's really hard for me to say my feelings, but I do love her."

Reluctantly I intervened again. "Jake, please say that directly to Susan instead of talking to me."

Long pause. Hesitantly, Jake tried, "I do love you, you know."

With tears in her eyes, Susan responded, "That's like manna to my soul, Jake. I love you too."

"Would the two of you give each other a hug?" I asked.

Hesitantly they did just that. And I could feel the spark of affection between them. So I waited a bit.

They rather hurriedly sat back down and resumed their posture of distance from one another. So I asked, "How did that feel to both of you?"

Jake was silent, but Susan said, "It felt really good. It didn't have the sexual undertone it usually has."

I thought Jake was going to react to that, but he remained silent. "Jake, how was it for you?"

"It was okay," he said. I waited. He added, "Okay, so we don't do the nonsexual thing very often. But that doesn't mean I don't love her. It's just that it's hard for me to be affectionate without it turning sexual."

There, the secret was out. So I said to Jake, "Then it must be hard for you to give Susan hugs."

"Yes," he said.

Susan was listening to all of this thoughtfully. Then she asked Jake, "Is it really that hard to be intimate with me and not sexual?"

He nodded. So I gave them a different prescription for this week. I asked them to give each other nonsexual hugs once a day until our next session. I told Jake that practice makes perfect and if he wanted Susan to respond, she needed to know that he loved her for the person she is, not just for her body.

I also gave Jake a hint from the boyfriend of a teenage girl who had trouble hugging without getting sexual. He handled it by taking a momentary time-out and trying to lift his car by the bumper. I said to Jake and Susan, "He told me it always worked. So I thought I'd pass that along." They both laughed, and a certain rapport that had been missing was reestablished in that brief moment.

Jake and Susan needed quite a bit of coaching and reassurance before they were able to enjoy affectionate, nonsexual touching. But once they mastered this skill, they felt closer to each other. Susan realized that Jake was really trying, and how hard it was for him. Jake realized that Susan had been feeling little to no affection from him because it was always sexually tinged.

Of course, this relationship had a happy ending or I wouldn't be telling you about it. Jake and Susan began enjoying their weekly night out and giving nonsexual affection to one another. Jake was proud of his self-mastery, which he assured me "wasn't easy!" And Susan felt loved for the first time in many years. Inevitably, they both asked if it was time for them to renew their sexual relationship.

I suggested they take a weekend away from the kids and do just that. So they got a babysitter and had a wonderful weekend! As Jake told me when they returned, "We really love each other after all." And Susan added, "He's my sweetheart again."

The couple came in once a month for several months until they felt sure that they wouldn't slip back into their old habits. The last I heard from them, they were sharing with each other, nurturing each other, and feeling comfortable with their sexual relationship.

As Jake put it, "I'd probably still like it more often, but I love Susan and I want us to be making love and not just having sex." Susan added, "Now that I feel Jake's love and don't feel pushed to have sex, I enjoy making love. It's really different, you know."

And that is very true. A sexual relationship based on genuine love for the other person is very different from having sex because the body demands it. A number of couples I have worked with have decided to be celibate for various periods of time in order to deepen their spirituality. And I always suggest that they continue to share their thoughts and feelings, appreciate each other verbally and use gentle words.

With respect to the karmic factor, Susan summed it up during our last session: "Our karmic lesson is crystal clear: to talk out our problems and express our love and appreciation for each other." Jake nodded and added, "I no longer feel like a modern Job! My life seems to have turned a corner."

Regenerating Love and Respect

When a couple comes in for marriage counseling, I usually discover that one or the other is under some kind of pressure and pulling back from the partner in order to get some space.

As one harried husband told me, "I need some breathing room! Every time I turn around, Kim is either telling me I don't love her because I don't show affection or telling me to go away because I'm oversexed! And she's always telling me what to do. I'm a grown man, and I'm tired of it. I feel like a yo-yo and she's pulling the strings."

Kim couldn't believe what she was hearing. And she was quick to defend herself. "Stan's just using that as an excuse not to relate to me!" she began. "Either he ignores me completely or he wants sex, and that's not my idea of relating. And as far as me pulling yo-yo strings, if he'd do his part around the house with the kids, I wouldn't be on his case."

"Okay," I responded, "it's obvious that you are both upset, but we are here to do something about that. Kim, would you please take a moment to reflect and then tell Stan what it is that you are most upset about right now."

Kim was quiet for a minute and then responded, "I love you, Stan, but I don't think you love me anymore."

I held my breath—talk about getting right to the point! But, then, Kim was obviously that kind of woman.

"Stan," I said, "would you please repeat back to Kim what she just said to you."

Stan looked uncomfortable but complied. "You said that you love me but you don't think I love you anymore. And that's not true. I don't know how to relate to you anymore, and I can't stand it when you nag me. So I pull back."

"Kim," I said, "would you please repeat back to Stan what he just said."

Kim sighed, "You said it's not true that you don't love me but you don't know how to relate to me and you can't stand it when I nag you so you pull back."

"Okay," I said. "You are both pretty good at hearing what the other person says they need. So that isn't the problem. What we need to do is figure out how you can meet each other's needs in a way that is comfortable for both of you."

They both looked puzzled. "How do we do that?" Kim asked.

"Okay, Kim and Stan, let's try something here," I responded. "Kim, I'd like you to hold Stan's hand, look into his eyes and ask him for something that he can do for you right now." Kim looked a bit bewildered. Stan looked curious but a bit uncomfortable.

"Stan," Kim said as she took his hand, "what I would really appreciate right now is for you to tell me you love me—if you do."

Silence. I waited. Kim waited.

Stan cleared his throat, looked straight into Kim's eyes and said, "I love you, Kim." It was a poignant moment. Kim gave him a radiant smile and responded, "I love you too."

As the moment faded but before embarrassment set in, I said, "Wow, you two are something else! And I mean that as a compliment."

They laughed, squeezed hands and turned to me for instruction.

It was Stan's turn. So I said to him, "Stan, I want you to hold Kim's hand, look into her eyes and ask her for something she can do for you right now."

Stan leaned forward, took Kim's hand and said, "Kim, I need to know that you respect me for who I am."

Kim put her hand against his cheek and said, "Stan, you are the finest man I know, and I do respect you for who you are. In fact, I'm proud of you as my husband."

Stan looked a bit bowled over but clearly delighted.

"You are?" he managed. "That's great! Will you marry me?"

"We're already married, you nut, but maybe I need to act more that way!" Kim responded. "You know, I'm realizing that I don't usually tell you how much I respect you. I guess I figure you already know that."

"Sometimes I do," Stan said, "but sometimes I don't. It would help me a lot if you would take me at my word instead of always asking me to explain or give evidence for what I'm saying."

"Oh," said Kim, "do you know why I do that?"

"No," he replied. "Why?"

"Because I really like to understand the details of what you are telling me—that way I feel included in your plans. And that makes me feel loved."

Stan looked shocked. "It does?" he responded. "I didn't know that. I always figured you were trying to find a hole in my logic."

Before Kim could react to that one, I intervened. "You guys are pretty much doing this session on your own, and I'd like to compliment you. How are you feeling right now?"

Stan said, "I'm feeling better knowing that Kim respects me and that she still loves me."

Kim said, "I am feeling a lot better now that I know Stan loves me. But I want Stan to know that when he thinks I'm trying to find a hole in his logic all I'm trying to do is understand where he's coming from."

"Did you get that, Stan?" I asked.

"Yes, but it's kind of new to me," he acknowledged. "I'll try to be better about listening and explaining."

Kim looked mollified and said, "Stan, what about everything you said about me not responding to you physically? I want to get the record straight on that. It's not that I don't love you, it's that I need a gentle, loving approach and a relationship with you on other levels before I feel like making love."

I commented, "Most women feel that way, Stan, and most men don't realize it. Men are quicker to be sexually aroused even if they aren't in a great mood, but women desire that kind of intimacy only when they feel loved and appreciated."

Both Stan and Kim took time to digest that one. And then they turned to each other. Stan asked, "Is she right about that with you?"

"Yes," Kim said quietly. "It would help me a lot if we had intimacy in our words and feelings before it gets physical."

"Hmm," I could see Stan's mind clicking away. "I guess that's what you mean when you say 'I'm not in the mood.'"

"That's right," Kim responded.

They talked back and forth for a while, with me intervening as little as possible because they were being very honest and caring. They had obviously been ready to make a change in their relationship but had been waiting for a safe place to do it.

As the session was coming to a close, I summarized what they had been saying and asked them to keep talking to each other and giving each other the benefit of the doubt. Part of what had happened in their relationship was that too much had gone unsaid for too long, and they had each made assumptions about the other based on their own hurt feelings.

"You are doing a great job, both of you!" I told them. "And I think this is a good point for us to stop for today. What I want you to do before you come in the next time is to practice what you learned. So that means you practice expressing your love in the language the other person understands.

"Kim, that means you listen to Stan and take him at his word. And if you don't understand something, don't interrupt. Just wait for the right minute, give him a kiss, tell him you love him and then ask about whatever it is you don't understand." They both laughed.

"Stan, this means you talk to Kim, tell her you love her, notice and tell her that you appreciate all the little things she does to make you and the kids happy. Share your day with her. And give her a hand with the kids." He nodded affirmatively.

"Yesss!" Kim exclaimed. Stan gave her a hug. And I waved them out the door.

This couple went through ups and downs as they worked to change their approach to each other. However, the major reason that Kim and Stan had a successful experience in marriage counseling was that they both were intent on preserving their marriage. Underneath their hurt feelings they loved each other, plus they had the courage to be honest and the fortitude to change.

They were willing participants in the regeneration of their mutual love and respect. Consequently, their marriage did a turnaround, and it didn't take that many months. What had been missing was their willingness to voice their appreciation of each other. It's been several years since I've heard from them. And they promised me that they would get in touch if they ran aground again. So I regard no news as good news!

Enmeshment and Disengagement

One more situation is worthy of mention. Couples and families sometimes have what we psychologists call "enmeshment" problems. This kind of family has a closeness and intensity in family interactions to the point where they are uncomfortably entangled in one another's lives. In extreme cases, the lack of individual differentiation doesn't allow any degree of separation from the family. Separating-out is considered an act of betrayal. Belonging to such a family can so dominate a family member's experience that it limits the development of a separate sense of self.

The problem is that enmeshed families are overdependent on one another because their personal boundaries are blurred. This results in confusion about the roles of father and mother and their relationship as parents to the children. Both parents and children suffer in this kind of situation.

On the child's part, the demands on the "parental child" (the child receiving the most parental attention) can clash with the child's needs and push him beyond his ability to cope. Then the child becomes rebellious or withdrawn or compliant to a fault. A further complication occurs when the boundary between the family and outsiders becomes so rigid that there is little interaction with nonfamily members.

We also see "disengaged families," where there is little or no family loyalty or interaction. Individuals coming from this type of family often lack the capacity for interdependence. They hesitate to request the support they need and are insensitive to their partner's needs. In such a family, communication is often difficult or nonexistent. The parents' role as protectors of the children is severely handicapped because they tend not to respond to the children's needs. And the children hesitate to express any feelings or desires. It's almost as if the karma is so heavy that they can't even see if the sun is shining or recognize a need when it's staring them right in the face.

Sometimes families move from being enmeshed to being disengaged. How does this happen? A child or youth may begin to feel threatened or smothered by the enmeshment, especially as he or she gains a broader look at the world outside of the family. At that point, the young person begins to rebel against family norms, which can result in disengaging from the family altogether.

Often this does not happen until the youth goes away to college or enters the work world. At this point the parents begin to get fewer or no letters or phone calls. They do not understand why their son or daughter is disconnecting from the family. This is a difficult situation for everyone involved.

Helping a Young Person Reconnect

The best way for parents to reconnect with their son or daughter is by accepting the reality that the young person needs to live his or her own life. That youth, now a budding grown-up, will reconnect when he or she feels comfortable doing so. Yet the young person still needs parental love and approval. Even when young people's values are different from family norms, it is important to love them and honor their right to separate out.

I remember Bruce, a college freshman, who informed me he was cutting off contact with his family after "escaping to college" on a well-earned scholarship. He came in for counseling because he felt he had been emotionally stunted from having been "smothered" by overprotective parents.

Since he had earned his way to college with a scholarship plus room and board, Bruce decided to stop interacting with the family until he felt ready for it. To his credit he did send a brief, polite letter telling the family he was fine but would not be corresponding for a while.

He did love his parents and missed his two sisters, but he was determined to make it on his own. Only when he had done that was he willing to reconnect. After he was doing well in his classes and had a number of counseling sessions, he asked me, "Do you think I have enough of a base within myself that I could contact my parents without getting overwhelmed?"

I asked him what he thought, and he told me he felt he was ready. He was just looking for encouragement to go through with it. He did it step by step: first by letter, then by phone call, and at the end of his freshman year, a brief trip home. That visit was challenging for all concerned, but Bruce held his ground and managed to be goodhearted with his parents. He enjoyed spending time with his sisters, and when he came back to school he was in good spirits.

We benefit when we respect our sons and daughters, all of whom are inwardly striving to fulfill a higher destiny. We can pray for our children, set a good example, and ask God to guide them. Once we have done so we need to trust that they will be guided by their Higher Self. When we couple our prayers with respect, a caring attitude and supportive behavior, we can create a bond of friendship within the family circle.

7

The Impact of Today's Changing Culture

Regardless of circumstances,
each man lives in a world of his own making.

—JOSEPHA MURRAY EMMS
Playwright

Many of the children born toward the end of the Piscean age or coming in now in the Aquarian age are souls who carry a tremendous amount of light and energy. However, they also need to develop the physical and emotional mastery that will enable them to express that energy in a productive way.

These souls receive counseling in the higher realms before they embody and they are aware that life on Earth is a challenge. However, knowing there will be the loving presence of their father and mother gives them comfort and courage. Born in a state of innocence, they look to their parents to guide them, to inspire them, and to help them mold their character and unfold their inherent spirituality.

These young people retain an inner awareness of their true nature and their connection with their Higher Self. Yet outwardly they are like any other children or teens. They need to be nurtured, instructed and disciplined. That is the role of parents and teachers and everyone who is devoted to assisting youth to develop their special gifts and highest potential.

Families, Youth and Children at Risk

Many of the issues for families, youth and children today are a result of major changes occurring in the worldwide culture. There are telling reports and statistics from the 1990s and early 2000s that indicate surprising shifts in family life. Here are some statistics that may be a surprise to you:

According to the National Center for Health Statistics, 957,200 divorces occurred in the United States in the year 2000. And this doesn't count the states of California, Colorado, Indiana and Louisiana, which do not track the number of divorces.[1]

Another shocker is the National Institute of Mental Health's report that in 2001 suicide was the third leading cause of death among young people fifteen to twenty-four years of age—following accidents and homicide.[2] Phil, the father of a seventeen-year-old boy who committed suicide in 2003, has researched the tragic phenomenon. And he states that for every two homicides in the United States there are three suicides and that teen and youth suicide rates have tripled since 1970. He says that among college students suicide is the second leading cause of death. I suggest you check out the Web site that Phil and his wife have put together to help teens who have suicidal tendencies.[3]

Doc Lew Childre, in his book *Parenting Manual: Heart*

Hope for the Family, offers additional disturbing statistics. He states: "Highway accidents are the leading killer of teenagers. All told, 33% of drivers ages sixteen to twenty who were killed in accidents in 1994 registered blood alcohol levels of .10 or higher. More than one-third of the nation's teens drink alcohol weekly, while nearly half a million are binge drinkers whose weekly consumption averages fifteen drinks."[4]

A bit of good news is that a government survey indicates that drug usage among teenagers has decreased by 11 percent among those between the ages of thirteen and eighteen. And the overall percentage of teens using drugs declined to 28 percent over the past two years. "Four hundred thousand young people are not using drugs today because of that decline," said Tommy Thompson, Health and Human Services (HHS) Secretary.[5]

Another HHS report states that birthrates among teenagers fell for the tenth straight year to a new record low in 2001. "This is an important milestone in our fight against teen pregnancy," Secretary Thompson said. "The research shows us that when teens postpone parenthood, they improve their lives and the lives of their children."[6]

The mix of positive and disturbing statistics is not unique to the United States. Families in other countries are also having challenges. Consider these 2003 statistics from Britain reported on the Good News Family Care Web site:

- More than 40% of marriages today will end in divorce....

- The average marriage lasts only 9 years....

- One in four single women aged 18–49 are living with a man to whom they are not married.

- Britain has the highest rate of teenage pregnancies in Europe. Legally induced abortions were carried out on 3,514 girls aged 15 or under in 2000....

- 5,000 children every week suffer the pain and anguish of a broken home.

- 15,000 children call Childline every day.[7]

The authors of this Web site believe that these statistics flag an eroding in the quality of British family life as a consequence of abandoning traditional family values. They encourage "a return to Christian family values and ... provide a 'safety net' for families in crisis." The Web site includes resources for families in distress.

The Role of Karma in the Teens

Karma can be the root cause of issues between parents and teenagers. Since one's personal karma frequently does not surface until a person is twelve, it is often a factor in the so-called terrible teens. During this time, the teenager is dealing not only with hormonal changes but also with karmic records and patterns that are returning from past lives.

Teenagers who understand this karmic factor can be successful in handling interactions with others when they realize that each situation involves a karmic lesson for their soul. Somehow, it seems more important to learn a lesson that not only benefits you but also benefits your soul. It's a double incentive.

Congruent with karmic cycles, the twelve-year-old begins to deal with the return of records of his birth and first year of life.* Whether or not he remembers being a baby (and some people do!), the emotional impact of events from

---
*See pp. 56–60.

infancy subconsciously influences his feelings and behavior as a twelve-year-old. And the karma of the first year of life, plus records from past lives, begins to surface. Sometimes when the budding teenager feels uncomfortable and doesn't understand exactly what's happening, it is because the records of infancy or a previous life have been activated.

One twelve-year-old girl, Amy, told her mother she couldn't stand to be around one of her uncles. She didn't know why. Her mother had an immediate alarm reaction since the uncle had been an occasional babysitter during her daughter's infancy. She and her husband confronted the uncle, and he confessed to losing his temper and slapping the baby around one time when she wouldn't stop crying.

The mother remembered coming home and finding bruises on the baby but the uncle had said that the baby had fallen off the changing table. He still felt terrible about what had happened and about his lying. He apologized to Amy in the presence of her parents and said he wouldn't blame her if she never spoke to him again. Amy was so relieved to know that there was a good reason that she felt the way she did that she forgave him. However, she also stated that she wanted no contact with him.

After the situation was as resolved as it could be, Amy asked her mother to help her because she still felt resentful. Her mother suggested they pray together to discover the lessons they needed to learn from this situation. Amy realized her lesson was not to hold onto the resentment, and her mother realized she needed to forgive herself for trusting her brother with the baby.

Spiritually, we can all ask our Higher Self to teach us the lesson from any hurtful experience. We can also invoke the action of the violet flame, the transformational action of the Holy Spirit, to transmute the records. We can center in our heart, visualize violet light all around us and give this mantra:

> I AM a being of violet fire.
> I AM the purity God desires!

As we continue to visualize the violet light and to give the mantra, we will begin to feel a shift in the energy. Why? Because the vibration of the violet flame changes the energy field and transforms the traumatic happening into a benign—emotionally neutralized—memory. In the process the young person begins to understand the lesson inherent in the experience.

Many young people are spiritually attuned and all they need is a way to handle uncomfortable feelings. When a mantra is given with complete focus, the individual often feels a tingling, liberating energy in the body and an uplift in mood.

Once a young person has neutralized the negative energy, how does he or she learn the karmic lesson? I believe we all do best to act as if each encounter is a teacher and on a regular basis ask our Higher Self, "What is the lesson for my soul?" When we get into the habit of doing that, we begin to see life as a series of lessons. And that makes life itself an education—the education of our soul and spirit.

Teaching Teens to Say No to Peer Pressure

Most parents teach their teenagers to take care of their physical body through nutrition, fitness and exercise. In today's fast-moving culture we also need to teach them how to relax, how to handle stress—and how to say no to peer pressure.

We particularly need to discuss the risks and consequences of sex, drugs and alcohol. Most teens today come face to face with the temptation and peer pressure and give in to it. We need to strategize with them how to stay out of trouble.

Some of the best antidotes are family rules and activities that give a natural high. And we can also determine to be a positive role model for our teens. While they may not always follow our example, our attitude and behavior will be there as a point of reference.

When we let our teenagers know we love them and also give them limits, we help them feel safe and emotionally secure. When we participate in our teens' lives and give them encouragement, they feel loved and appreciated. When we keep our commitments, they trust us. And when we give high-fives and pats on the back, they feel good about themselves.

Teens who are pursuing a passion usually make it through without serious problems. That's because they have a goal, they have an all-consuming interest, and they respect themselves.

Parents need to be supportive of their teenagers' interests and of the healthy pursuits that appeal to them. This means showing interest in their projects, suggesting ways to earn money to support a venture, carpooling them to activities and cheering them on.

All of this is best begun before the teenage hormones are fully activated. If a youngster is already involved in the pursuit of a goal that he or she is excited about, the hormones will fuel that pursuit instead of creating excess energy that can get a young person into trouble.

I suggest parents stay involved in a way that is supportive but does not take away budding independence and self-accomplishment. Give praise where praise is due. And give correction through consequences.

Correction through Consequences

Consequences need to be clearly defined before correction is necessary, rather than after the fact. For example, if you are requiring a teenager to be home by 10:00 P.M., make it a house rule with the consequence of lateness clearly stated. And follow through! Sometimes parents give way to a teenager's logic, and this is a mistake, even if the logic is sort of reasonable, such as:

"If I can't go to Rick's sleepover just because I was a half-hour late getting home last night, everyone will think I'm a nerd!" "If I have to stay up to get my homework done, I'll be wiped out at school tomorrow." "Nobody else has to get home by 10:00." You can add to the list. The point is that a rule is a rule and a consequence is a consequence. It's non-negotiable after the fact.

You will not have to do this many times before your teenager will get the point. If he breaks the rule, he bears the consequence. And if he continues to break the rule, the consequence gets tougher. If he goes by the rules, there's no problem. And he can always tell his friends, "Sorry, I've got to go. House rules." In other words, rules give him a relatively comfortable out with his friends.

Through all of this we want our teens to know that we accept them for who they are, for their special individuality. How do we accomplish that? By telling them they are special, praising their accomplishments and letting them know we are proud to be their parents. We encourage them to develop their talents when we support their interests, champion their curiosity, assist the learning process and reward them for achieving their goals.

We want our sons and daughters to know that we love them and that this is the reason we have rules and standards. And yet they may still mull over the question, "Why can't I make my own rules?" We can remind them that the time will come when they will be making their own rules, setting their own standards. House rules now will prep them to make better decisions when they are on their own.

Dr. Kathleen Moorcroft, a Canadian education expert, offers words of encouragement from her successful teaching career and interaction with elementary, secondary school and college students.

She describes the point of view of her students and offers her own perspective:

> In working extensively with teens in recent years, I have seen evidence of changing attitudes among many of today's teens. They lecture their teachers and classmates about unhealthy habits. One student persuaded the principal to quit smoking because it would "ruin his health," and besides, "It makes you stink."
>
> Some students called their parents "stupid" for using alcohol, tobacco and other harmful drugs, and "unfair" because they were too permissive and didn't set and maintain boundaries. These students felt that permissive parents put too much responsibility on them at an early age.
>
> I find it very heartwarming when I see, as I often do, the friendly, companionable way that so many teens interact with people of all ages and from every cultural, social and racial group and when I see them work

together to raise money for community projects. It warms my heart when I know that they are giving up their holidays to go and do volunteer work in Third World countries. In spite of the problems, I see much to admire in today's teens.[8]

Outwitting the Impact of the Media

Today many parents unwittingly turn their children over to the TV set, and the potential impact is startling. Statistics presented in February 2004 by U.S. Senator Fritz Hollings indicate that the average child will witness 100,000 acts of violence on TV and 8,000 TV murders before completing elementary school.[9] And this is not necessarily safeguarded by viewing TV programs as a family. A study in 2003 reported that 61 percent of children have a television set in their bedrooms.[10]

The truth is, for many children TV is taking the place of parents. Children are going to TV for love, for comfort, to learn. If parents plug their kids into the TV, they are going to raise TV kids, not real-life sons or daughters. It is essential that parents play their role as parents and not let TV become a surrogate parent.

Most of us are concerned about the quality of media programming, but another problem with TV watching has nothing to do with the content of the program. It has to do with the way the brain works. When we watch TV, the pattern of brain waves we emit is similar to those emitted when we dream. It is as if we are propelled into a dreamlike state where we do not necessarily distinguish reality from unreality.

That's how many children react to TV. They become part of the scene. They absorb what they watch. And they play it out. Furthermore, they get a speeded-up idea of life. TV characters take about twenty minutes to settle major conflicts! And children raised on TV can get frustrated when they can't solve their problems as fast as their favorite television character.

Thus, it is important that parents be selective about what their children watch and also avoid using TV as a time-filler or babysitter. Parents can provide videos they know to be wholesome and enjoyable for the whole family. And they can initiate activities and family outings that have real-life interaction instead of the vicarious experience of the media.

What is going to happen to our young people, to the millions of souls being born today? Will they buy into the unreality of TV socialization? Will they fall prey to the lure of alcohol, drugs or suicide? It is up to all of us to do the best we can to help the children and youth entrusted to our care avoid these pitfalls.

We can make certain our young people are informed of the risks in today's culture. We can encourage them to choose healthy activities, to build on their special talents and to develop friendships with young people who have similar interests. We can monitor their progress and if they come under the influence of adverse elements in their school or social life, we can initiate a discussion about how to stay away from the wrong crowd.

Teens are sensitive to their friends' and parents' reactions and vulnerable to the energetic impact of media images. No matter how they act outwardly, they want to know that their friends like them and their parents are proud of them. Media images influence them because they offer excitement and adventure. The problem is that the media exaggerates what actually happens in the world.

Young people who spend hours playing video games or watching a lot of TV and movies can get an unrealistic view of life as it really is.

Although young people may be advanced intellectually or physically, they have strong emotional needs. Those needs are best met by thoughtful, caring adults who engage their teens in dialogue about world events and make it a point to be encouraging and supportive. Be selective about the information and emotions you share with your teens and how you share it. Do not assume that they can integrate all sorts of shocking information about traumatic events. When they feel overloaded or frustrated about a difficult situation, they are likely to react emotionally and behaviorally.

The world at times is very challenging. And none of us can afford to be an ostrich with its head in the sand. What we can do is pray about difficult situations, share our perspective and discuss possible solutions. Once we bring a scary situation out in the open and talk about it, we feel more in control. And the same is true for teenagers.

We can also share our faith with our teenage sons and daughters. It is comforting to know that difficult situations are soul lessons and that God and his angels answer our prayers. Teens are open to spiritual solutions once they know how to find them.

What If You Discover Your Teen Is Sexually Active?

Most parents hope and pray their teenager will not get involved in a sexual relationship before marriage. And they do their best to take a positive approach if they discover differently. However, parents who have faced this situation recommend taking action in advance of dating—they advise talking to your teens about sex and its rightful place in marriage.

A father of five that I know told me of going to his elder daughter's high school graduation. He was walking along a corridor at the high school with his very attractive eighteen-year-old daughter on his arm and several of the boys of her age were whispering to one another and pointing to her, obviously commenting on how beautiful she was.

My friend said, "I managed to restrain myself from causing them grievous bodily harm and made the decision then and there that she wasn't going to date until she was twenty-eight!" As the fates would have it, she married a very nice young man just a few years later.

Adults can teach teenagers how to work out a strategy to keep premarital sex from ever happening. When this is done in a positive manner, teens feel supported and are more likely to seek parental support when tempted.

Young men experiencing the increase in testosterone need guidance on how to handle their sexual energy so that it doesn't get the best of them. Parents can explain that this is a natural physical development that a young man gradually learns to master. They can require group dating and suggest activities that do not lend themselves to sex play. In the event that your teenage son's energies do get stirred up, tell him to take a walk until he cools down. But the best course of action is not to get into heavy necking or petting. A hug or kiss goodnight at the front door is the safest approach.

An important reason for teens not to indulge in sex play is the fact that we are seeing a major increase in sexually transmitted diseases (STDs). Dr. Meg Meeker says we have an epidemic among our teenagers and that half of all girls are likely to be infected with an STD during their first sexual experience. Nearly one in four sexually active teens is infected.[11] And Pam Stenzel, founder of Enlighten Communications and proponent of teen abstinence, states that today's teens need to hear "straight talk ... about sex, about the consequences, about the life and death choices that they meet every single day."[12] STDs can be treated but not always cured. And this is a fact of life that many sexually active teens do not fully understand.

A number of teens these days are having what they consider "safe" sex—meaning oral sex. What they haven't been taught is that STDs can be transferred through oral sex too. Whatever form of sex a couple engages in, so-called safe sex is not safe. If a couple is planning to marry, the same is true and both partners benefit from being tested for STD if they have had sexual activity of any kind.

The good news is that teen pregnancy rates are dropping and parental values and rules make a difference. Education experts tell parents emphatically: Have rules and enforce them.

A positive way to do this is to hold a family council where you discuss and agree on house rules. Here are some rules that families have agreed on:

- Homework comes first

- Outings to be approved by parents

- Be home by 10:30 P.M.

- Group dates until the sixteenth birthday

- Driver training required for driving privileges

- Once the teen earns a license, parental permission necessary to borrow the family car

- No teenage passengers while driving, to be reassessed in a year

- Smoking, drinking or doing drugs revokes all privileges

Parents have the responsibility to protect their teenagers; what the teenagers do with the rules is their accountability. Most teens admit that family rules make it easier to stay out of trouble.

Spirituality Helps Teens to Resist Sexual Pressure

Sex outside of marriage is typically a no-no in traditional family life, and young people who are anchored in a spiritual faith seem to be handling abstinence better than other teens. Haley, a teenager who recently did a 180-degree turnaround in her sex life, asked me, "I'm not doing sex anymore, but what kind of karma have I made already?"

Now Haley was already aware of the spiritual teaching that the bonds of marriage form a protective circle for the union of man and woman and their exchange of sexual energy. But she didn't quite understand how sex outside of marriage is karma making.

I explained to Haley that it's all about the exchange of energy. Sexual energy is sacred fire, spiritual light that is stored in our chakras, our spiritual centers. And we have only so much available to us each day. When we are promiscuous with the sacred fire, we do not have it for use in creative activities.

That sacred fire is exchanged during sexual relations. So in sex outside of marriage we not only deplete our store of sacred fire with no depth of commitment to balance it out, but we also take into ourselves a little bit of everyone with whom we have sexual relations. And since it's all about energy exchange, we not only take on the energy of our partner but also the energy of everyone he or she has slept with. This has an impact upon a person's sense of identity and is a karmic debt that is felt at the level of the soul.

I told Haley that whatever karma she had made could be balanced by future right decisions plus the action of the violet transmuting flame—and that she could make some good karma by passing along to other teens what she had learned.

I suggested that Haley pray for forgiveness and guidance, call upon the Holy Spirit to cleanse her soul and body, and give the violet-flame mantra "I AM a being of violet fire. I AM the purity God desires!" to transmute the karmic residue. I reminded her that Jesus loves her and will give her the strength to refrain from activities that are not beneficial to her soul.

I also told Haley that if she felt tempted, the best thing to do would be to leave the situation quickly. That would take courage but would be a completely effective strategy. Haley agreed. She started doing her prayers and felt relief from her feelings of guilt. She promised God that she wasn't going to let her crowd tempt her into making the mistake again. And she asked Jesus to give her the right words to say to her friends.

When Haley confessed all of this to her mom, this smart mom gave her daughter a hug and told her she was proud of her. She also gave her a cell phone and volunteered to pick her up anytime she needed to be rescued.

Teenage Pregnancy

What does a parent do if you find out your teenager is sexually active or is pregnant or has gotten a girl pregnant? The most important first step is to handle your shock privately and then reassure your teen that you love her or him and are concerned about the welfare of everyone involved.

If this has been unprotected sexual activity, the next step is to see that your teenager is checked for sexually transmitted disease. If the test results indicate STD, your teen needs to start treatment—and it is necessary to inform the other teen and parents so that his or her treatment can be initiated. An important aspect of all of this is that the teens feel loved and supported by their parents rather than abandoned because of their misbehavior.

Any young girl who is sexually active needs a good gynecologist, and most girls are open to this once they understand the possibility of being infected from sexual activity. The follow-up from the first visit is a Pap smear every six months to track any possible problems. It's important to realize that a sexually transmitted disease is a serious situation—a lifelong problem in some cases.

Even if STDs are ruled out, a pregnancy may be involved. If this is the case and it's your son and someone else's daughter, help the young people tell the girl's parents so that she can get the appropriate tests and prenatal care. Be as comforting and reassuring as you can—this is a critical time for both families.

If your daughter is pregnant, she needs all the love and support you can give her to bring that baby into the world and make the decision either to be a mom or to give the baby up for adoption. This is a serious decision that will affect both young people for the rest of their lives. How many times have we heard of mothers who had given up their babies trying to find them years later? Or about people who had been adopted searching for their birth mother and father?

All of this underlies the wisdom of acquainting young people with the issues involved in premarital sex and doing all we can to help them remain celibate until marriage. In a world where sex is glorified in practically all of the media, it takes a lot of gumption for a young person to be celibate. And yet, the long-term benefits are a blessing to the heart and soul.

I have known a number of young people who have refrained from sex outside of marriage. And they tell me they are happy they did. I remember Audrey, a bright young girl, who turned to her parents and church for guidance in maintaining her standards in the face of peer pressure. She and her friends put their attention on doing their best in school and enjoying extracurricular activities—tennis, swimming and folk dancing.

Audrey completed her college education without giving in to the temptation to have premarital sex. She told me she had been pressured by several boyfriends but followed her mother's advice to stay out of potentially risky situations by simply saying, "No!" with no further explanation or discussion. She married Vance, a young man of her own faith who also had withstood the temptation. He said his dad's advice to compete in sports had made it possible for him to handle his energies and that was an important factor in his not getting involved in sex before marriage.

When they came in for premarital counseling, the couple told me they were happy that they could come to the altar and take their vows with a clear conscience and a joyful heart. And today, five years later, they have a son and daughter of their own. They will be in a strong position to guide their children through the "terrible teens" because they understand the temptations from personal experience and know how to deal with them.

The Value of Spiritual Principles

As parents, teachers and friends of children, we are meant to guide the souls entrusted to us to become mature individuals who can embark on their own path of self-discovery and service to God and mankind. This is the great challenge that is set before us today.

Many experts echo these sentiments. I remember Jack Kornfield's words from the 1990s: "By bringing the principles of spiritual practice to childrearing, we can end a crisis that plagues us all."[13] Have we done so? If not, why not start right now?

Perhaps the greatest gift we can give young people is to be clear about our higher principles and be a living example of what we believe—and this includes being respectful and loving toward our children. When we exercise self-discipline, wise decision-making and generous behavior, our children take it for granted that this is the way life is meant to be.

Although they are individual souls in their own right, our children unconsciously imitate what we do, how we laugh, smile or frown, how we talk, what we like and dislike. They tend to absorb our emotions and our attitudes—for good or for ill.

Most of us do our best to rise to the challenge of parenting or being a friend to children and youth. And yet, everyone can get a bit short-tempered or insensitive at times. Even as our parents and teachers sparked reactions in us when we were young, so we may unwittingly ignite rebellion or argumentation in our children and teenagers today.

What do we do when that happens? We hold the line without becoming punitive or vengeful. If we have jumped to the wrong conclusion or reacted in a hurtful way, we apologize. Once everyone has cooled down, we discuss with the young person what it is we are trying to accomplish. A positive example is more powerful than a lecture!

In addition, family strengths—such as expressing mutual love and respect, sharing spiritual beliefs, having fun times together and establishing community ties—keep young people on the right track. When we give our children this kind of foundation, they are not as apt to follow the negative ways of the world when they reach the turbulent teens.

Children and youth continually test their skills with other people. They build character as they learn how to cooperate with other people while staying true to their own values. And by so doing they prepare for adult responsibilities: a career, relationships and a family of their own.

Young people are sensitive to fair play. They want to understand why we want them to behave politely or complete household tasks. They are pleased and reassured when we compliment them on their achievements. They expect concern when they are upset and enthusiasm when they are excited. And they appreciate respect even though they may not always be respectful.

If we want a teen to do something for us, we do best to make eye contact, use a pleasant tone of voice, get right to the point, state the reason and give specific directions. The worst way to try to get teens to do something is to accuse, blame, or shout at them for not having done it in the first place. And this holds true for adults too.

I remember Dan, a supervisor who always yelled orders, interrupted the person trying to comply, and bawled his staff out for not doing a task the way he would do it. Then the day came when he had a new boss who was the spitting image of Dan. Talk about payback time! Dan couldn't please that guy, even when he was trying his best.

When Dan came in to see me, he was at his wit's end. But as we discussed what had been going on, he began seeing his boss as his mirror image—and he didn't like it. To his credit, he realized he had met his "karmic comeuppance." Dan decided to turn himself around. He began to behave more diplomatically, and he and his boss gradually came to terms with each other.

Once he got it, Dan was able to laugh at the irony of the situation. As he told me, "I guess I asked for it, the way I have been treating other people. I suppose the universe did me a favor by sending it back. That kind of boomerang is a real wake-up call!"

Young people, like adults, respond to respectful requests and the opportunity to give input. They resist accusatory demands and insulting feedback. When we are bossy and demanding, drill on their mistakes or are physically hurtful, they turn off. Even if they do what is demanded, they will do it with a resentful attitude.

We do well to set a good example by relating to other people diplomatically and giving others the benefit of the doubt. When you get right down to it, most people are trying to do the best they can.

Response to a Teenager Interested in Spirituality

Over the years I have received e-mails from teens interested in spiritual psychology. One teenager wanted to know "how spiritual psychology works." Here is part of my response:

> When I was a teen I was also interested in understanding how spiritual psychology worked, although I didn't know what to call it at that time in my life. We had a great youth group in the Baptist church I grew up in, and that is probably what got me through my teens without major problems.

We would do our own Sunday evening youth services and then we would play volleyball or go skating or square dancing. On Saturdays we often went to a nearby lake or the mountains and did boating and swimming and hiking. All of these activities with other Christian teenagers helped me integrate my spiritual and social life.

Later on I got interested in the world's major religions, particularly the Buddhic concepts of nonattachment and *metta*, which means loving-kindness. And I tried to practice those in my life. Nonattachment means that you observe yourself at the same time you are doing something or feeling something instead of getting all wrapped up in whatever is happening. When I practiced nonattachment I started understanding people better and wasn't as reactive to negative stuff.

Loving-kindness means wanting the best for others, thinking of their good qualities instead of what we don't like about them, treating them the way we want to be treated. I believe that the Buddha's metta and Jesus' Golden Rule, "Do unto others as you would have them do unto you," are very similar teachings.

When I think about it, all my life I have taken whatever I learned that was spiritual and tried to see if I could make it happen in my own life. And when I realized that psychology meant the study of the psyche, the study of the soul, I tried to understand my own soul. I would ask myself, "Why am I doing this? What would God think about it? Do I feel right about doing it? Is it good for my soul?"

The really exciting part of my life began when I started to realize that I had lived before in other lifetimes. I understood reincarnation is real and that a lot of my problems were about karma, which means whatever we give out to others we get back. As we used to say in the sixties,

"What goes around, comes around." That was a real eye-opener for me.

Another wake-up call was when I began to study energy and to realize that everything is energy, including me. And it made sense to me that whenever we are talking to someone else or interacting in any way, we are exchanging energy. I realized if that's true I'd better be careful about who I was spending time with. There's a lot more about this in my book *Sacred Psychology of Change: Life as a Voyage of Transformation.*[14]

I learned a lot from my prayers, meditations and contemplation, and I found books and scriptures that made sense to me. Sometimes I would go into a bookstore and ask God to show me a book that was right for me, and I'd find exactly the right book. I still do that today.

One inspiring book I found several years ago is called *Grandfather.*[15] It is about a Native American who has many exciting experiences with nature and the Great Spirit. It was written by Tom Brown, Jr., who runs one of the biggest wilderness and survival schools in the United States.

I also recommend James Redfield's books, especially *The Secret of Shambhala.*[16] He writes spiritual adventure stories, and this is one of my favorites. I think you would appreciate all of his books because they are written for those who have an exploring mind and an interest in spiritual awareness and synchronicity.

What I realized in responding to this young man and from discussions with other young people is that they are seeking deeper answers to life's problems. I believe that many teenagers and young adults are interested in spirituality and in knowing more about their soul.

As parents, teachers, counselors and friends of youth,

we can inspire young people by being up-front with what we believe. Teens make critical decisions every day, and they need spiritual awareness as well as mental, emotional and physical tools.

An Inventory for Parents and Mentors of Teens

Ask yourself the following questions. Take time to write your answers and reflect on any changes you might want to make. This kind of self-examination can help you improve your parenting or mentoring skills:

1. What is my philosophy of parenting?

2. Is my philosophy based on my spiritual values and principles?

3. Is it based on expectations my parents had for me?

4. Is it based on the demands of my career?

5. Is it based on how I was raised or my reaction to how I was raised?

6. Is it based on how my friends are raising their kids?

7. How is it working for me, my spouse and my children?

8. Is this the outcome I hoped for? If not, why not?

9. Are my spiritual values and principles reflected in my behavior?

Now ask yourself what you would like to do differently and how you might do that. Write it down. Practice the changes you decide to make and they will gradually become your natural response. You can become the parent or mentor you really want to be.

Here is a decree that you can give for the protection of young people everywhere to help them successfully navigate the troubled waters in today's complex world.

PROTECT OUR YOUTH

Beloved heavenly Father!
Beloved heavenly Father!
Beloved heavenly Father!
Take command of our youth today
Blaze through them opportunity's ray
Release perfection's mighty power
Amplify cosmic intelligence each hour
Protect, defend their God-design
Intensify intent divine

I AM, I AM, I AM
The power of infinite light
Blazing through our youth
Releasing cosmic proof
Acceptable and right
The full power of cosmic light
To every child and child man
In America and the world!
Beloved I AM! Beloved I AM! Beloved I AM![17]

8

The Inherent Genius of the Soul

Find a purpose in life so big
it will challenge every capacity to be at your best.

—DAVID O. MCKAY
Church leader

How do our children learn? How can we maximize their inherent genius and capabilities? Although the answers to these questions are multifaceted, parents and children in the twenty-first century can benefit greatly from the work of a remarkable woman of the nineteenth and twentieth centuries, Maria Montessori.

Through careful observation and intuition, Montessori developed a unique and successful method of teaching children, which ultimately brought her fame as a world-renowned teacher and educator. Today many children attend Montessori schools, and other private and public schools are carrying on her work.

Leslie Britton and others have spoken about Maria Montessori's life.[1] Curiously enough, Montessori did not start out to be a teacher. In fact, she absolutely refused to comply with her parents' intention for her to become an educator. Instead, she did battle with her family's opposition and in 1890 entered medical school to become a doctor. She became Italy's first woman doctor.

Maria Montessori and the Inner Teacher

Montessori began her practice as a physician in the San Giovanni Hospital in Rome, and she began volunteering in 1897 as an assistant at the University of Rome's psychiatric clinic. While working there, she came into contact with children who at that time were known as "idiot children." These children were placed in asylums with the criminally insane because their families didn't know how to cope with them. The special needs programs we have today hadn't even been thought of, much less developed.

As a doctor who was passionately concerned about social reform, Maria Montessori was touched by the children's wretched living conditions. As she watched them crawl around on the floor feeling for crumbs of food, she sensed that exploring with their hands was a way of trying to understand their environment. As she carefully observed and put two and two together, she determined to see if these children could learn through working with their hands.

Montessori's compassionate heart, intuitive understanding and intellectual courage led her to confront the standard mind-set of the times concerning these children. She started working with them in the psychiatric clinic and also began to examine the work of two now famous men, Jean Itard and Edouard Seguin.

Montessori was intrigued by Itard's book *The Wild Boy of Aveyron*. Itard was a French doctor who succeeded in socializing a wild, mentally retarded boy and teaching him through sensory stimulation. She also studied the work of Seguin, one of Itard's students, who developed a physiological method (exercising the muscles) to induce behavioral change and thereby teach the child.

Maria Montessori combined the two men's ideas—"education of the senses" and "education of movement"—with contributions from other educational thinkers and her own synthesis of medical and educational methods. She continued hands-on work with retarded children, observing and developing methods of teaching these youngsters.

To the surprise of many, children previously thought to be impossible to educate not only learned to read but also did extremely well in the State primary examinations. This educational phenomenon coupled with Montessori's lectures on the subject proved her expertise in education as well as medicine.

Montessori's next step was to set up "infant schools" in a project where families were being rehoused after slums were cleared. Her initial school, known as *Casa dei Bambini* (Children's House), opened its doors in 1906. In this school for youngsters three to six years old, Montessori was able to set up her learning environment and test her methods with children of normal intelligence. Consequently, she opened several other schools and successfully demonstrated her belief that *every* child is capable of learning.

As a result of her pioneering work, Montessori developed and refined what is known today as the Montessori method, a learning path that develops the mind through the work of the hands. Combining the insights she gleaned from observing children with her own inner genius and sense of practicality, Montessori focused on the child's inherent capabilities and on "how to awaken the man that lies asleep within the soul of a child."[2]

She documented what she called "sensitive periods"— cycles of life when a child intuitively explores a particular dimension of learning. And she discovered that parents and teachers facilitate and maximize what is already built in as a readiness to learn.

Montessori demonstrated that children go well beyond what we normally expect when an observant adult helps them maximize these learning periods. Yet it takes art and skill on the part of a teacher or parent to assist the child in a way that is productive and enhances the child's sense of self-mastery.

Maria Montessori was clearly on the mark, spiritually and developmentally. She recognized the soul's potential in the child's inherent capabilities. She understood the inner teacher, an aspect of the Higher Self. And what she called sensitive periods is an accurate description of the soul's built-in readiness to learn. Even as Montessori taught that each child has inherent genius, we can think of this genius as who the person *really* is, the Real Self.

The Impact of Who We Think We Are

Who do you think you are? Do you identify with your own inner genius? Or are you weighed down by the opinions of others? We do well to remember these cryptic words: "You are who you are no matter who you may think you are!" In other words, our unique identity does not change as a result of human opinion. However, who *we think* we are does influence our lives.

Our human sense of identity tracks back to early life experiences, how we are raised and how we are treated as children. Every child's sense of "who I am" is influenced by the attitudes, mind-sets, emotions and physical behavior of parents, teachers, siblings and others who are close to the family.

As babies and young children we do not learn in a linear fashion. We simply absorb whatever is going on around us, particularly in the first five to seven years of our life. Montessori aptly labeled this period of development "the absorbent mind." We continue to develop and refine what we have absorbed, but what we take in as infants and small children remains a major component of who we think we are.

We particularly absorb whatever influences us emotionally, both the positive and the negative. When we have happy times, an exciting adventure, a glimpse of a rainbow, we laugh with glee. When we are hurt or scared or frustrated, we cry and wail. Even if we are distracted from the pain we are experiencing, we absorb the whirl of energy at subconscious and unconscious levels. Essentially, we have no real control over what we absorb until we are old enough to avoid hurtful encounters or to put them in perspective in light of what we have already experienced and learned.

It is interesting to note that certain young geniuses do this at a very early age. They seem almost like adults in little bodies. For the rest of us, we learn at a more gradual pace as we move along in life.

Once we broaden our horizons from home to school, we have a lot more information to juggle. We model ourselves after people who are significant in our lives—parents, older siblings, teachers, friends and neighbors. How many times have we seen children consciously copying their father or mother, an older sister or brother?

I remember some years ago watching two little girls doing a ballet lesson together. Julie, age seven, was watching her sister Celia, age twelve, and doing her best to mimic her sister's performance. The teacher let it go at first because both children were performing beautifully. However, at one point she had to intervene because the older sister did a movement incorrectly and the little sister faithfully followed her example even though she had done the movement correctly earlier.

The teacher's correction seemed to come as a surprise to seven-year-old Julie. So the teacher explained that although her sister Celia was a good dancer, everyone makes mistakes sometimes. She had them watch her do the movement and then asked each of them to follow her example, separately. And they both corrected. This teacher didn't simply correct the ballet movement, she was also teaching the younger child to think for herself.

Let's think about our own formative years. As children we had our own personality and likes and dislikes, yet we also tried to copy our siblings and friends. Or if we got mad at them we decided to do the opposite. And sometimes we copied our parents by experimenting with cooking or telling our little brother to behave. And we tried to learn what our parents taught us.

When we reached the teen years, we began to reexamine our attitudes, ideas, beliefs and behaviors. Sometimes we kept them because they were comfortable and familiar. Sometimes we changed them to adapt to our expanding world. And if we went away to college, we experienced another metamorphosis as we developed a broader view of the world and its possibilities.

Many of us struck out on our own after high school or college, entering one of the trades, working for a business, or taking a professional position. We began to create our adult life, adult values and adult ways to handle the present and address the future. Maybe we married and started our own family. And now a peculiar experience occurs when we return home for a visit.

Almost as quickly as we go through the front door of the old family home, we find ourselves reacting pretty much the same way we always did when we lived at home. We may think we have our adulthood well in hand, but when we interact with our birth family we might as well be twelve years old again. We find ourselves teasing our sister, taking a backseat to our father, and feeling uncomfortable if we don't volunteer to help our mother. And we have emotional reactions coming up that we haven't felt for years!

Why? This is the hidden power of the absorbent mind and the influence of our family life experiences. However, these reactions are not indelible behavioral traits. As mature adults we can make it a point to change our knee-jerk reactions. We can train ourselves to relate to our family in a mature and congenial manner.

Gifted Souls, History's Geniuses

In addition to early-life experiences, we also have our genetic inheritance and a soul memory of earlier embodiments. In gifted people their "genius" may very well come through the genes or from past-life accomplishments.

Wolfgang Amadeus Mozart

I have always been moved by the story of Wolfgang Amadeus Mozart, a gifted child who became one of the world's renowned composers. Born in 1756, in Salzburg, Austria, Mozart lived only thirty-five years, yet his ageless musical works have created a profound impact on generations of music lovers.

By age five Wolfgang began writing minuets and progressed to composing symphonies by the time he was nine. In
addition to his skill on the keyboard, he also mastered the
violin. When Wolfang was six, he and his sister Maria Anna
embarked on a European concert tour, performing for the
sovereigns of Vienna and Versailles and audiences in Paris,
Germany and London.

At the age of eight, the young musician introduced his
first musical compositions, sonatas for clavier and violin. At
the age of twelve, he completed *La Finta Semplice*, his first
opera, and over the next few years composed three more
operas. At the age of sixteen he became a concertmaster.
During this time, although he was given only a pittance of a
salary, he wrote symphonies, operas, string quartets and several sacred works. We might well ask ourselves, could
Mozart have been a composer in previous lifetimes?

In 1778, at the age of twenty-two, Wolfgang visited
France, where he wrote the *Paris Symphony*. After his
mother's unexpected death, he went back to Salzburg and
over the next few years completed a series of sacred works
and the famous opera *Idomeneo*.

Mozart was invited to Vienna, where he gave a number
of concerts and became court composer for Joseph II. He
was well known and successful in the eyes of the public. And
in 1782, ignoring his father's advice, Mozart married a Ger-
man woman, Constanze Weber. She bore him six children,
two of whom survived.

In the years that followed, Mozart wrote a number of
magnificent piano concertos and string quartets as well as the
popular operas *The Marriage of Figaro, Don Giovanni, Cosi
fan tutte* and *The Magic Flute*.

In 1791, Mozart began to compose a requiem, music for

the repose of the souls of the dead. As fate would have it, this work remains unfinished due to Mozart's illness and subsequent death that same year. He had the premonition that the requiem would be a self-fulfilling prophecy, and so it proved to be.[3]

Were there any flaws in this man of genius? Yes. Wolfgang was known to be stubborn, which irritated some of his patrons, and he was actually dismissed by one of them after a series of arguments. Perhaps his stubbornness was in the service of his genius; geniuses are often insistent on having their own way.

Parents who have genius children benefit from trying to understand their children's willfulness while at the same time not allowing them to tyrannize other people. Since they are extremely bright, these children frequently respond to dialogue and an explanation of what is in the best interests of the family.

Ludwig van Beethoven

Another of my favorite composers not only had genius but also a handicap in his later years. Ludwig van Beethoven was born in Bonn, Germany, in December 1770, fourteen years after Mozart. He came from a family line of musicians and by age twelve was assisting a well-known organist who was his music teacher.

At the age of sixteen, Ludwig moved to Vienna to further his training but returned almost immediately when his mother fell ill and subsequently died. Two years later, Ludwig had to request the retirement of his alcoholic father, who was a musician in the service of prince elector Max Frank. This circumstance left the care and responsibility for his younger brothers to Ludwig.

In November 1792, when he was twenty-one, Ludwig again set out for Vienna, this time to further his musical training with Franz Josef Haydn. His father's death occurred shortly thereafter. And when the French occupied a portion of Germany in 1794, Ludwig's financial support ended.

By 1795 his two brothers had moved to Vienna. And in 1796, Ludwig took an extended trip to Prague, Dresden and Berlin. He returned to Vienna to spend the remainder of his life, except for vacations and concerts in the local area.

Beethoven faced difficult situations in health and personal relationships in his remaining years of life. The most serious setback was his loss of hearing. He began to notice symptoms of deafness before he reached the age of thirty and wrote despairingly about it in several letters to family and friends. However, he resolved to defy the fates and went on to compose a series of masterful musical compositions.

He also faced heartbreak with the loss of the woman he addressed in a letter as the "Immortal Beloved." Biographers believe she was married and therefore unavailable to him. His life was further complicated by the fact that the loss of hearing had progressed so far that his public performances had to stop.

Beethoven's works are typically grouped into his early, middle and late periods. Beginning in 1792 and through his early period, he studied the best music of the time and mastered Hadyn's and Mozart's classical form. And he composed primarily piano and chamber music. A composition for voice from this period is the oratorio *Christ on the Mount of Olives*.

His middle period, 1801–1814, brought forth dramatic symphonies and sonatas, which have been described as having "a heroic cast" arising from the trauma of deafness that Beethoven was suffering. During this period he also composed piano and violin concertos, piano trios, and the incidental music (music played to heighten the mood or effect on the audience in a dramatic presentation) for Goethe's drama *Egmont*.

Beethoven's style in his late period, 1814–1827, has been described as generally introspective, a style that undoubtedly echoed his mood. He wrote a piece of music, *To the Distant Beloved*, which we might suspect was connected with his earlier letter to the "Immortal Beloved." He composed a number of string quartets and sonatas for the piano and cello, the *Missa Solemnis* mass, and the well known *Ninth Symphony*, completed in 1823.

Understandably, Beethoven isolated himself socially as his deafness increased. In poignant words in a letter, Beethoven described the pain of his deafness: "My misfortune pains me doubly, in as much as it leads to my being misjudged. For me there can be no relaxation in human society; no refined conversations, no mutual confidences. I must live quite alone and may creep into society only as often as sheer necessity demands; I must live like an outcast. If I appear in company I am overcome by a burning anxiety, a fear that I am running the risk of letting people notice my condition. . . . Such experiences almost made me despair, and I was on the point of putting an end to my life—the only thing that held me back was my art. For indeed it seemed to me impossible to leave this world before I had produced all the works that I felt the urge to compose, and thus I have dragged on this miserable existence."[4]

Parents of handicapped children can be heartened by Beethoven's accomplishments. Even in the face of impossible odds, he fulfilled his musical destiny. We can encourage our children never to give up, no matter what the odds. Every child is special in the eyes of God—and infinitely more than his or her handicap.

All of us as parents and mentors can encourage young people to maximize their talents. And we can offer encouragement and support when they feel discouraged. Who knows? Perhaps your child or someone you are mentoring will excel in a way that creates a better tomorrow for the next generation.

King Tutankhamen

If we go farther back in time, we find that ancient history also had its remarkable children. For example, Tutankhamen, who was crowned king of Egypt in 1361 B.C. when he was nine years old. He reigned until he died, at the peak of his youth, at age eighteen.

Tutankhamen left a notable legacy in his underground tomb, over five thousand items, some of the greatest treasures the world has ever known. Many pieces are made of gold and decorated with semiprecious stones. And as was the custom of the times, the tomb also contained many items for the king's use in his afterlife, including clothing, board games and seeds for a garden.

On Web sites that describe Tutankhamen's life, you can view the golden mask that was placed upon him when he was buried so long ago. The mask has been displayed at the Cairo Museum in Egypt.[5]

Mozart, Beethoven and Tutankhamen were young geniuses who left a rich legacy for the world. How can we help the geniuses of our generation do the same?

Today's Young Geniuses

Today's children who have the characteristics of genius may also start careers when they are young. Three young girls featured in The Kids Hall of Fame exemplify the kinds of talents and interests of bright youngsters who are helping to shape the world of tomorrow.[6] Many children who haven't yet been cited in The Kids Hall of Fame are also busily creating their own legacy.

A Young Poet

Before the age of five one little girl became interested in poetry—she was fascinated by the words on gift cards. She started composing her own poems and earning awards for them. At one point she sent a copy of her published book of poetry to the president of the United States. And he encouraged her. This young girl loves to give poetry readings, has held book signings and has appeared on TV. She tells people through her poems that all children are important, no matter who they are or where they live.

A Young Linguist

Another young girl's ability was evident before the age of three. She was learning several languages at once, and by the age of five had appeared on TV. She decided to illustrate a little book she wrote and ultimately became a published author. When people ask this young girl how she got so smart, she tells them it came down the family line and she works at it a lot.

A Young Craftsman

A third young girl loves crafts and has written a book to teach other children how to make special items out of everyday things. She also gives demonstrations of how to do it. A true humanitarian at heart, this child happily donates some of her proceeds to charity. And she tells young writers that even though writing a book is hard work, if they write a few pages a day their book will soon get done.

Home-Schooling Genius Children

The first important step in nurturing a child's genius is identifying the gifted youngster at an early age. And this is often problematic because genius children are a challenge to teach in the ordinary classroom. They catch on quicker than their classmates and are soon bored because their minds are moving faster than the instruction. Teachers may very well think of them as hyperactive troublemakers rather than kids with genius potential.

Most parents cannot afford private tutors for these children. However, other options are being taken by parents who are determined that their children's gifts will not sit in a dusty corner of the mind. Home-schooling is one excellent alternative.

Charlotte Mason, a nineteenth-century educator, is perhaps the best-known originator of home-schooling methods. She was an inspiring, modest woman with a great sense of humor. Most important, she loved children with a passion. And she wanted to strengthen their love of learning so that it would stay with them for life. Her philosophy was based, as was Maria Montessori's, on the concept of *educare*, meaning to train or develop knowledge.

In Charlotte Mason's time, education was quite different from what it is today. Schooling meant learning the basics of reading, writing and arithmetic and spending many hours writing on slate tablets, cleaning them off and using them again. Children were expected to memorize major cities, historical dates and the spelling of difficult words. If a lesson wasn't properly done or mischief took the place of diligence, a strapping or banishment to the corner was a typical consequence.

Charlotte's educational methods were anathema to the society of the time because she was nontraditional. However, her innovative methods worked. She understood the child's mind and had the capacity to inspire her students to strive for the highest of which they were capable.

Her approach was based on mastering the three R's, with an additional smorgasbord of broad areas of study, including drawing, painting and sculpture. Children learned directly from the practice of music and art and from timeless stories that touched the mind and heart. They were trained to recite to the teacher what they had learned, a forerunner of today's essay exams. The teacher's emphasis was on what the student knew and could describe.

Charlotte's students kept a nature diary and their own "Book of the Centuries"—a few pages of important facts, historical personages and major events for each century. They studied entire books of the best literary works available. And Charlotte was careful not to expose them to "twaddle," her name for literature that was too simplified. Charlotte's method involved brief periods of instruction, which promoted concentration. And her students thrived.

The children kept their own journals, recording their activities, thoughts and feelings, favorite sayings, poems, personal mottoes and reflections. They also copied memorable poems, prose and quotes, which gave them practice in handwriting, spelling and grammar. And each day included free time to pursue crafts, leisure activities or other areas of a child's personal interest.

They took daily walks and special weekly nature walks and kept a notebook that included their own drawings of flowers, trees, plants and animals with the Latin names, poems related to nature, and notes on the weather. They learned art by studying a particular artist, being shown his or her work for five minutes and then relating what they had seen. And when they had internalized the work of that artist, Charlotte would introduce a new artist.

Charlotte Mason also emphasized forming good habits, one at a time. She described habits as "ruts in a path from a wheelbarrow going down the same trail again and again." She knew that when a child formed a good habit, both school and home life would go more smoothly. This brilliant teacher instilled an exploratory spirit and a sense of practicality in her students. Thus did she nurture the inner genius of the child.[7]

Innovative Education in the Twenty-First Century

A modern innovative approach links public schools with colleges and universities that provide campus initiatives that meet the needs of children and teachers as well as college students, faculty, and the wider community. These initiatives include remedial instruction, tutors, mentors and advanced study for gifted kids.

Since the 1970s Hartford, Connecticut, has exercised this option. A letter from the Hartford Consortium for Higher Education describes this collaborative approach:

> The member colleges/universities of the Consortium operate a range of innovative programs in partnership with public schools from tutoring to professional development for teachers to science and technology enrichment

for students.... Thousands of youngsters ... benefit from these activities.... Two members of the Hartford Consortium ... have magnet schools on their campuses that are enriched by their connections to higher education leadership and resources.[8]

Along with these programs, the Consortium offers Career Beginnings to young people in the Hartford area. This program provides guidance to students as they consider educational opportunities and career choices.

Another innovative program awards federally funded grants to "magnet schools," schools that offer a wide variety of instruction and options. Schools participating in the Magnet Schools Assistance Program are required to offer educational and cultural activities that

- improve the racial balance among area schools;

- provide innovative education practices and methods;

- achieve systematic reform within the school, providing all students with the opportunity to achieve high standards; and

- use high-quality classroom instruction in the curricular areas of the magnet program.

One such magnet-school program is being conducted in North Carolina with great success. Beginning in 1982, Wake County initiated magnet schools. They developed a curriculum that provides a variety of choices, helps students maximize their creativity, and stimulates higher achievement.

Wake County public school officials have this to say about their cutting-edge programs:

> Our network of magnet schools offers parents a choice of instructional programs such as Creative Arts

and Sciences, Gifted and Talented, International Studies, Global Communications, International Baccalaureate, Language Exploration, Community Model, Leadership, Montessori, Museums, University Connections, Accelerated Studies and Year-Round.[9]

Magnet Schools of America, the national association of magnet schools, honored the Wake County Schools with its National Champion of Public Choice Award in the year 2000.

Whether parents choose public schools, home-schooling, collaborative programs with universities, or magnet schools, options are out there these days. And most important of all is parental involvement in the education of youth and children. The better educated a young person is, the more facile he or she will be in the arena of returning karma, which begins to unfold for most young people at age twelve, when they are in middle school or beyond.

Entering the Arena of Returning Karma

Many times we find ourselves feeling uplifted for no particular reason or downhearted for no good reason. Sometimes the downhearted part is because of physical or emotional circumstances. Yet at other times we throw up our hands in shock and say, "That must have come from another life!"

We may be saying more truth than we realize. From experiences of my own and those of clients and friends, I have come to understand that the soul has been through many lifetimes and old traumatic experiences have left their mark. Thus, even as the soul is prepared by the angels and the Higher Self and looks forward to new opportunity in a new embodiment, she may find herself hesitant as she reenters the portals of life. Why? The soul realizes she is reentering the arena of returning karma.

Each lifetime the soul is born in a new body to a family necessitated by karma (both the good and not-so-good karma). And the soul of the developing child goes through all kinds of experiences—some rewarding and some traumatic. The positive experiences are comforting and inspiring, while the traumas are a wake-up call—a reminder of soul lessons to be learned and dimensions of soul growth to be attained.

All of us can get enmeshed in the memory of painful experiences and distracted by the emotional pain that comes with that recall. And our soul can be hampered from learning her lessons by defensive habit patterns we develop to survive mentally, emotionally and physically. We gain insight when we realize that traumas in this life often relate to karmic lessons still to be learned from past lives.

The soul cries out to be healed from painful encounters and yet is impelled to repeat them until the lessons are learned. Thus, we need to exercise patience and compassion for the soul's predicament—our own soul and the soul of each family member. As fathers and mothers we are called to mentor our offspring, and we in turn may call upon our Higher Self and the angels to help us mentor our own soul.

As we move through life experiences and pick up dropped stitches of lessons not mastered earlier in this life or in previous lifetimes, we gain greater mastery over life's challenges. And the sense of relief we experience in doing so is coupled with the joy of the soul—"I passed my test!"

Cinderella: A Story of the Soul

Classic fables and fairy tales often tell a story about the soul, and there is always a spiritual interpretation of these stories. The fairy tale of *Cinderella* can be seen as a story of the pain of the soul, the tests of the soul, and her redemption.

While the original Grimm's fairy tale and the movie versions differ, the theme is the same: a soul of light assaulted by the forces of darkness. Let us look at the Cinderella story from a spiritual point of view.

In the classic tale, a rich man's wife falls sick and she tells her daughter to be "good and pious," that God will protect her and that she will be watching over her daughter from heaven. After she dies the husband remarries. The stepmother brings with her two daughters, who look beautiful but have vile hearts. And we begin to see the work of evil forces.

The stepmother and stepdaughters take away Cinderella's nice clothes and give her an ugly old dress and clunky wooden shoes. She is at their beck and call as the maid. From daybreak to nightfall Cinderella lights the fire in the fireplace, carries the water from the well, cooks and washes. And her stepsisters make fun of her every step of the way. She has no place to sleep except in the cinders by the fireplace, and they mockingly call her Cinderella.

From a spiritual perspective we can view Cinderella's story as a metaphor of the soul caught in her karmic predicament. And the stepsisters and wicked stepmother represent forces of evil assaulting the soul.

One day the father goes to a festival and asks the three daughters what they would like him to buy for them. The stepdaughters want fancy clothes and jewelry. Cinderella simply asks for "the first branch which knocks against your hat on your way home." When a hazel twig does exactly that, the father breaks off the branch and gives it to Cinderella. She plants the branch on her mother's grave, where it grows into a beautiful tree.

Cinderella often cries as she sits under the hazel tree and a little white bird brings her whatever she wishes for. We can think of the white bird as symbolic of the Holy Spirit, the Comforter, often portrayed as a white dove.

As it happens, the King announces three days of festivity to which he invites every young girl in the kingdom so that the King's son may choose his bride. Cinderella happily looks forward to attending. However, the cruel stepmother makes her help the stepsisters get ready but refuses to let her go.

When everyone has left for the festival, Cinderella runs to the mother's grave under the hazel tree and cries out,

> Shiver and quiver, little tree,
> Silver and gold throw down over me.

The little white bird tosses down a beautiful gold and silver dress and slippers embroidered with silk and silver. Cinderella attends the ball and no one recognizes her, including her sisters, who think she is at home working or sleeping in the cinders.

The prince is captivated and will dance only with Cinderella. And when she wants to go home, he tries to accompany her. She escapes by jumping into a pigeon-house and just as quickly jumping out the back. She puts the beautiful clothes on her mother's grave, and the little white bird removes them.

The second day Cinderella appears at the festival in an even more beautiful gown. The prince dances with no one but her and determines to find out who she is. He follows her when she leaves, but she climbs a tall pear tree and jumps down the other side. When the family returns home, she is sitting in the ashes.

The third day Cinderella arrives at the festival wearing an even more elegant gown and golden slippers. This time the prince has cleverly had the staircase daubed with a tarry substance, and one of Cinderella's slippers gets stuck as she flees the ball. The prince announces, "No one shall be my wife but she whose foot this golden slipper fits."

The two stepsisters are certain theirs will fit. And when the eldest sister's foot is too big, she cuts off her toe and forces her bleeding foot into the shoe. As the King's son rides away with her, they pass the hazel tree and two pigeons cry out:

> Turn and peep, turn and peep,
> There's blood within the shoe,
> The shoe is too small for her,
> The true bride waits for you.

The King's son realizes he's been tricked. So the other sister tries on the shoe. Her toes fit but she has to cut off a bit of her heel. As she and the King's son ride away, the pigeons cry out:

> Turn and peep, turn and peep,
> There's blood within the shoe,
> The shoe is too small for her,
> The true bride waits for you.

The King's son sees blood running out of the shoe and takes her back. He asks if there is another daughter and the father says only a kitchen wench who couldn't in any way be the young woman he's seeking.

The prince insists on seeing her and Cinderella bows to him. She puts on the golden slipper, which fits her perfectly. He recognizes Cinderella as the lovely girl he has danced with at the festival. And to the horror of the wicked stepmother and stepsisters, he announces, "This is the true bride!"

Analyzing this fairy tale metaphorically, we view the Prince as the Higher Self, seeking reunion with the soul. And Cinderella is the soul seeking to free herself from the cinders of her karma. No matter what plots and ploys they concoct, the forces of evil represented by the wicked stepmother and jealous stepsisters do not win out. When the soul is pure in heart, evil ultimately has no power. Thus the soul, portrayed by Cinderella, outwits the evil forces and weds her Higher Self, depicted by the prince. And they live happily ever after.[10]

The concept that Cinderella is symbolic of our soul and the prince is a representation of our Higher Self relates to the spiritual teachings of Gnosticism. Gnosis, from which the term *Gnosticism* derives, refers to an intuitive understanding of the mystery of the self. Many Gnostics taught that the soul or spirit was held captive by evil forces until awakened to her true nature in God by the redeemer, who quickens the soul and points the way to self-discovery and salvation.

In her book *The Gnostic Gospels*, Elaine Pagels explains that in ancient times those who embraced Gnosticism believed in God as both masculine and feminine. Although this ancient teaching on the spiritual mysteries has been a subject of controversy over the centuries, it appears to be gaining support among biblical scholars today.[11]

We Are Students of the Soul

Elizabeth Clare Prophet teaches that not only are we parents and teachers of the soul, we are also students of the soul:

> The ascended masters have referred to the soul as the child who lives inside of us. Psychologists have dubbed the soul "the inner child." The soul by any other name is still the soul. And we are her parents and teachers even

as we are her students.

It is our responsibility to daily impress upon the soul (1) what is right—what is real and of enduring worth and therefore must be kept; and (2) what is wrong—what is not real and not of enduring worth and therefore must not be kept but cast into the sacred fire.

As parents, we can lovingly care for our souls as we would care for our children, or we can neglect our souls and become creatures of our own self-neglect, i.e., soul-neglect. Proverbs says, "Train up a child in the way he should go: and when he is old, he will not depart from it."[12] These words refer to one's soul as well as to one's offspring.

The ascended masters do not intend that we should be led around by every whim of our souls, even as they do not intend that we should be led around by every whim of our children. Since the soul is our child until she comes of age, we must love and protect, instruct and discipline her on the spiritual path.

El Morya says that we should not place our emphasis on being obedient to the soul as the inner child, but rather that we should place our emphasis on teaching the soul to be obedient to God and to her Holy Christ Self. You would not allow your children to dictate the terms of your household or your comings and goings, so why would you allow your soul, your inner child, to dominate you and tell you, "Go here. Go there. Do this. Do that"?

The soul is the little child who is destined to become the Christ Child. Let us lead our souls even as we are led by our Holy Christ Self. Moreover, let us remember that as parents and teachers we are responsible for the protection and education not only of our children but also of our souls, that we might mold both the souls of our children and our own souls after the heavenly patterns.[13]

We need to remember that we are spiritual beings on an earthly journey. We have lived many lifetimes in physical bodies as we have sought to fulfill our soul's mission. And this is the lifetime when many souls are intended to complete the journey victoriously and return home to God.

Thus it is important that we recognize our soul as the living potential of God within us, the spiritual being we inwardly know ourselves to be, the part of us that has lived long on planet Earth and yearns to return to the heaven-world. We are called to cherish and champion our soul and to fulfill her raison d'être—even as we nurture and guide the souls of our children to fulfill theirs.

As we awaken to who we really are, we contemplate the karmic lessons we still need to master. Those lessons become apparent in our flaws of character, our secret sins or vices, and our unwitting reactions to other people. When we catch ourselves being negative toward our self or other people or difficult situations, we do best to take a time out and ask our Higher Self: "Why am I so upset? What is my lesson? What do I need to change in myself? How can I move beyond this negative reaction? How would my Higher Self respond to that person or handle this situation?"

Often when we do this we discover to our discomfort that a part of us is the troublemaker. And that troublemaker seems almost impossible to get around. The feelings are so strong, the instinct to lash out so compelling. We are now face to face with our own dweller-on-the-threshold. If we're smart we'll get down on our knees and implore God to help us. That's step one.

Step two: We lasso the troublemaker dweller until we

can redeem it. The best way I know to do that is to give the decree "I Cast Out the Dweller-on-the-Threshold"* for the binding of these negative patterns that seem to have a life of their own. We know we don't want to behave badly, but we find ourselves doing it anyway. When we give this decree, we invoke God's angels to bind that pesky dweller.

Step three: We need to come up with a positive solution. And remember that God never gives us a test we can't pass. So we pray for guidance and then ask ourselves, "What would my favorite hero or saint do?"

Step four: We walk ourselves through what we know that hero or saint would do. We rehearse it in our mind and out loud. And we practice it as if we were going to perform on stage.

Step five: We take the action in real life making certain we are balanced, firm but soft-spoken.

Step six: No matter the result, we choose to be upbeat.

Step seven: We thank God and our Higher Self for the opportunity to increase our self-mastery.

As we pass our spiritual tests and grow in inner strength, wisdom and compassion, we ready ourselves for our return to the octaves of light. In accordance with our love for God, compassion for others, the balancing of our karma and the fulfillment of our soul's divine plan, we can ultimately achieve our victory, whereby we, one with our soul, reunite with the Spirit of the living God, the beloved I AM Presence. This ritual, known as the ascension, is the culmination of the soul's sojourn in time and space. It is the final initiation and divine destiny intended for every son and daughter of God.

---

*See "Spiritual Formulas for Family Harmony and Soul Liberation," pp. 123–30.

Teachings on Family Karma

Elizabeth Clare Prophet taught her students about the role of karma in family relationships and how love and forgiveness heal the soul and liberate the spirit:

> This is an imperfect world, and we descend into it because we have our own karma of being imperfect.
>
> Many parents try very hard to do their best for us. They make mistakes, thinking they are doing good for our souls and for our beings. Many of them are influenced by all kinds of philosophies and psychological systems of child-rearing and they make mistakes. And we have to forgive our parents their mistakes, even as we will forgive ourselves for coming into a situation and bringing our own mistakes of the past with us....

Exercise Compassion

> We can have compassion and not come down upon our parents as though they should have been omniscient and known every possible technique of dealing with us— and dealing with us not just as a baby like every other baby but as a unique person, the unique person that we were in the womb, already burdened, already having scars, already having genius, already having talents, already knowing how to manipulate parents. We have to realize that parents would have to be absolute geniuses to know from day one exactly how to deal with us every step of the way.
>
> So I think we need to come off of this and recognize: "Okay, there were those elements, but I am who I am and I am a soul in God and I am an immortal God-free being and I am determining my course in this life.
>
> "I understand what it means to have dysfunctional parents; I will send them mercy and forgiveness and

healing. And I will make certain that I correct those elements in myself, give my own children a better opportunity to become who they are, and in the process of trying, I may make mistakes. People who do nothing are the only people in the world who make no mistakes.". . .

The Four Lower Bodies

You always have to remember that these four lower bodies* are merely coats of skins, as it is referred to in Genesis. We wear them. They affect how our soul expresses itself, but we will not wear these bodies and their momentums forever. We have an ascended master light body. And we will cast off these coats of skins when we have worked through them and brought ourselves into resolution and brought them into submission to the living Christ.

So you have four children—you have four lower bodies. You are already a parent while you are still a child. Your four lower bodies are your four horsemen, and as you train them, so they will function for you. As you indulge them, so they will be indulgent, and so forth. As you are divisive in your thinking and feeling, so your four lower bodies will not work as a harmonious whole.

So we already have a laboratory of self and those of us who have tried it out know just how much those four lower bodies can perform when we determine that they are going to perform—and just how lazy the mind, the physical body, the memory, and even the desire [emotional] body can get when we give it no stimulus, no encouragement, no goading to move forward, and no exercise.

---

*The four lower bodies are the etheric (spiritual), mental, emotional and physical aspects of our being.

So we can see a parallel here in the bringing-up of our children. I believe that if you count the children you have, the first child represents [the patterns of] your etheric body, the second your mental, the third the emotional, the fourth the physical, and it starts round again depending on how many children you have....And you'll find that your children each have a greater development in those areas according to the order of their appearance in your family.

Pass Every Test!

There is no question about it that the law of God requires that we work through relationships which we have with people with whom we have karma. We just don't walk out on relationships. We determine that whatever is the problem, we are going to resolve it. If we have to change ourselves, we will change ourselves until we can be completely harmonious and loving and able to work with a certain individual.

That individual may not change, but we will know when we have brought to him or to her everything that we have of our God-free being and when we truly have conquered our pride, our stubbornness, our rebellion, our resentment, our envy, our jealousy and all of those things that go into interpersonal relationships.

When we can truly stand at the altar before God and say, "I have nothing toward this individual but love, and I am loving no matter what this individual does or says," we know that that is coming toward the resolution which is the liberation, desiring nothing of that person but only to serve the Lord, the Christ, in that one and to help that soul.

We come to a point of personal love and impersonal love, and we find that when we have passed all of our tests with that individual and served to the level where the karma is also balanced, God will change our circumstance.

And it's very important that we see that and that we not be so quick to move away from those individuals where the karma is not balanced. And when it is not balanced, we will have to meet that one again or do some mighty work at inner levels and in our physical embodiment of violet flame to transmute it.[14]

Over many lifetimes we have created karma that culminates in our problematic experiences in this life. The karma propels us into circumstances that allow the soul to undertake and pass certain spiritual and physical tests. Our karma is like a neon sign flashing what we need to learn in order to handle our life situations and encounters with other people. Karma is a teacher.

Thus it is important to reach the point of responsibility where we say, "I take responsibility for myself, for my karma and for my psychological take on life. My parents, family and the friends I have grown up with are responsible for their actions. But I am responsible for my own actions and reactions; I am responsible for who I am and what I choose to do today."

When we choose to take responsibility for our own motives, thoughts, feelings and actions, we become as beacons of light to guide our children and youth. And we feel an inner joy in knowing we are balancing our karma and helping our family along the way.

Helping Young People Become Their Best Self

We can help young people become their best self. How? We can tell them about their wonderful qualities. We can teach them how to overcome negative thoughts and desires and abstain from hurtful behavior. By word and example we can show children and youth how to be respectful of other people's feelings. We can demonstrate unconditional love—which doesn't mean permissiveness. It means, "I do not necessarily like what you just did, but I love you and I'll help you do better next time."

We teach our youth emotional resilience by handling our own emotional reactions in a constructive way. And we inspire respect for body and soul by living our higher values. In order to be successful as parents and teachers, we also need a certain sense of humor about the ups and downs of life. As we lighten up we brighten the day for everybody.

All of us have had the experience of watching children learn, grow, mature and move beyond what we have taught them. This is the joy of parenting and teaching. We rejoice as young people entrusted to our care unfold the gifts of their soul and spirit, their unique individuality and the building blocks of their character. We thank God for the next generation!

As youth strive to fulfill their destiny, they place their feet firmly on the path leading to the summit of the mountain of selfhood. And that summit is often beyond our wildest hopes and dreams. We watch with awe as young people stretch to fulfill a human destiny and to forge a destiny divine. And we determine to stretch to fulfill our own soul's destiny.

I'd like to share with you an exercise to accelerate the healing of soul and spirit. My clients have found it helpful and rewarding. I suggest you do the exercise in a quiet place at a time that you will be undisturbed.

A Dialogue for Healing the Soul and Spirit

1. Ask your Higher Self and the angels to help you in the work of healing your soul and spirit.

2. Tune into whatever uncomfortable feeling is bothering you. It could be a feeling of hurt, fear, vulnerability, sadness, resentment, anger, shame. Name the feeling that troubles you and make a note of it.

3. Ask yourself: When is the earliest time in my life I remember feeling this way? How old was I? What happened? What person or event triggered this feeling? Write down your answers to these questions.

4. Put your arms around yourself as if you were hugging that younger self as you talk about what happened. As the loving adult, try to express the qualities of your Higher Self.

5. Tell your younger self that you want to help heal that hurtful experience. Ask that wounded self: How can I help you? What do you need me to do for you right now?

6. Listen to whatever your younger self asks for and respond directly to the request. If it's something not possible to do at the moment, set a definite time when you will do it. Be a strong and comforting adult that your younger self can depend on.

7. Answer truthfully whatever questions your younger self asks. Ask your Higher Self or the angels for help if you get stuck as to what to say or how to help this wounded part of you.

8. Tell your younger self: I love you for who you are. I love you when you make mistakes, when you're

scared, when you're hurt or angry. And I will do my best to help you heal this hurt. Our Higher Self will help us, and we can do it!

9. Listen to the response from your younger self and continue the dialogue until you feel a sense of peace and inner resolution. Give your younger self another hug, agree to meet again, and ask your Guardian Angel to escort him or her to the secret chamber of the heart [15] and take care of both of you until the next visit.

Jot a few notes to yourself after the dialogue so that you will be able to follow through with what you have learned and agreed to do. And make it a point to talk to your younger self once a week or whenever you feel you need the connection.

PART THREE

Integration of Soul
and Culture

9

The Care of Discipline
Is Love's Fulfillment

The true beginning of wisdom
is the desire of discipline,
and the care of discipline is love.

—ECCLESIASTICUS
The Apocrypha

*D*o your children or teens enjoy being at home? Is your family a haven to come home to? If not, ask yourself, why not? And consider making some changes. Children and teenagers need to know that they are loved and their gifts are appreciated in the family circle. They feel supported when they can come to parents for guidance and advice. And they look to parents and older siblings to help them when they face difficult situations.

When we look at raising a family from the perspective of what we accomplish in a lifetime, we realize family is a major part of the balancing of karma and the fulfillment of dharma. And we have such a short period of time to give our children the love, support and discipline they need to be successful in their own lives.

Helping the Child Develop Key Qualities

We could list many traits that are important for children to develop. When I reflect on what I have learned as a mother, a psychologist and minister, I believe that the key qualities young people need to develop are a giving heart, a thirst for wisdom, emotional control and self-discipline. And these qualities begin to develop in the home.

How do we help our children develop these qualities? First and foremost, they learn from our attitudes and behaviors. And second, they learn from their experiences.

The Joy of Laughter

A child's heart is nourished by the joy of laughter and by tenderness and loving appreciation within the family circle. He learns from interactions with family and friends the importance of being loving and kind to others. His heart opens up to a pet, such as a puppy or kitten or little bird, that is a source of joy in his life. And he learns the joy of giving as he helps his mom clean the house and his dad wash the car, when he hugs his little sister and gives his brother a hand with mowing the lawn.

The beauty of nature helps all of us open our hearts to the love of the Creator. Whether it's watching a beautiful sunset, looking in wonderment at the stars at night, enjoying the beauty and uplift of a rushing waterfall, or driving through beautiful pines or tall redwood trees, we see the wonder of the universe everywhere in nature. We naturally respond with a burst of joy in our heart and praise to our Maker—and it's somehow easier to be kind and loving toward one another.

A Thirst for Wisdom

Every child has a natural curiosity, which turns into knowledge as he explores his world and the adults around him take his questions seriously and help him discover the answers. Even if we as parents think we know the answers, it's a good idea to teach the child to look up information in an encyclopedia or other library books or on the Web. Additional insight is often gleaned by combining life experience and the information available in modern times with the knowledge of the ancients cited in reference books.

The family also nurtures the exploring mind of the child through nature walks, family excursions and games that expand the mind. Exploring the world through books, the travel channel and programs such as NASA's Education Hour also nurtures a child's curiosity. The knowledge a child gains begets wisdom as these bits of information lead to reflection and a sense of mindfulness within the child. Spiritually, wisdom has been described as "wise dominion," meaning the wise ruling of our self in relation to the way we live our life and interact with other people and the environment.

Emotional Control

What about emotional control—how does a child develop that quality? Most of us understand the power of emotions and how much of our life is emotionally driven. We could write an entire book on emotions, and in fact many books have been written, one of them by this author.[1] Perhaps the most important point for parents and teachers to understand is that emotions are a powerful instinctive force that can be used for good or for ill. We want to teach our children to harness their emotions for good.

Perhaps the most important way a child develops emotional control is by imitating parents or teachers who exhibit that kind of self-control in the home or at school. Of course, none of us are perfect, but parents need to exercise balance and restraint as best they can. Demonstrating emotional control is a more powerful lesson than simply talking about it. Children need to learn how to handle their emotions when they are stirred up.

This process takes patience and loving discipline on the part of parents. Over and over a parent may need to help a child take a time-out, to take several slow, deep breaths, remember a happy experience, and seek a creative solution to the crisis. But it's worth it. The result for parents and children is not only a more peaceful household but also the fruit of higher consciousness. As Dr. Christine Page describes it, "Liberating the golden seed that sits within some of the most difficult emotions can produce greater light energy and consciousness than the individual has ever experienced before."[2]

Self-Discipline

What about a child learning self-discipline? How do we teach that? In the first place, we need to realize that loving and protecting children includes giving consequences for physical acting-out, e.g., punching your sister, throwing a tantrum, running across the street instead of coming when called, or refusing to do your chores. However, discipline needs to happen once everyone has calmed down instead of in the heat of a reactive moment. Discipline is meant not only to teach the child the logical consequences of behavior but also to help the child learn to exercise self-discipline.

When we observe a child trying to self-correct, it is

important to acknowledge and appreciate the effort. And creating a system of logical rewards for a child's self-discipline is also a useful tool. For example, if after a discipline the child refrains from punching his sister, he might earn a privilege. However, if he repeats the infraction, the discipline would be given again. When we discipline a child thoughtfully and kindly, explaining as we go, we help that child take a step forward toward self-discipline.

If we look at discipline from a spiritual point of view, the soul of the child expects parents to stand in for God and to teach boundaries and limits on the physical plane. This knowledge assists the soul to fulfill her spiritual mission on Earth. Thus, during childhood and the teenage years, the soul is in training to become the disciplined one. Parental discipline that is loving and appropriate to the infraction helps children to mold their character and to unfold the majesty of their soul.

The Seeds of Character

Here is a wonderful story that highlights the importance of self-discipline in molding a young person's character:

> Ling was excited. The Emperor had invited young people in the land to a palace assembly. When they arrived, each was given a seed. They were to plant it, water it faithfully and return in a year with the fruits of their labor. The Emperor said the successor to his throne was among them.
>
> Ling hurried home. He planted his seed, watered it and placed it in a sunny window. Nothing grew. He fertilized it. Months went by. Nothing happened.
>
> Hesitantly Ling returned to the palace at the appointed time. He was embarrassed when he saw the

other children's plants and flowers. He picked a spot in the back.

The Emperor spotted him and called him forward. Ling reluctantly approached as the kids snickered. The Emperor asked his name. "I am Ling, your majesty."

The Emperor bowed and said, "One year ago I gave each of you a boiled seed that could not grow. Yet, today I see every kind of plant that grows in our land. Ling is the only one among you with enough honesty to bring back an empty pot and face possible ridicule and reproach. That kind of integrity shows nobility. All bow to your next ruler, Ling!"[3]

Discipline Is the Fulfillment of Love

The ascended master Paul the Venetian, known as the chohan of the ray of divine love,[4] gave a compelling dictation* about discipline being the fulfillment of love. Here is a part of his message to our soul and the souls of our children:

> As love is the flowing essence, the ephemeral quality of God, as it is the movement of the wind and the flowing of water, it requires the greatest of discipline to be able to retain—to have and to hold that love that is so tender, so gentle, and yet the ultimate expression of creative fires. Those who are the greatest artists, poets, and musicians who use the flame of love to implement an idea of God are those who have the greatest discipline—discipline of self, energies of self, of life, even of time and space.

---

*A dictation is a message from an ascended master, an archangel or another advanced spiritual being delivered through the agency of the Holy Spirit by a messenger of the Great White Brotherhood (*white* refers to the light of the Christ and not to race).

I come, then, to bring to you an understanding of this discipline so that you will understand that discipline is not something to be feared, but discipline is the Law, the fulfillment of love. Discipline is a grid, a forcefield that is necessary in order to have the flow of love and to retain the flow of love.

You notice all around you where there are undisciplined lives how love flies out the window, how love is compromised and perverted and then lost. Where energies in motion are undisciplined, where there is not a chalice that can contain the fire of love, mankind lose that love. . . .

To continue to receive love you must give love. But love is given in rhythm, in measured harmony, in increments of gratitude and a bursting forth of joy—a bursting forth that seems uncontrolled yet that proceeds from the bubbling fountain of the heart, the heart that knows that it is in that God-control of energy flow.

Understand, then, that when you discipline your energy, your supply, your expression, the hours of your day, your service to life, you are increasing your capacity to release love. The more you are disciplined the stronger are the grids of consciousness. And to have a strong consciousness, as strong sinews, enables you to balance megatons of the light-force that you call love. . . .

Open the Gift of Love in Your Heart

All of the science of the Aquarian age, given at the hand of the alchemist Saint Germain,[5] is channeled to mankind as the flame of God-love. For out of love is the fulfillment of the Mother flame of every invention, every aspect of divine reality that is waiting to be lowered into manifestation through the creative genius of many among you and many among mankind.

Unfortunately, due to the educational systems of the world and the equation of certain mass concepts and certain omissions of concepts that ought to be taught from childhood, mankind have a misunderstanding of creative genius and they are not taught of the talents of the LORD given to each one, nor are they taught how to release those talents and those flames of their innate God reality. People feel a sense of worthlessness and that only the few have the ability to invent and to create.

But I am here to tell you that locked in the heart of every one of you is a unique idea of love that you can bring forth for the benefit of your fellowman and the progress of the culture of the Divine Mother. It may be an invention, it may be a poem, it may be a geometric design, but it is a gift, which only you can bring forth. Unfortunately, many of you have held that gift in your heart for a succession of embodiments simply because no one has told you that you could release it, that you could bring it forth, that you are beings of ultimate creativity.

Why, creativity is the nature of God—your Father, your Mother! If God be creative, then you are creative. In your hands, in your eyes, in the movement of energies through you there is creative flow. And if you have the discipline here below you can realize beautiful thoughtforms in Mater.* You can release those things that are not for profit nor for the trade and merchandising in the world that are here today and gone tomorrow. But you can release something of enduring worth, a pearl of great price, something that will transcend the fads of the times

---

*Thoughtforms are images that represent spiritual concepts. *Mater,* or *Matter,* is a synonym for *Mother,* in this context, Mother Earth or the physical universe.

and move across the centuries as a permanent contribution to the race of mankind.

And so . . . in analyzing what my message should be, it was first of all to tell you that the art of living love is to be creative. And the art of being creative is to be self-disciplined. . . .

Receive the Impartations of Genius

Now self-discipline becomes a point of enlightened self-interest. To move toward the fulfillment of your divine blueprint and your divine plan can be accomplished in the greatest beauty and joy of the fire of love if you will only take me into your daily invocations and give generously of the "Introit to the Holy Christ Self" * so that you can receive directly from your Christ Self the impartations of genius that are native to the "droplet of identity"—and this is what you are in this vast ocean of God's being.

To come into union with the Christ flame is to move with love.

Why cannot you walk the earth as Christed ones? What is hindering your manifestation of the Christ? Only the ignorance, the banality, and the sleep of the ages; only because your billboards and your media are not constantly telling you that you can become the Christ. They tell you other things and you fulfill them out of the hypnotism of the mass consciousness.

Well, I tell you, the media were given to mankind as a means of disciplining self, selfhood, and of releasing to mankind the messages of the ascended masters, the Elohim,[6] and the angelic hosts.

Can you imagine if every time you turned on the television set the announcer said, "You can become the

---

*See pp. 128–29 for this prayer.

Christ"! You would begin to believe it. It would become a common fact—no longer startling or astounding. Well, turn on the television set of your inner being, of your etheric body, tune in to the teachers in the retreats of the ascended masters and hear these teachers as they teach classes in ascended master law.

Here I am releasing an opportunity for you to realize that there is an invention right within you already functioning, a means of contacting through the etheric body—by a mechanism and an electronic frequency far above the physical plane—the octaves of the ascended masters.

Journey to the Etheric Retreats

The ascended masters have retreats on the etheric plane,[7] do they not? This you know. You also know that you have an etheric body. You also know things equal to the same thing are equal to each other. If you have an etheric body, you have a body that is functioning at the frequency of the ascended masters and their retreats. You have been told that your soul, using the vehicle of the etheric body, can journey to those retreats while your physical temple is at rest.

Well, then, since there is in reality no time and space, realize that you can be at any moment of the hour or day in the presence of your teacher. You can be in that retreat through your etheric body because there is no time or space at that plane. And you are where you will to be, where you think you are, where you feel you are.

It simply takes the practice of projecting the mind's eye to that physical point, that geographical location in time and space that is the coordinate of the retreat, which is on the etheric plane. And then, by an inner key which I will allow you to receive from your own Christ Self, you can be transported in frequency, in consciousness, through the ear and the eye and a congruency of your chakras with the ascended masters to their inner retreats. And so, you see, creativity can flow, flow, and flow through you.

Broadcast the Simple Truths

There are so many simple truths that ought to be broadcast across the radio waves. I am delighted to hear the "Hail Mary" coming forth, entering the atmosphere. And do you know that the elementals (nature spirits, beings of fire, air, water, and earth) are tuning in their radio sets to play that "Hail Mary" and to give it with the Mother of the Flame* and the sons and daughters of the flame as that recording is played each morning?

Do you know, then, that the elementals rejoice to see the media, the airwaves, used by the frequencies of the ascended masters, for they know that this will lead to their freedom, to the resurrection and the life within them whereby one day there will be imparted to them that threefold flame† which will be the gift of immortal life? And so, let the waves of the air, let the plane of the mind conduct now that which is in the mind of God that is transferred to and through your mind....

And so, let our experiment be the transfer of frequencies through the lobes of the brain and through the mental body. Let there be a transfer through your minds by the momentum of my love that is God's love, by the momentum of the emerald ray of precipitation—yes,

---

*Mother of the Flame is a title given to Elizabeth Clare Prophet.
†The threefold flame is the flame of the Christ; the spark of life that burns within the secret chamber of the heart (a secondary chakra behind the heart); the sacred trinity of power, wisdom and love that is the manifestation of the sacred fire.

let there be a transfer of energy of God's mind to all minds on the planet and to the mental belt. And let there be a permanent recording in that belt this hour of the geometry of love.

Fashion a Chalice for the Elixir of Love

The geometry of love is the art of living love according to the sacred science, the science that was taught by Melchizedek, priest of Salem and priest of the Most High God—the science that is practiced by artists and artisans of the Spirit.

So let the chalice that was released many years ago as a thoughtform now be given here below as a chalice for the mental body, as a chalice for the mental belt. And let that chalice be for the elixir of love. Let the chalice be a disciplined forcefield given to you at my hand and yet which you yourself must fashion. For this chalice will not remain with you unless you reinforce it by daily application to the discipline of the flame, specifically with calls to the white-fire core made with Serapis Bey and the ascension flame.* For this chalice is composed of ascension fire.

As water seeks its own level, so the flame of perfection seeks its own level. And since the level of mankind's consciousness is at the level of imperfection, all that is perfect that is lowered into form must either be reinforced each twenty-four hours by those in embodiment or, if it is not, it will return to the higher octaves.

You might say, then, that this is a decay rate in reverse, for, of course, perfection does not decay, it simply withdraws. Particle by particle, then, the chalice will return to the level of your Christ flame unless by invocations to that Christ flame you continually reinforce in

---

*Serapis Bey is an ascended master, the chohan of the ray of purity. The white-fire core is the sacred fire of creation and of the ascension.

the physical octave the atoms and molecules of fiery light that compose the chalice.

Now isn't this an interesting experiment? It's almost like going the opposite way on a moving conveyer belt. If you don't keep moving..., you will lose the ground that you have gained. And that is almost how it is prior to your ascension, as though you were on an uphill climb and as though that belt were continually moving, so that once you get on the belt you can never stop, for to stop is to move backwards with the automatic reverse trends of civilization that move down, down, down the mount of attainment.

And that is why progress is the law of being in infinity. Unless you are forever transcending yourself, you are not coming into the perfection of the Christ flame that is continually gathering more of itself, more of God's Self-awareness, continually becoming more and more of God until God in you is the All-in-all.

So I come to release creative fires. I could release much more. But I am limited, not by the laws of cosmos but by karmic law—the law of your own being. For your own being has a law of its own, and each individual has made that law of himself according to himself and his own self-discipline....

Turn Your Chalice Right Side Up

In reality, you are chalices filled with love. But you have inverted those chalices and made of them the entire complement of the electronic belt—the record, the memory of all past misdoings contained in the subconscious at the level of the astral plane.

Now, then, if you think about it, all you have to do is turn that chalice that is upside down right-side up: let the sacred fire pour in, let the misuses be consumed, and you will have megatons of cosmic love at your disposal and a new law of your being, the law of infinity won here below as you become the electrode for the sendings, not only of angels and elementals, but of mighty cosmic beings, Elohim, Mighty Victory,* and the very God of very gods himself.

See, then, karma as the opportunity of God's own love to fulfill his science and to learn the art of living love.

Will you not think of me as you come across those jagged patterns and emotions in your world? Think of the rose of my heart and the delicate petals. Think, then, of taking that energy and fashioning the beautiful rose, even as the lotus grows in the swampland and out of the mud comes forth the beauty of the light of living fire.

So, you see, you can plant a garden that grows from the energies of the electronic belt. You can sow love continuously. You have a reservoir of light on high in your causal body. It has been told to you. But I would remind you that every erg of energy that is transmuted in answer to your call is 'money' in your cosmic bank account. It is 'money' that can be drawn forth and multiplied for the bringing in of the kingdom of God.

Therefore, accept the challenge of the hour to go back and undo those misqualified energies that you left behind on the trail of life. Where you have walked away from karma, go back and fulfill that karma. Be the one who has dominion. Accept the challenge of life to liberate God's energy, to use that supply for the bringing into manifestation of the city foursquare.

If you have walked away from a situation, a karma,

---

*Cosmic beings are beings of God who have never descended below the level of the Christ, have never taken physical embodiment, and have never made human karma. Mighty Victory is a cosmic being who is devoted to the flame of victory and the victory of the lightbearers evolving upon planet Earth.

a marriage, a family, a job, a business where you should have fulfilled the transmutation of love, you still have time in this life to go back and be the living presence of the Christ. And then you will see that to "go back" does not mean to compromise, but to go back means to take your stand with the sacred fire, to compel all human creation to move into that flame. And let the flame take that energy and place it upon the altar of the LORD. This is the cosmic honor flame as it is outlived in love. . . .

Mesh Consciousness with Your Christ Self

Do you not understand that all of the problems of the planet on a planetary scale can be transmuted in the flame of love? This will take place more and more as you bring your consciousness into congruity with your Christ Self. In some of you that Christ Self is hovering perhaps an eighth of an inch or a hundredth of an inch from full congruency with all of your chakras and your mind and heart.

Call, then, for the transmutation of the blockages to the meshing of your consciousness with the consciousness of the Christ. Call for that Christ flame to press in and through you. Call for that Christ consciousness to take over your life, to purge you of all darkness.

I want your hands to be the hands of your Christ Self. I want your very skin to pulsate with the frequencies of the fire of that transparent one. . . . I want you to be, through and through, the frequency of the Christ. For by that love, the planet will be transformed and mankind will know that love has returned. For your own Logos, your own self-awareness in the Christ consciousness is the fulfilling of Law, as Above, so below. It is healing. It is science. It is victory. Love is the All-in-all.[8]

Principles of Loving Discipline

Here are principles that will help you discipline youth and children in a loving way:

1. **Share spiritual principles.** Introduce your children and youth to their spiritual Father and Mother. Tell them about God's love. Teach them to follow the Golden Rule, "Do unto others as you would have them do unto you." Explain that doing this will help them get along better with their friends, family and teachers.

2. **Give clear messages.** Give clear and specific directions. Describe and demonstrate exactly what you want the young person to do.

3. **Use specific consequences.** If you are giving a consequence, be specific. Choose one that has the power to change behavior, which means it's something that matters to the child or teen. Use a positive consequence to encourage desirable behavior and a negative one to stop problem behavior. Be clear, be consistent, be brief, and follow through.

4. **Correct problem behaviors.** Calmly get the young person's attention. Give a clear instruction. Describe what happened or is happening. If necessary, give a consequence. Describe specifically what you want the child to do instead. Give a reason why he or she should do it. Practice the new behavior together. Offer encouragement during practice.

5. **Voice your approval.** Young people need to know when they have done well. Praise is powerful. It nourishes the young person emotionally and helps build self-esteem. Show your approval. Describe specifically what was done well.

6. **Use interactive learning.** Give the child or teen a chance to show what has been learned. Give praise. Be an active part of the learning process and work together toward a common goal.

7. **Be a coach.** Coach the young person by having him or her practice and role play. Be the cheerleader. Follow Ben Franklin's advice: "An ounce of prevention is worth a pound of cure."

8. **Help young people develop self-control.**

   - Step 1: Tell the child or youth what he or she is doing wrong. Clearly describe the correct behavior. Give options for calming down.

   - Step 2: Allow time for calming down. Leave the area for a few minutes. Come back and check on the young person's readiness to continue.

   - Step 3: Describe what the child or teen might do differently when he or she is upset. Rehearse what to do next time. Give feedback and praise for right action during practice.

Teach Problem-Solving Skills

Problem-solving skills are important in changing behavior. For example, you can help young people address problematic situations by talking it over and asking open-ended questions: What happened? What did you do then? What happened after you said that?

Brainstorm together positive ways of handling the situation, focusing on those most likely to have a positive outcome. Discuss the pros and cons and honor the young person's choice of a better solution. Give praise for the positive moves he or she makes in the process. You are helping the young person develop problem-solving skills as well as setting the stage for discussing difficult situations in the future.

Children and youth can also develop problem-solving skills by helping to set family rules. Here is a process that families have found useful:

1. Sit down as a family and discuss whatever problems have been coming up. Make it a point to include the young people's point of view.

2. Discuss together what rules might be helpful and why.

3. Decide as a family on specific rules. Write them down and post them in a convenient place, on the bathroom wall by the mirror or on the refrigerator door.

4. Include both positive and negative consequences, e.g., "If you clean up your room you may watch your favorite TV program." The negative consequence: "If you don't clean up your room, you may not watch TV."

5. Review the rules as necessary or requested by anyone in the family. Since everyone has input in making the rules, it takes a good reason for a change.

6. Praise the young people for following the rules, and follow through with consequences when they do not.

Of course, youth and children are unlikely to sit through family discussions or problem solving without objecting or getting distracted. What do you do? Here are a few suggestions:

- Count to ten very slowly, and ask everybody to do it with you.

- Ask everybody to take a deep breath and let it out slowly. This is a safety valve for pent-up emotions.

- Take a time-out together. Have a snack or a cold drink. Then come back to the family discussion.

In summary, determine a positive course of action, follow through, and keep your cool. Remember, your attitude and behavior are key to the young person learning the lesson. Children and youth learn from the people they live with— and they live what they learn.

Classic Words of Wisdom

All of us would do well to frame in our minds this wonderful message from Dorothy Law Nolte:

The child who lives with criticism learns to condemn.

The child who lives with hostility learns to fight.

The child who lives with ridicule learns to be shy.

The child who lives with shame learns to feel guilty.

The child who lives with tolerance learns to be patient.

The child who lives with encouragement learns confidence.

The child who lives with praise learns to appreciate.

The child who lives with fairness learns justice.

The child who lives with security learns to have faith.

The child who lives with approval learns to like himself.

The child who lives with acceptance and friendship learns to find love in the world.[9]

10

The Education of the Heart

The soul takes nothing with her to the other world
but her education and culture; and these, it is said,
are of the greatest service.

—PLATO
Dialogues

What can we do to maximize spirituality in the family? Rev. E. Gene Vosseler, spiritual leader, writer and former director of social service programs for disadvantaged youth, delivered a lecture for "Festival of the Family," a gathering held several years ago in Toronto, Canada. He made a number of important points in which he emphasized the spiritual nature of the family.

Rev. Vosseler stressed the importance of understanding the nature of the soul and recognizing the role of the family in providing a spiritual foundation for children and youth:

> In the first place, I believe we have to promote a true understanding of what the family is intended to be: a unique spiritual training ground for each of its members. Contrary to what today's mass media and popular culture

are trying to tell us, we must restore the understanding that each family member has his or her own indispensable role to play and that each gains immeasurably in personal growth if these roles are fully realized.

The Grand Design of Destiny

To understand our role in the family, we must first understand who we are as a unique human being, a unique individual soul. We must understand God's grand design for the destiny of souls and every soul's individual calling from God. The ascended masters teach that the timetables of the conception and birth of every child are directed by Almighty God and his angels. Our divine parents choose the very special moment in history for each soul to return to Earth to take part in the divine plan of the decades and the centuries.

Just think how wondrously you were made, how God cared for you personally, how your own divine Father and Mother watched over your conception, your parents, your life, your purpose, your reason for being, and carefully oversaw the nurturing of your soul and body in the womb. And you were born at that precise moment in cosmic history.

Even before a child is conceived, the divine plan of a soul has been worked out in intricate detail. The grand design of God is so exact that at the moment of conception the genes in that tiny embryo are already suited to the specific soul who will inhabit it. Before conception ever takes place, a board of spiritual overseers (the Karmic Board) together with the Higher Self of the soul, determines when and where and under what circumstances the soul will embody. These circumstances are tailored to the individual's needs in order to give the soul the best opportunity to work out her karma.[1]

The Law of the Circle

For those of you not familiar with the term *karma*, let me briefly explain. *Karma* is a Sanskrit word meaning "act," "deed" or "work." Karma is energy/consciousness in action; it is the law of cause and effect and of retribution. The law of karma is also known as the law of the circle, which decrees that whatever we do comes full circle to our doorstep for resolution.

The law of karma is inseparable from life upon Earth. It implies reincarnation, even as reincarnation implies karma. Karma contains positive and negative momentums—momentums we have set in motion by our free will, by actions, by words, by deeds, by thoughts, by feelings, and also by inaction, not speaking out when we should, not taking action but simply sitting back and being an observer, taking life as a spectator sport.

Karma is reaping what we have sown—yesterday, five minutes ago, and ten thousand years ago. Many of us do not reap in a given lifetime what we have sown in that life. We don't know if it will take a thousand or twelve thousand years for that karma to come full circle.

Every one of us who is preparing to come into life is charged with that sense of going back to pick up the dropped stitches, set our house in order, and then give the world something of ourselves, that great creative gift, that gift of love and sweetness, of kindness or some great monument of achievement we are meant to bring forth.

And so before conception, the parents of every child—whether they are aware of it or not in their outer consciousness—have agreed at inner levels to receive that soul.[2] And who is that soul?

The Nature of the Soul

God is a Spirit and the soul is the living potential of God. The soul's demand for free will and her separation from God resulted in the descent of this potential into the lowly estate of the flesh. When the soul descends into earthly existence, she is clothed upon with the four lower bodies.

The four lower bodies are four energy fields, inter-penetrating sheaths of consciousness. Each of these bodies vibrates in a different dimension. They surround the soul for her journey through time and space—they are our vehicles of expression in the material world of form.

The body you see is your physical body. Your mental body is the cognitive body, your thinking and reasoning mind. You have an emotional body that is called the astral, or desire, body. It is the body of your feelings and your desires. The etheric, the highest vibrating of the four, is the memory body. It serves as "the envelope of the soul." The etheric sheath is the gateway to our three higher bodies, which are the Higher Self, or Christ Self; our Divine Self, or I AM Presence; and the causal body. . . .

The ascended masters teach that it is the ultimate destiny of all of us on Earth to so purify ourselves, our souls, and to so accelerate in consciousness that we will become immortal, God-free beings. The first step is to learn to listen to the Christ Self, our Higher Self, which functions as our guardian angel and guide in this life. . . . Our great example for attaining union with our Higher Self is Jesus Christ. Jesus demonstrated complete oneness with the Christ mind while still in human form. And as we follow in his footsteps we are meant to do the same.

The ultimate goal of the path taught by the ascended

masters is our soul's union with our God Self, the I AM THAT I AM, in the process called the ascension.... Once we are ascended, our soul becomes an immortal atom in the great body of God and there is no further need for reembodiment.

Every soul knows deep inside that the path of growing and perfecting the self is her personal mission on Earth and that immortality is her goal. We also know at a soul level that in order to reunite with our Divine Presence, we must reincarnate again and again until we gain mastery over the lower aspects of self. Thus, the soul travels from lifetime to lifetime in her etheric body, or memory body, which contains the patterns of her karma as well as the details of her divine plan. And with each new incarnation we don the remaining lower bodies—mental, emotional and physical—and embark upon a new adventure in physical form.

The Impact of Karmic Ties

What many parents do not understand is how karma operates to reunite souls who have known each other in previous embodiments.

An enlightening little book is *Life between Life*,[3] by Dr. Joel L. Whitton and Joe Fisher. Whitton, as you may know, is a Toronto psychiatrist who has done extensive research on the mechanisms of reincarnation by means of hypnotic regression. Many of his case studies show how negative karma draws souls together again and again in the same families in order to work out their old adversities and finally free themselves from those karmic ties. When raising a family, it is essential to understand that much tension between family members may originate in the outplaying of old karma. This fact shows us the need to analyze and comprehend these patterns in order to avoid creating even more karma.

Whitton's research also shows how karmic tests not passed compromise the individual's progress. For example, a person who committed suicide in a previous life learned how she had aborted her opportunity in that life to fulfill her karmic plan, which included a brilliant musical career. Speaking of her previous life, she said: "If only she had been patient and persevering, she could have had it all."[4]

Whitton and Fisher state that "time and time again [subjects] have asserted . . . that they must undergo certain experiences in order to purge imperfection and to further personal growth." One account tells of a man named Ben who in past-life regression "reexperienced a succession of male and female lives in which he participated in vicious exchange by killing those who treated him badly.

"In this life, he has been plunged once more into a repugnant situation in which he has been tempted to opt for a violent solution. Severely brutalized as a child, Ben grew to hate his father so intensely that, at the age of eighteen, he came very close to killing him. . . . Then, listening to the promptings of an inner voice, he changed his mind. . . .

"This decision to desist became a major turning point in Ben's life. From that moment on, his characteristic aimlessness was replaced with ambition, he grew more outgoing, and he went on to pursue a career that brought administrative responsibilities." Through past-life regression, "Ben learned that he was embroiled in karmic circumstances that were designed to teach him to withstand extreme provocation without recourse to violence."[5]

How many of you feel like you've been placed in family situations where you have had to withstand extreme provocation? There's probably nobody here that's an exception to that, including me.

Ben discovered that prior to taking embodiment he had chosen his difficult childhood "knowing he would be severely tested by a father who had figured prominently in a series of antagonistic relationships in previous incarnations. . . . Ben was aware of a voice which said, 'If you do it right this time, things will work out all right.'" Luckily for him, he still had an ear for the voice of conscience, the voice of the Holy Christ Self. It's a saving grace when we can listen to that voice.

The voice of conscience said to him, "If you don't do it right, you will require a learning environment of even greater intensity." By acting with restraint toward his father, he "had wrestled a karmic predicament into submission. By passing his . . . test, he had finally extricated himself from the pattern of error in life after life."[6]

Whitton and Fisher also point out that "Group reincarnation, in which the same set of souls evolves through constantly changing relationships in different lives, recurs frequently."[7] This corroborates the teachings from the ascended masters. They tell us that we have all been male and female, friends and lovers, teachers and students, employers and employees, parents, husbands, wives and children to the same souls many times over in order to work out our karmic differences and to gain mastery in each of these roles and relationships.

The ascended masters teach that a newborn child is a fully developed soul, a complete and whole being, mature as we are. Our function in relation to this child is to assist the child in having the soul make the adjustment to her four lower bodies. This is our role as parents. We are acting for and on behalf of the Creator for this child, who is not ours but God's child, and our job from the moment of conception is to assist the child to integrate with the new temple, the new four lower bodies.[8]

One of parents' most important tasks is to be sure that children understand the hierarchy of the family—the father and the mother respectful and loving of each other and the child as a soul they love and teach. No matter how many children are in the family, each one should be valued as an individual. Each one is special in his or her own turn. And we must be very careful to give equal time and attention to each child and equal love, for does not God love them equally?[9]

The Role of Father and Mother

As members of the family strive to become more of their Higher Self, or Christ Self, they begin to fulfill the role that God intended them to play. Let's take a look at these roles.

The father in the household needs to have the dignity, respect and presence of God the Father and to be so acknowledged by the mother. She needs to uphold him so that the children know that he is the one to whom everyone turns, the rock of the Christ and the Buddha.

A wife and mother supports her husband and his position insofar as he follows the path of the Universal Christ. . . . A husband and father likewise supports wife and mother as she too follows the promptings of the inner Christ Self. And both parents uphold their children when they are bonded to Christ.

Paul said: "Let the husband render unto the wife due benevolence: and likewise also the wife unto the husband."[10] In this role the father is called to raise up the Christ in himself. In Jesus' words: "And I, if I be lifted up from the earth, will draw all men unto me."[11] The father needs to be true to his calling so that the mother can defend his honor and his actions.

The mother bears a great responsibility to protect the family, to pray for each member, to assist them in gaining control over their lower nature. At the same time she sets the example of walking in the presence of God, the Mighty I AM Presence and the Christ Presence. It's simply not possible to conquer the lower nature unless the Real Self is made plain.

The Real Self needs to shine through us every day, not with fanfare but just being that sweet presence of the mother or that firm presence of the father, depending on which role each of the parents is expressing at the moment, for, of course, both can be sweet or firm.

Regardless of whether the mother has an outside job or not, it is absolutely essential that she tend the Mother flame on behalf of the entire family. Keeping this flame in prayer and invocation, in holiness and a closeness to God makes her the listening one. Mother Mary, the blessed mother of Christ, was always listening and she listened to God and kept this inner guidance in her heart. Listening to God in this way, the mother can give strong direction to her family.

The light of the Divine Mother that the mother raises up in her meditation on God is the foundation of the parenting process. Every mother is a world mother in her own household. Through her invocations to God, the souls entrusted to her care are strengthened and uplifted.[12]

Your Children Will Wear Your Psychology

Parents, of course, need to demonstrate harmony and love in the home. When they share a mutual commitment to God and his Christ and this is reflected in their interaction with each other and their children, each child develops a profound devotion to the parents and the parents become a pane of glass through which the child can see and love God. The child is a reflection of the levels of attainment of the parent. When it comes to the parent's self-indulgence or what the parent allows himself to get away with, the child will follow the patterns of the parent's emotions and desires.

Most of us let ourselves get away with something now and then. We think we can get away, at times, with ignoring or disobeying God's laws. As long as we're good most of the time and do everything else right, we think we can cut corners a little here and a little there. Whereas we may be able to keep ourselves in control by skipping around the edges of the law, our example may be multiplied without restraint in our children. . . . If you do something once in their eyes, they may make it a habit and decide, "If daddy or mommy does this, it's okay."[13] . . .

Children tie into their parents' emotional bodies and the patterns of karma that are communicated through the parents' subconscious. And the parents transmit their unspoken self to the child.

We've all seen a father and mother duck waddling along with their baby ducks all in a row behind them. They waddle the same way. They quack the same way. And like little mirrors, the ducklings will incorporate the same emotional strengths or weaknesses as papa and mama duck.

Your children will put on your psychology and they will wear it. They imitate everything you are—how you walk and laugh, smile or frown, your speech patterns, your likes and dislikes, what you eat or don't, your tastes in entertainment, sports, politics, et cetera, et cetera. And so the greatest gift you can give to God is to understand parenting, parenthood and parental responsibility.

If you follow a path of discipline and set standards of sacrifice, surrender, selflessness and service, your children will take for granted that this is the way life is.

So what parents find in their offspring is many times what they have not challenged in themselves. For example, if you have a habit of losing your temper, you may see this habit manifesting in your children.

On the other hand, children have their own unique karma for which they are solely responsible. Parents can only do their best and set an example of excellence for children to do their best.

Even if you do not have excellence in every area, you can make very clear in many, many ways every day of your life that mediocrity itself is a sin, that laziness is a sin, that there is no room for self-indulgence that allows us not to give the best of ourselves to every job we undertake. This level of excellence is the level for which a child should be praised.[14]

The Need for Discipline in the Household

Let's look now at the need for discipline in the household. Some parents think that whenever anything goes wrong it's the parents' fault, that when children misbehave the parents should not become angry or punish them but should try to show more love. To me what that is doing is rewarding anger with love, misbehavior with love.

Now, there is an unconditional love for a lifestream, for a person in his evolution toward God. But there is *not* unconditional love when it comes to *behavior*. We don't unconditionally love someone who is a perpetual alcoholic and who is destroying everyone in the family, including himself. We may love the soul that is there. We do not love the behavior and we do not love the person when he is engaged in that behavior.[15]

The important thing to remember about discipline is that the child will develop devotion to the Father-Mother God in direct proportion to what his parents give him as love and wisdom and the discipline that he is yearning for.

When we give children an understanding of why something has to be a certain way and not simply exact blind obedience, we find that children without exception are little philosophers; they can reason and they can understand if we give them a logic as to why something is important to do or not do.

What are the reasons? Is it for their health or their safety, for the principle of trust, for the principle of obedience? There are many, many reasons why we ask children to do things. We are not obliged to tell them, but it does help. It does help them to be obedient.

And remember, we are all trying to avoid that ultimate confrontation that demands the spanking. We try to lead the child so that he will never have to get to that point and we will never have to get to that point. But we don't shirk it and avoid it when the time comes.

If we bring up our children properly, they will become devotees who love the Father-Mother God all of their lives and who can accept themselves as a dearly beloved son or daughter of God.[16]

So you can see yourself in this loving relationship where you are teaching the child and the child is actually your disciple—disciple meaning "the disciplined one." The child is really the disciple of God, but for now the child sees you and so you are the child's teacher.[17]...

Television, the Pseudo-Teacher

Before we talk about parents as teachers, let's take a look at the subject of television—the great pseudo-teacher.... Television presents a distorted picture of society. That's the conclusion of the book *Watching America: What Television Tells Us about Our Lives*, by Robert and Linda Lichter, of the Center for Media and Public Affairs, and professor Stanley Rothman.[18]

A review of the book reports: "According to *Watching America*, millions of TV viewers nightly are visiting a nation where sexual infidelity is the norm, where citizens are murdered at a rate 1,400 times higher than actuality, where the rich commit most of the crimes, where businessmen almost always are bad guys, where only liberal politicians operate in the public interest ... and where religion is a silly superstition."[19]

So what can we do about this situation? If you have children, the first thing you must do is to get control of the television in your house. If you can't monitor the TV set twenty-four hours a day, you can buy and install a lockbox that blocks the flow of electricity to the TV.

Marie Winn, author of *The Plug-In Drug: Television, Children, and the Family*, comments on the dangers of using video as a baby sitter: "It interferes with socialization, the long and tedious process that teaches children the rules of acceptable behavior." She says that when parents use video to solve child-rearing problems, their opportunities to teach their children the daily lessons of life are diminished. They could end up with kids they can't control and who can't control themselves.[20]

The Role of Parent as Teacher

A primary role of parents is to be a teacher. Your child *wants* to relate to you as teacher. From the moment the child is born he cannot wait for you to teach him. That is what is on every baby's mind the moment he is born. He doesn't just want you to cuddle him and love him and coo to him. He wants you to sit down and have a formal lesson to teach him. He also wants you to teach him the boundaries of cosmic law. He wants you to teach him about the world we live in, the world he has come to by your grace.

You can talk to your baby about everything, about your favorite subject. If you're an engineer, sit down and have a discussion with him about what you're doing at work and be animated, and he will smile back and get all excited because that baby is totally in touch with his adult being and his Inner Self. He is absolutely delighted that you know this and that you're talking to him about adult subjects. You can go on and on about anything that is on your mind—just don't tell your baby your problems!

So if you want to make your child feel loved, it is just as important to talk to him and teach him as it is to touch him and hold him.[21] And as your child grows, you will of course want to continue this interactive process.

It is up to you to surround your child with constructive choices. He may be an adult within, but he is a child now and he's coming into integration with his four lower bodies and his Holy Christ Self. You do not leave him to his own devices at a young age to choose right and wrong. It's your job as a parent to help him learn to discriminate.

Surrounding your child with constructive choices is the foundation of the Montessori method. You preselect the environment of your child because the child must first learn to discriminate by your example between good, better and best. You give the child the tools and the equipment that allow him to unfold the petals of the mind and heart and to develop spirit, soul and body. In these early years you don't expose him to things that you don't want him to choose. For example, you may not want him to listen to heavy metal or rock music or spend hours playing video games.[22]

The Value of Community

As we ponder the value of the nuclear family,* we realize how important it is to raise our children in such a way that they are ready to become constructive, creative members of society. In order to be able to do so, and to hold the fortress against the onslaughts of a civilization that appears to be rapidly breaking down, I believe that parents who are fighting for traditional values can be greatly supported by affiliation with like-minded individuals—in other words, by *community*, where values and beliefs are shared for the sake of mutual reinforcement.

We all know that our values and beliefs are important to us. They become a way of life as we internalize them and live them. We are drawn to others of like mind and heart because we can share our thoughts, feelings and ideals. Community in this sense is essential for sound physical, mental, emotional and spiritual growth.

Throughout history, communities have been recognized as strong social units, especially those with shared religious beliefs or convictions. We can think of historic communities, such as the Essenes or the early Christians, who banded together in the face of great persecution. We know of the Hindu ashram and the Buddhist sangha. In more recent times, the communities of the Hutterites, as you know, are well-known here in Canada. In the United

*A basic social unit consisting of parents and dependent children living in one household.

States, we think of Quakers, Mormons, Amish, and many other groups. History has shown us that such groups are strong and often better able to withstand outside pressures for undesirable change than isolated individuals or families.

Prepare Young People to Make a Difference

Whatever way of living we choose, I think we all agree that caring for children and supporting them with strong family ties must be our major concern. We simply *have* to prepare our young people for the harsh realities of modern civilization. We *have* to equip them with the tools with which they can make a difference in today's challenging society.

We can't define our children's future. They will have to make their own choices. But we can provide a firm foundation of positive values, which they can fall back on in times of trouble.

Our children are a God-given gift to us—but this gift is not for keeps. We must reciprocate and return that gift to God—with increase. Our children must be given back to God as mature individuals who are ready to embark on a path of spiritual self-discovery and service unto God and their fellow men. This is the great challenge that lies before us, and all of us, whether we are parents or not, should consider how we can assist and guide the next generation.

I'd like to close with the words of Elizabeth Clare Prophet: "Remember, the servant is not greater than his lord. You, the parent, are the servant of the Holy Christ Self of your child. You are also the servant of his soul. But you are role-playing in the role of teacher and of parent and authority figure. You never forget who that child really is."[23]

11

Impartations of the Soul and Spirit

As fires of creativity flow
From this sacred God I know,
I bring to you an impartation of the soul—
'Tis the fragrance of Alpha and Omega
That will make you whole.

—PAUL THE VENETIAN

ost of us hide parts of ourselves until we feel secure
about letting them show. Eventually we start to wonder,
"Who is the real me?" Yet we all have a sense of our soul,
our intuitive being, who we are minus our defensive armor.
And most of us have a sense of our Higher Self. Who we
really are is a combination of both. And our soul and Higher
Self are often expressed through our hopes and dreams.

What are your hopes and dreams? What do you see as
your destiny? Are you fulfilling it? Or do you get in your
own way or allow circumstances to hold you back? Take a
few moments to identify the inner obstacles, stumbling
blocks in yourself. Once you identify the blocks, you can
remove them, be your Real Self, and take a giant step forward

in fulfilling your destiny.

Encourage Young People to Be Their Real Self

Even as we have a destiny to fulfill, so do our children and youth. As parents, teachers and friends, we are meant to encourage young people to recognize and develop their gifts and talents. We do this by championing their Real Self and helping them outwit the not-self.*

Young people need to understand the Real Self and the not-self. And they need to know they can rely on our support to be who they really are instead of what other people think they should be. How do we support them? By encouraging their imagination and sense of wonder, helping them explore ideas and information, valuing their joy and enthusiasm, helping them develop their talents, and being a shoulder of comfort and support when life gets tough.

In doing this we need to keep in mind that inwardly our children are mature souls. And each soul entrusted to our care is imbued with the living Spirit of God. How do we help our children express their soul? When we teach our children spiritual truths, we quicken their souls. When we pray or meditate, they notice. When we live our beliefs, our children are encouraged to live theirs.

Remaining true to one's spiritual nature is not easy in today's world where the emphasis is placed on earning money, piling up material goods, achieving prestige, and currying favor with other people. Yet, heroes and heroines, spiritual leaders, great men and women over the centuries have set a higher example. In the words of Shakespeare, "To thine own self be true."

What does this mean today? I believe it means to honor

*The dweller self, unreal self, synthetic self.

God, to be true to our Real Self, to develop our special gifts and to contribute to civilization. The same is true for our children. To forge their destiny in the Aquarian age, they are called to tap the inner resources of their soul and spirit.

Teaching an Adult Soul in a Child's Body

Mrs. Prophet discussed the topic of teaching the soul of a child in her memorable lecture "The Challenge of Teaching an Adult Soul in a Child's Body." She taught this subject in the context of the spiritual nature of the soul and the Montessori method of teaching the child:

> We've talked about the foundations of the Aquarian education as having been drawn out of the past, in golden-age civilizations even before the descent of consciousness. We have talked about that thread, that golden thread of light of a religion that is common to all mankind and of truths that underlie all religion. We've talked about the penetration of the child and the concentration of the child. And we've spent two hours this morning on Maria Montessori's system, her materials and how she received a plan for education for the Aquarian age that orders and draws out of the soul that which is inherent within it.

The Concepts of Socrates and Plato

This evening I'd like to talk to you about the concepts of Plato and Socrates ... because the method of the dialogue is most important in Aquarian-age education—the questioning, the questioning, the questioning. It is important to understand what value this has from the premise that in educating a soul we are appealing to the untapped resources of that soul and drawing them out—*educare*, meaning to draw out. We are looking for methods of drawing out that which is within rather than superimposing upon the soul something from without.

Socrates' intense questioning revealed that men don't know what they think they know. And therefore the method of questioning guards against the deception of others and of one's self.

For instance, on the topic of virtue, he says that you can't know a specific virtue or how to get it until you know what virtue is. In this particular dialogue he says, "I have no knowledge of virtue at all. And how can I know a property of something when I don't even know what it is?"

This method of inquiry on the part of the teacher is not to withhold the information from the students, but he presents a state of perplexity with the goal of infecting others with perplexity. He guards against what is a universal problem in education and it is this: that when we have the *words*, we think we have the *knowledge*.

Words are only cups. They're matrices for consciousness to flow into. Having the words does not mean we have the understanding. Learning by rote—as our children are often taught to do in school today, repeating words back which have been given—is by no means even the beginning of education or understanding. It is producing parrots or robots or computers that spit out what has been fed into them.

Dialogue and Questioning Evokes Soul Memory

Socrates speaks of the necessity to know and of the possibility of knowledge. This, to me, is the heart of the teaching of Socrates, recorded in this quote from Plato:

"The soul, since it is immortal and has been born many times and has seen all things, both here and in the other world, has learned everything that is. So we need not be surprised if it can recall the knowledge of virtue or anything else which, as I see it, it once possessed. All nature is akin and the soul has learned everything so that when a man has recalled a single piece of knowledge, learned it in ordinary language, there is no reason why he should not find out all the rest if he keeps a stout heart and does not grow weary of the search, for seeking and learning are, in fact, nothing but recollection."

This is the teaching of the ascended masters and of all the great teachers who have walked the earth. Evoking soul memory is the purpose of education....

And here we see that Socrates and Plato, of course, acknowledged the law of rebirth, of reincarnation, whereby the soul comes again and again to be clothed upon with a new form, a new body awareness, in various places in time and space so that she can master life's energies, so that she can bring into the forcefield of Matter that which is contained within in Spirit. Now here's the great key to this form of teaching: *The method of the dialogue, of questioning and probing, evokes soul memory.*

I cannot tell you how many times this has happened to me, that I have sat in meditation and asked God a question, "God, why is this so?" And then I would release the question as a thought matrix into the mind of God and seal it and go about my way. Perhaps within a fortnight or forty-eight hours the computer of the mind of God would release into my [mind's] computer the answer to my question....

The mind of God is like a computer, and the mind of man is like a computer. And we can use the computer of our mind to tie into this giant computer. In fact, tying into that fiery core of light, to that flame in the heart that is real, you can have the answer to any question. And that is truth.

The Bursting of the Thousand-Petaled Lotus

This is why the world's greatest lights, those who have really plugged into the cosmos, who have their chakras tuned into God, have never had to study. And, of course, the bursting of the thousand-petaled lotus in the crown is that moment of all-knowledge, all-wisdom. In this light, if virtue is a kind of knowledge, it must be teachable or something we recollect. If it is there within the human soul ready to be learned or recollected by a kind of education, it means that virtuous men are made, not born.

What this means is that when the soul comes forth clothed upon again with a new body and body consciousness, she has locked within her the secrets of a cosmos. These secrets will not come forth unless that soul is placed in the proper environment so that they are drawn out. . . .

The whole purpose of the Aquarian-age education is to draw out of the soul what the soul already has within. The dialogue is the key method, and the questioning. Therefore, children should be taught to question. Most children do question unless their creativity has somehow been stifled by a false sense of discipline by the parents.

I can remember when I was a child, it seems as though for a period of time I went around night and day saying "why?" and then a sentence. And I think I went from neighbor to neighbor until each one got fed up with me and put me out or couldn't answer my questions. But I can remember that experience, the whole world being this great wonder and somehow the soul inside having to continually ask "why?" because "why" was the means whereby that soul tied into God. And eventually the answers came forth in the right cycle, in the right time.

Maximizing Periods of Soul Sensitivity

Now without education, the proper education, these faculties, these virtues, all of the accomplishments of past lives, remain dormant. These momentums of attainment that are locked in the causal body do not come forth because the key is not turned and the opening is not created.

Maria Montessori, in her program of education, has a set of materials and methods and concepts whereby periods of a soul's sensitivity to her inner being are maximized. And during a period of sensitivity to certain forms of creativity, the child goes through certain exercises calculated to bring out this inner being. Her whole method teaches the child to go within, to go within to contact reality. She even teaches the child to listen to the inner voice. She speaks of the inner voice. . . .

When the children first understand that there is a voice to listen to, they think that that voice is going to be audible inside. And then she explains to them that it is a sense, an inner sense, that they are listening for. The inner sense is innocence. The innocence of the child makes the child capable of having the inner sense. In essence, she is teaching ESP long before its time, the extrasensory perception that is natural to the child because of his innocence. In his innocence he has practically no veils keeping him from contact with his own soul.

The essential premise, then, of Plato and Socrates is that the problems of man can be dealt with through education, specifically through this form. Rather than lecturing or preaching at people, the best form of education, then, is the dialogue, is the questioning. Each time a question is asked of the individual, especially a question that does not pertain to bringing back textbook knowledge or something that has been discussed but an original question that makes the soul have to go back and then back and back and finally find the original premise of being, this questioning is that which leads to creativity.

The Wisdom of God in the Child

Montessori says that the challenge of teaching is to discover the laws of the child's development. And to discover these laws would be the same thing as to discover the Spirit and wisdom of God operating within the child. This is the true mentality for the educator—the recognition of the divine wisdom as the necessary element in his work as an educator. She says that the child has a real sense of the supernatural, a real intuition. Everything in his soul carries him to God.

The whole purpose of education, then, is the converging of the soul of man and the Spirit of God at the point of contact that is the Christ consciousness, the consciousness of your Real Self. If we can accomplish this in education, we will inaugurate a golden age [an age where mankind's actions are congruent with God's divine plan]. If we cannot, we will remain in the darkness of a rote mechanized consciousness that is the very death of life on this planet. There is nothing more important today than education pursued in its highest sense and true educators willing to call the children into that inner awareness, into that inner knowing....

When I opened our Montessori school in Colorado Springs, I spoke to parents from all walks of life and I said, "Your child has genius." Every child has genius, has elements of God's consciousness that must be drawn out....

I can remember when I was three and four, having a map over my play chest and memorizing these places by continually asking my mother, "What country is this?" And I can remember when I would touch the map and the country, I would get a vibration, and I had the feeling in my soul, without any other pictures, of what kind of people lived there, what kind of countries these were, what the karma of these people was.

Now, you may not remember what you thought when you were one and two and three. But I know that you had thoughts of awareness, of life, that you do not retain in this time. And it is blocked out of your memory by the training, the outer so-called education that we have experienced, blocking the soul's memory....

Developing the Intuitive Faculties of the Heart

The proportions of a cosmos can be felt through the hands, the chakras in the hands, which are the secret-ray chakras. These are developed in children and then they cover over. You know how the soft spot in a baby's head eventually closes over. That soft spot has a pulsation. It's the pulsation of the I AM Presence releasing energy and it's to the rhythm of a cosmic heartbeat.

That child is touching measurements for the time when his own soul will be measured against the cosmos. This is a part of initiation and its path; it is called co-measurement. And this is something we need inside of ourselves, a measuring rod to measure our own progress against the progress of the universe.

Look at the eyes and look at the mind and see if you can't see that that child is having an experience far beyond what we can describe. Mathematics, the entire laws of a cosmos; sound, the tones of the Elohim of creation—all of this relating the inner man to the outer man, integrating the soul for life. Just by meditation on pure geometric forms the child develops the discrimination of the Christ mind to know right and wrong because the child will sense a dissonant vibration. When the child is older, the child can discriminate between discord and harmony....

Harmony is the goal of the soul's integration. By being sensitive to vibration, the child is developing the intuitive faculties of the heart. And the child will be able to discern what action leads to harmony, what action leads to discord, because the impressions of the geometric forms and the pure sounds are upon the mind. They are at the subconscious, and they are regulators of consciousness in later life. When the child is surrounded with an ordered environment, which we call a disciplined environment, he has the matrix for the full release of his inner creativity.

The Building Blocks of Creation

The child is not able to distinguish these factors at birth. The child comes in helpless. There is a philosophy of education that says, "Just let the children grow as they're wont to grow and when they're adults they will choose right and wrong, they will choose their religion, they will choose everything." There's a tremendous burden placed upon the child by parents who think that in giving the child total freedom, the child will arrive at the correct inner discipline.

That concept is not true. The child has to be acquainted with the building blocks of creation. This is not imposing upon the child your own thoughts, your own consciousness. It is giving him the tools that are inherent in nature. By having the tools as order, the child has a cup of consciousness, and then the full fire of the creativity of the causal body can be released to him at the correct age.

Maria Montessori said that the classroom should be an environment that includes the total life-experience of the child. And this includes religion. And therefore she made provision for a section of the classroom or a room apart to be a chapel where the child could go and give his devotions and commune with God. . . .

"Oh, I Love Jesus"

Dr. Cavaletti, the woman who under Montessori's direction developed the religious program, said she once stood outside the atrium of a school and listened to a small child stand before a picture of Jesus, singing a song of love over and over and over again for an hour and twenty minutes. The child was four years old. The child came out smiling affectionately, saying, "Oh, I love Jesus."

Do you actually think that child would have stood there if the child had not established a contact and felt a flow and an energy? Do you really think a child would stand there of his own free will and sing a song for an hour and twenty minutes if there weren't something more going on than what appears to the outer, what we as adults interpret as rote, what to the child is the glorious ritual of communion?

I'm certain that that child was so aware of Jesus that it was superfluous to say that she was talking with Jesus. She simply said, "Oh, I love Jesus," assuming that the adult would realize that Jesus was standing before her.[1]

The wonder of the child is a holiness and bliss beyond words. We can learn so much about God from little children if we simply take the time to listen and observe. And we tap into a limitless reservoir of divine love as we practice behaving lovingly.

We open our own fount of joy and happiness by giving and sharing ourselves with our family. In seeking to understand, we learn empathy. In allowing our sons and daughters to develop at their own pace, we learn patience. In determining to meet their needs, we learn endurance. If we are smart we will learn to listen, not only to the words but also to the tones of the child's voice, to her feelings and subtle behaviors.

Children teach us to live more consciously, to become wiser and more loving, to set our priorities, to be efficient and effective, to communicate clearly and to be assertive as necessary. The joy we experience in caring for our children can become a catalyst for renewing and deepening our faith. And as we help young people plumb the depths of life's mysteries, we deepen our understanding of the fragility of life and the power of the soul.

The Dictates of Karma

Our soul and life itself show us that karma is a powerful force. Karma dictates genetic characteristics and physical vulnerabilities. Karma draws us together and thrusts us apart. There is perhaps no better arena in which to study karma than in relationships, marriages, families and the drama of families split apart by divorce.

Many people today marry with the intention of a lifelong partnership only to watch the bonds gradually disintegrate or abruptly break in a situation of violence or emotional turmoil. Gone are the days when the majority of people married for life no matter what kind of personal or economic adversity occurred.

There are many reasons for today's skyrocketing divorce rate: unfaithfulness or abuse, disagreement over values, widely different interests, shifting goals, financial reverses. Sometimes divorce is simply the result of the separating out of two people who married as adolescents or young adults before they had coalesced and refined their individual life goals.

And no longer do families necessarily stay together "for the children's sake." When karma gets the upper hand, family break-up is often the result. Many children today live with one parent and go back and forth to visit the other, who may or may not have remarried.

Consciously or unconsciously, we tend to create situations that can help us balance our karma. Some parents adopt children, and still others enter bereaved or divorced families as a stepparent. Both of these situations are emotionally challenging. And they involve a complex mix of karmic factors that family members may not understand.

Energetically we draw to us people with whom our soul needs to learn karmic lessons or settle karmic debts. Many of us understand this principle in relation to our birth family, and it is equally true in adoptive families and those that have a stepparent. Everyone we meet, especially family and friends, offers us a lesson to learn. Whatever situation we are in, we are wise to take a moment to ask our Higher Self, "What is my karmic lesson?"

By focusing on our lesson, we take the onus off other people and assume responsibility for our own behavior. We get excited about mastering the lesson because we are forging an aspect of our soul's destiny in the process. And once we learn whatever lesson is associated with a particular circumstance, the situation either changes for the better or we find ourselves better able to cope. Life becomes our schoolroom when we realize that every situation we encounter is an opportunity for soul growth.

Families with Stepparents

Our major life lessons have to do with our soul's adaptability and growth during cycles of change. And one major change for families is the loss of a parent and the remarriage of the remaining parent. Since many people have this kind of situation, let's explore the lessons inherent in stepfamilies.

When a family loses a parent through death or divorce and the remaining parent remarries, the children often have difficulty accepting the stepparent. And the situation is further complicated when two families of children or teens are meshed together in such a situation.

What can parents do to help children adjust? In the first place a parent needs to realize that the new marriage partner and his or her children may not necessarily receive instant love and acceptance. The children, who may still be grieving, need to be reassured that their own father or mother still loves them and they are not expected to stop loving the parent they lost. The children need the mothering or fathering they are missing, but acceptance of a new parent takes time and patience.

A client of mine, Sylvia, mother of two teenage boys, lost her husband, father of the boys, in a car accident. Around the same time, Jeff, father of two teenage girls, lost his wife to cancer. After several years, Sylvia and Jeff met, began dating and fell in love. They wanted to be married but were apprehensive about how the children would respond. Both of them talked to their teenagers, and the reaction was about the same: "Why do you have to get married again? I don't want another parent!"

Jeff and Sylvia persevered, but the marriage had a rocky beginning. None of the four teenagers were happy about it, but they handled it in different ways. Jeff's younger daughter withdrew into her world of teenage friends, while Sylvia's younger son retreated into hobbies. The older son and daughter were attracted to each other and expressed it by teasing each other unmercifully.

When Sylvia and Jeff realized that all of the teens were acting out in their own way, they called a family council and the underlying resentments came out. As Jeff put it, "It was a real blowout! We couldn't believe what our kids have been thinking and feeling, but at least they all had their say. They told us they were hurt, angry and embarrassed about their 'instant new family' and yet they wanted us to be happy. They just didn't know how to cope with the whole situation." Sylvia added, "We told them we didn't expect them to be instant friends, but we did want them to be kind to each other and to give us a chance."

They went on to explain that after the blowout life had been better because the teenagers were less reticent to talk about their feelings. Both Jeff and Sylvia realized they had underestimated the impact the marriage would have on their kids. They talked it over and decided to have another family meeting where they would ask the teens individually what they wanted and needed. When they did this, the teens, each in his or her own way, said they needed to know that their birth parent still loved them.

Jeff and Sylvia decided the best way to show their love was to spend one-on-one time with each of their own children on a regular basis. At the same time, they initiated a monthly outing for the whole family, and everyone took turns choosing the kind of outing. After a month of one-on-one time and a rafting trip they all enjoyed, one of the teens said, "It's like we're a family now instead of just a bunch of people living together!" They had a family hug and Jeff and Sylvia heaved a sigh of relief.

What Jeff and Sylvia learned is that putting two families together can be challenging, but we all have an unlimited reservoir of love. We just need to rediscover it and turn on the faucet. Perhaps the greatest gift we can give our children is simply to love them.

The Power of a Child's Unconditional Love

Why is it that everyone smiles at a baby, and the baby smiles back? It is the power of unconditional love. Only when a child is hurt over and over again does a child develop emotional defenses that stand in the way of being a loving person.

Children inspire within us unconditional love, as mothers and fathers know from cradling their newborn infant. And many are the stories of love in little children. One of these stories, as reported in the news, is about four-year-old Michael and his love for his baby sister.

Michael's mother prepared him for the birth of a sister, and one of Michael's favorite activities was singing to the baby in mommy's tummy. He already loved his little sister.

Karen's pregnancy was normal; however, the baby was born a little bit early. And shortly after birth little Marlee had trouble breathing. When the doctors found a tiny hole in her lungs, she was moved to a special neonatal unit.

Michael asked to see his little sister, and the doctor allowed him to do so. When he came to his baby sister's crib, his dad asked if there was something he wanted to do. Michael fixed his eyes on his little sister and began to sing, "You are my sunshine, my only sunshine, please don't take my sunshine away."

The baby responded to her brother's song, and from that point on her condition improved dramatically. To everyone's joy, she came home to her family a few days later. Her grandmother says it was God's grace and Michael's singing that saved the baby. That was more than ten years ago and Marlee is now a healthy, active young lady.[2]

One can't help but wonder if Michael and his little sister had been soul friends before they were born—either on Earth in a past life or in the heaven-world. Certainly, the power of their love-tie was enough to keep the little one in embodiment.

Love is the essence of who we are as spiritual beings. And that essence is potent in little children. Love is the way that we connect with the mystery of life and with our innate spirituality.

Nurturing Children's Spirituality

Children are born with a sense of wonder. We help them develop that intuitive response when together we watch a shooting star, baby birds and animals, a glistening waterfall, a beautiful sunrise or sunset. We share a sense of wonder when we observe the complexity of nature and the rhythm of the seasons. And we experience wonder and grace when we contemplate the mystery of life, of the angels, of God.

Every child has a unique spiritual essence that emanates from the soul and spirit. And parents are called to nurture that essence in everyday family life. One of the most natural ways is through appreciation of nature. We can take our children on walks, hikes and trips into the countryside. We can raise plants and cultivate gardens. We can lie on the grass and watch the clouds form into interesting shapes and dissolve and form again.

A child's love for pets, whether birds, fish or animals, is another expression of the child's inner nature. Children have such fun with them and willingly take responsibility for their care. They are happy to learn how to care for their beloved little friends because they love them so much. Pets of all kinds can be a wonderful addition to the family. The family loves them, and they return that love without condition.

When we share experiences with our children, we make it easier for them to share their hopes and dreams. We help them open the door to self-knowing. And self-knowing is the core of creativity, innovation and invention. When adults appreciate and encourage their children's talents and aspirations, they play a major role in their future accomplishments.

We can also listen to and appreciate the dreams that children have during sleep and tell us about in the morning. Every dream contains a message for the dreamer, whether that one is a child, an adolescent or an adult. Dreams are inner contemplation and often a message from the soul and Higher Self. If you are interested in understanding your dreams from a spiritual perspective, you will likely enjoy my book *Dreams: Exploring the Secrets of Your Soul*,[3] in which you learn how to interpret your dreams.

Rituals nurture children's spirituality. The simple rituals of lighting votive candles, blessing the food at the table or saying bedtime prayers give the family an opportunity to pray, to feel the presence of God, and to transcend the problems of the day. This is especially valuable for little children, whose souls have so recently been in higher realms.

According to Search Institute, a research organization, family spirituality combined with church affiliation provides a firm base for teenagers' faith. And statistics show that teens asked to choose the top five positive influences on their faith ranked mother, father, pastor, church youth-group, and church education, in that order, as the top five.[4]

Perhaps the most important way we nurture young people's spirituality is by example—how we live our life. When we pray, they learn how to talk to Father-Mother God. When we ask God for help and thank God for blessings, they are reminded to ask for help and think of their blessings. When we thank God for the family and the grace of living in a free country, they feel warmed, comforted and reassured. And when we live up to the ideals we pray for, youth and children are inspired to do likewise.

The Archeia Charity* reminds us of the power of divine love, the ultimate source of our blessings and ideals:

> Look up into the heavens and realize that as far as you can see there is manifesting the power of divine love in infinite concentration and consecration to the fulfilling of the divine plan in all creation. The stars themselves sing of fulfillment and victory, of desire satisfied in the hearts of those who are blazing their light throughout cosmos as an activity of divine love.[5]

---

*An archeia is the divine complement and twin flame of an archangel; in this case, Archeia Charity is the twin flame of Archangel Chamuel.

12

The Soul's Restoration
of Innocence

*The windows of my soul I throw
wide open to the sun.*

—JOHN GREENLEAF WHITTIER
"My Psalm"

*I*f we would master the lessons
of divine love in the age of
Aquarius, we are called to restore our soul to her original
innocence. Many describe a saint as one who retains the
innocence of the child, the child mind, the child heart, the
child's state of consciousness. As has been said, "God himself is a child playing in a playpen."

Whether or not we consider ourselves saints, we benefit
by asking ourselves, "What has happened to the sense of
innocence that we had as little children? How do we restore
it in our heart and soul and cultivate it in our family?"

To the Child of the Heart

In a dictation given to the messenger Elizabeth Clare
Prophet, Master Jesus instructed the soul, saying:

I for one prefer the image of God as *child* because so much virtue and freedom and love and light can be conveyed in concept when one has the image of the child. And the Divine Manchild is the presence of the Christ, and the fullness of that child is the mature son and daughter of God.

I speak to you as you knew the innocence of God in your cradle, in your mother's arms; as you heard the birds chirping in your window, . . . the music of the breeze flowing through the trees; and watched the stars in the heavens and the sun and the rolling of the waves; and all of these things as they conveyed to you the consciousness of the Holy Spirit and the presence of love.

All that has been superimposed upon you since you were that child—the sophistications of the world, the struggle for supply, the struggle that is political, social and economic, the complications of egos vying for positions of power—all of these things have buried the child and the soul until you no longer identify as the child beloved of the Father-Mother God, but you identify with the struggle and the sense of the struggle.

Suffer the Little Children to Come unto Me

If you would teach these little ones "suffer the little children to come unto me and forbid them not, for of such is the kingdom of heaven," if you would teach them, you must be like them; your consciousness must be translated into the freedom, the nonattachment of the child. The child is not worried or concerned of the morrow what it shall eat or drink, for it trusts wholly in the father and the mother to provide. . . .

It is a return to this innocence that will restore a golden-age culture, for there is one thing that the childlike innocence always demands—it demands the presence of the mother, it expects the mother, it waits upon her voice, her song, her comfort. When mankind lose their identity as children, they also lose the mother and they lose that need, or seemingly so, in the outer consciousness. But you see, precious hearts, mankind always need the mother, for the mother comes to comfort and to impart the grace of the father, the knowledge of his law.

Mothers: Impart Light and Love to the Hallowed Circle of the Family

The function of the mother in every home, in every household, is to receive the father and the children, to demagnetize their worlds from the shocks and the burdens and the weight of the consciousness of the mass mind and of the encounters with that mind during the daily striving to overcome, to be educated, to provide for the family and for the needs thereof.

The mother's flame must be great enough, then, to receive the father and the children and to absorb from them the substance of the world and to take that substance into her heart, which is the very hearth of the home, and there, by the action of the sacred fire of love, to consume that energy, to transmute it, to restore the light and love and to return it to each one, to each member of the hallowed circle of the family.

The mother, then, must see to it that the lamps of her being are kindled and bright and trimmed and well-oiled. For the fires that are necessary to keep the flame on behalf of her family and then her community and her nation must be great enough to absorb the shocks, the densities, and the discord and the strife and the turmoil of the outside world....

There is no end to opportunity for the women of this world for service, public and private, for to serve is to become all that you are. In service there is a ripening of the inner talents and the fruit of the Tree of Life. The mother, then, is the source, as she takes from the father the energies of strength, the energies of power, the energies of courage, the energies that are the light of Alpha and translates these into the comfort and the ministration and service that represent the ideal of home in America and the world.

Mothers, bake the bread for your families. And as you bake the bread impart the word, impart the vibration, for it is light on which your family is nourished. And the wheat and the flour are only a small percentage of that which your family needs for sustainment.

Mothers, be the personification of the woman who took the leaven and hid it in three measures of meal until the whole was leavened.[1] So take the measure of the Father, the Father consciousness, take the measure of the Son and the Son consciousness, take the measure of the Holy Spirit and the Holy Spirit consciousness and convey them through love into the food, into your household.

And let plants adorn your household and let them be for the focus of the ray of truth and for life and elemental life [the nature spirits]. And welcome the elementals of the field into your home to help you with the housework and the chores, to sing with you, to invoke the violet flame, to play with the children and to dance a merry jig.

Let the angels also be in the rafters and in the ceilings, hanging there as ethereal intelligences, hanging there carved of wood or terracotta; let them be there smiling to remind the little children as they look upward that God is watching over them and that you are his handiwork, his instrument.

"Behold the handmaid of the Lord" was the reply of

Mary to the annunciation of the archangel.[2] Behold the handmaid of the Lord. So be the handmaid of father, as in heaven, so on Earth.

Fathers: Be the Sure Arm of Courage and the True Counselor

And you who represent the masculine ray, as you celebrate the influx of the light of father, see how mother and children depend upon your counsel, the sure arm of courage, of vision, of strength, of determination to conquer this world and to set the example to your children of father as law; and yes, father as compassion, as great wisdom; father as the balance of mother; father as all of the energy available to create, to bring forth ennobling ideas.

Father, take your children into your arms and show them how they can attain to the fullness of the stature of Christ, and play with them and frolic with them and know that your children will know God upon your very countenance when you smile, when you laugh, and when you are stern in the true discipline of a hierarch of the will of God.

So be unto mother a sure shield of defense, a protector, a guide and a teacher. Be unto each one the true counselor. Be, then, prophet and king and priest and poet and philosopher, and show each child a work of the hands as Joseph showed me how to be a carpenter. Show your children, O fathers, how to accomplish one thing with their hands that they might feel the mastery of this plane of Mater... and know that they have learned from the hand and heart of their father how to accomplish something that is good, of worth and beautiful.

Teach your children how to work with plants and how to garden, how to care for that place where then the

Christ will come into the garden of the heart, into that place set aside for the elementals. Teach your children the arts of communion with nature, with the Holy Spirit, how to make a place in the wilderness, how to go camping in the woods, how to build a fire, how to do so many things that will compel them higher in their understanding of [divine] law.

And you know, the child will always remember and always say, "My father taught me how to do this and so I teach my children also." And from generation to generation the precepts of the law are transferred.

I Will Not Fail You, O Child of My Heart

As I recall the moments when I sat upon my mother's knee and felt the purity of her soul entering into my being, so remember that your children treasure the moments when they can be held close to your heart. And you also treasure that moment, for you know that the impartation of love to a child is one of the highest and purest experiences that you can have in an entire lifetime.

For you know that to smile upon the face of a child who looks up to you with hope, with courage, with faith and to return that gaze with the confidence and with the vow within your heart "I will not fail you, O child of my heart"—that this is a mutuality of flow, of cosmic cycles that reenact the flow from father to son, from mother to daughter and the fusion of the family in the grace of the Holy Spirit.

Allow Your Child to Tell You All Things

Remember when you call your children to table that it is always the Lord's table and the Lord's supper. And I tell you that there is not a table in the world where if there is dedication to the Christ that I am not also seated there present to break the bread of life, to listen to the stories of the children as they recount the day's experiences.

It is so important to the child to be able to have the ear of the parent listening to what is so important to the heart of the child as the day comes to the end and some of the difficulties of the world and life must be heard. For you see, blessed parents of the new age, to allow your child to speak and to tell you all things is allowing the child to be relieved of subconscious patterns, energies and problems that unless they are spoken will remain there to cause disturbances later in life.

If you allow your children and encourage them to tell you of their day's activities, their joys and their sorrows, they will feel comforted. And because they know you as God, they will believe in their hearts that because mother and father have heard them, then all will be well.

And they free themselves in this manner and they are unburdened, much in the same manner that you are unburdened when you confide your problems to a friend. Somehow you give that friend your problems, and in this ritual there is the consuming of the problem by the action of the threefold flame of the friend. And so each day there must be opportunity for the child to speak, for the child to listen, for the child to ask questions.[3]

Tend the Child's Garden of Consciousness

Think of your child's consciousness as a beautiful garden that needs cultivating, watering and weeding. As an infant he or she is born with seeds that have already been planted, beautiful flowers that are hiding just under the surface of consciousness.

As the child experiences both positive and hurtful life

experiences, he develops both flowers and weeds. So we needn't be surprised when we discover weeds in the garden. They are simply the result of certain genetic influences and difficult life encounters. However, as parents and teachers and friends of children, we are called to be the gardener and to teach the child how to garden.

The wise parent is the gardener who is intent on creating beauty and health in the garden of consciousness of the child. He cultivates by tending the child's needs and nurturing the child's body. And he plants seeds of self-worth by loving the child unconditionally. When the child misbehaves, he views that action as a little weed in the garden of the child's consciousness.

How does he deal with the weed? He catches it when it is small and helps the child pull out the weed and plant a flower instead. For example, when a child tells a lie, the thoughtful parent helps the child face the truth and praises him for being honest.

If the truth unveils a misbehavior, another weed, the gardening parent helps the child pull that weed out too. In other words, he shows the child how to correct the misbehavior and helps him practice the correction until he masters it. The new behavior becomes another flower in the garden of the child's consciousness.

A child's self-confidence, which we can think of as a beautiful fruit tree in the garden of consciousness, is built on the image of self. When a young person has a positive self-image, he thinks of himself as a good person and behaves that way. If he makes mistakes or misbehaves, he quickly self-corrects. And the tree bears good fruit.

If, instead, he develops a negative self-image, the tree becomes stunted and doesn't bear fruit. Consequently, the child doesn't like himself and behaves in unlikable ways. In so doing he reinforces his negative view of himself and builds a momentum on not trusting himself.

The way to help the stunted tree grow and bear fruit is to water it with good intentions and fertilize it with loving behavior. How do we help our children do that? We let them know that we love them. We help them change their negative behavior, which typically comes from not feeling good about themselves. We teach them how to behave in a way that expresses the person they really are.

We become coaches dedicated to helping our children build a positive self-image. We focus on their talents and on activities that promote a sense of well-being. And we continue to nurture their positive potential, even when they are misbehaving.

When we think of children's misbehavior as weeds to be pulled out of the beautiful garden of their Real Self, we shift our own consciousness. And we are better able to teach our children how to behave appropriately.

When we think of what makes up a person who cares for self and others, we think of such qualities as conscience, being sensitive to the needs and rights of others, and having the ability to make wise choices. As young people take responsibility for their actions while they are growing up, they prepare themselves to make right choices as adults.

Perhaps one of the most important interactions we can have with our sons and daughters is to listen with our heart and mind as they talk about school, their activities, their friends, their hopes and desires. And listening doesn't mean correcting, it means absorbing what they are saying and what they mean. Listening is one of the most loving activities we can participate in with anyone.

Many times young people talk all around what they really want to say. And often, as they feel their way along, they are trying to mobilize the courage to share deeper feelings. If we listen to their tone as well as to the words, we'll get some clues as to what they are really trying to tell us.

Sometimes they are simply practicing self-expression, and that's a good thing. At other times they want input or advice. And then there are times when they are simply blowing off steam. Whatever is their motive, if we listen with our heart we will know what kind of response will be helpful and encouraging.

Most young people, especially as they get into the turbulent teens, are experimenting with self-expression. They appreciate honest feedback as long as it is given with kindness. And they accept correction when it's given respectfully. Here's an example of this kind of dialogue between a father and son.

A Dad Teaches His Son Responsibility

Andy, a sixteen-year-old who had just received his driver's license, had quite a conversation with his dad. He started out by talking about how dumb other drivers on the road are. He went on to describe what dumbness meant from his point of view. And he was clearly leading up to something more specific.

His dad was smart enough to listen instead of interrupting and finally Andy got to the point. He had been driving too fast and came upon a car going much slower than he was. He couldn't stop in time and ended up bumping the other car from the rear. He had the good sense to stop and there wasn't any damage but the other driver was furious.

As Andy put it, "This guy just wanted to rub it in and rub it in! And all I wanted to do was get out of there when I found out there wasn't any damage. I mean, I realized I was going too fast, but it didn't do any damage and he was just a jerk about the whole thing."

When Andy stopped for breath, his dad queried him, "What are you really upset about, Andy?"

Andy didn't respond for a minute. And then he said, "I guess I'm mostly upset with myself. I didn't realize I was going too fast to stop, and that kind of scared me."

His dad said, "Andy, I realize you were scared, and that's probably what was going on with the other driver. When you get scared, you tend to flip into being upset and angry. Right?"

"I guess so," Andy replied.

"How are you feeling now?" he asked.

"I'm still kind of shaky, I guess. He was really mad," Andy responded with a sigh. "And I suppose you are too."

Andy's dad reflected before he answered. "Andy, are you ready for some feedback?"

"I guess so," Andy sighed.

"Okay," his dad responded, "this is more about what you did than about the other driver's reaction. What got into you to be driving too fast?"

Andy was silent and then responded, "I don't know exactly. I guess I was just enjoying the wind in my face, and I wasn't actually over the speed limit. I just didn't realize how slow that guy was going until it was too late."

"It sounds like you were going faster than your ability to stop, even if you weren't over the speed limit," Dad replied.

"I guess so. Does this mean I can't drive the car?" Andy asked.

His dad raised an eyebrow quizzically. "What do you think?"

"Yeah, I thought so," Andy responded. "But how am I going to learn if I don't drive?"

His dad thought for a moment, "Okay, Andy, you have a point there, but I'm not about to let you off the hook. You have to prove to me and to yourself that you can drive safely, and that means to drive slowly enough not to hit a car that's going slower than you are. I think we had better sign you up for some special driver's training before you drive by yourself again."

Andy took a deep breath. "Okay," he said, "I actually would appreciate getting some help on this. When I think about it, I don't blame that guy for getting mad at me. It was my fault. I don't want to scare myself that way again."

Andy's dad found an expert driver to teach Andy how to judge the relation between speed and distance. What it came down to was putting his attention on the traffic as well as on his own driving. He had to earn back his driving privileges, but he did so. And he hasn't had an incident since.

As Andy said, "I watch out for other cars as well as paying attention to my own driving. I guess that's a big part of being a good driver, isn't it?"

Andy's dad didn't make the mistake of blowing up at his son and damaging their relationship. Instead he listened to him and responded in a way that allowed Andy to look at himself. And he came up with a commonsense solution to help his son self-correct.

Changing an Attitude or Behavior

Here are seven basic steps for changing attitudes and behavior. Try it yourself first and then suggest it to your teens.

1. Decide on a specific attitude or behavior that you want to change.

2. Tell yourself exactly what you want to do, and tell yourself what will be your internal benefit, e.g., "I'll feel more in charge of myself. I'll respect myself more. I'll like myself better."

3. Practice the new attitude or behavior daily until it feels like second nature.

4. Correct any mistake immediately.

5. Congratulate yourself for your effort.

6. Record your progress in writing at the end of each day.

7. Keep it up until the new behavior is a habit.

Practicing these steps can be a demonstration project that helps the family. As you change an attitude or behavior, they will take notice. And when you correct yourself, you are in a better position to help your children and teens self-correct. The family can also gain a positive understanding of consequences:

- The consequence of a mistake is a negative outcome.

- The consequence of a negative outcome is a correction.

- The consequence of a correction is a positive outcome.

For a teenager like Andy, the consequence of driving carelessly is losing the privilege of driving the car. The correction is learning to drive safely. And the positive outcome is becoming a better driver and having access to the family car.

How about another family issue, such as getting a teen up in the morning? Consequences work the same way. The consequence of staying up late is it's hard to get up in the morning. The correction is getting to bed on time. And the positive outcome is it's easier to get up and start the day.

We give young people a major tool when we help them understand the law of cause and effect—that although they can't control the consequences of their actions, they are fully in charge of the actions that lead to the consequences. And they can self-correct.

Most young people want to be responsible. They want to succeed in life and they know responsibility is a major factor. So they look to their parents and teachers as mentors and guides. When we give correction with humor and affection, we prime our youth to respond positively.

A Mother's Way:
"A Little Patience and We Are There"

A friend sent me the following poem that was passed on from a Native American friend. The author is unknown. The poem beautifully describes the journey of the mother who understands her calling to teach her children patience and endurance.

THE JOURNEY OF LIFE

The young mother set her foot on the path of life.
"Is this the long way?" she asked.
And the guide said:
"Yes, and the way is hard.
And you will be old before you reach the end of it.
But the end
will be better than the beginning."

But the young mother was happy,
and she would not believe that anything
could be better than these years.
So she played with her children, and
gathered flowers for them along the way,
and bathed them in the clear streams;
and the sun shone on them,
and the young mother cried,
"Nothing
will ever be lovelier than this."

Then the night came, and the storm,
and the path was dark,
and the children shook with fear and cold,
and the mother drew them close and covered them
with her mantle, and the children said,
"Mother, we are not afraid,
for you are near,
and no harm can come."

And the morning came, and there was a hill ahead,
and the children climbed and grew weary,
and the mother was weary.
But at all times she said to the children,
"A little patience and we are there."
So the children climbed and when they reached the top,
they said, "Mother, we would not have done it
without you."

And the mother, when she lay down at night,
looked up at the stars and said,
"This is a better day than the last,
for my children have learned fortitude
in the face of hardness.

Yesterday I gave them courage.
Today, I have given them strength."

And with the next day came strange clouds
which darkened the earth, clouds of war and hate and evil,
and the children groped and stumbled,
and the mother said: "Look up.
Lift your eyes to the light."
And the children looked and saw above the clouds an
everlasting glory, and it guided them beyond the darkness.
And that night the mother said,
"This is the best day of all,
for I have shown my children God."

And the days went on,
and the weeks and the months and the years,
and the mother grew old and she was small and bent over.
But her children were
tall and strong,
and walked with courage.

And when the way was rough, they lifted her,
for she was as light as a feather;
and at last they came to a hill,
and beyond they could see
a shining road and golden gates flung wide.
And the mother said:
"I have reached the end of my journey.
And now I know the end is better than the beginning,
for my children can walk alone, and
their children after them."

And the children said, "You will always walk with us,
Mother, even when you have gone through the gates."

And they stood and watched her as she went on alone,
and the gates closed after her.
And they said: "We cannot see her,
but she is with us still.
A mother like ours is more than a memory.
She is a living presence."

I am always with you.
I am the whisper of the leaves as
you walk down the street.
I am the smell of detergent in your freshly laundered socks.
I am the cool hand on your brow when you're not well.

I live inside your laughter.
And I am crystallized in every tear drop.
I am the place you came from,
your first home;
and I am the map you follow with every step you take.

I was your first love and your first heartbreak,
and nothing on earth can separate you from me,
not time,
nor distance,
not even the end of my days.

Setting the Sail for the Upward Journey

Mother Teresa gave timeless instruction on love, and her life was a pure example of her teaching. She said, "Spread love everywhere you go. First of all in your own house . . . let no one ever come to you without leaving better and happier. Be the living expression of God's kindness;

kindness in your face, kindness in your eyes, kindness in your smile, kindness in your warm greeting."[4]

We can be the hands and feet of this loving saint of our times. And surely she will be smiling and radiating light from the heaven-world as we and our families move forward, our consciousness and decisions guided by the Father-Mother God and our Higher Self.

We as fathers, mothers and friends of youth have the blessed opportunity to help young people set their sail for life and the upward journey. We are the nurturers and mentors who will inspire youth to excellence by our character and behavior. When we accept the challenge, we initiate one of the most rewarding experiences in life: assisting young people to maximize their gifts and talents, and knowing we have made a difference.

The advanced souls who are coming into embodiment today are inherently spiritual. If the youth of today uphold their higher values, we will see a spiraling upward of spirituality and soul integrity. What joy will fill our hearts as we see our children, grandchildren and great-grandchildren creating a better world, a world in which each soul fulfills a higher destiny.

We are the authors of a divine destiny if we so choose. And young people growing up all over the world are called to accelerate an upward spiral of higher consciousness that correlates with the mind and heart of God. How each of us plays our role on the stage of life will greatly determine whether the Aquarian age is recorded in history as an age of violence and destruction or fulfills its destiny as an age of divine love.

Let us call to the angels for assistance to fulfill the mission of the Aquarian family. Let us advance in enlightenment every step of the way and accelerate our heart flame to expand and glow to lead the way for succeeding generations. Let us raise the consciousness of planet Earth. By grace, determination and effort, we and our children and grandchildren will write a defining chapter in Earth's cosmic history.

LULLABY TO THE SOUL

Lullaby, lullaby

Guardian angels are hovering near you
Elementals surround you to cheer you.

May the violet flame
Be your cradle so bright
In the arms of the Mother
Your dreams of pure light.

Blue-flame angels so gently descending
While the music of spheres is ascending.

Lullaby, lullaby, lullaby*

---

*Adapted from "AUM Lullaby," in *The Book of Hymns and Songs*
(The Summit Lighthouse, 1996).

Questions and Answers
with Dr. Marilyn Barrick

A Mother-to-Be

Q: My husband and I are expecting our first child. We're excited and happy, but I'm emotional and nervous too. Is this normal?

A: Congratulations! Yes, it is normal to be emotional when you are pregnant, and most women are kind of nervous about having a baby for the first time. After all, you haven't ever done this before—at least in this life. First of all, I highly recommend that you and your husband read *Nurturing Your Baby's Soul: A Spiritual Guide for Expectant Parents*.[1] This beautiful book by Elizabeth Clare Prophet, edited by Nancy Hearn and Dr. Joye Bennett, will inspire, comfort and reassure you both that you are embarking upon the greatest adventure of your life—motherhood and fatherhood.

Just think, you are welcoming a soul who has specially chosen you and your husband to be mother and father. You may very well have been together in previous lives, and all of you have special gifts to exchange. I'll tell you a little secret: whether boy or girl, this incoming bundle of light is also looking forward with a mixture of joy and jumpiness to what is to come. As a family, you are about to celebrate the journey of life in a whole new way.

Parents-to-be have their work cut out for them. Lots of books have been written on the subject, and everyone you know will have a great piece of advice for you. I'd like to take another tack. *It's okay to trust your inner guidance and intuition.* Let your baby guide you as well. Remember, the only words the baby has at first are his cooing and crying, but those are pretty good signals. When a baby cries, he or she is usually either hungry or in need of a diaper change. If you rule out these two items, the baby may simply want to feel cuddled and loved. And that's a good thing to do!

Most couples worry about repeating their parents' mistakes. Actually, you probably will, and you will make some of your own. However, you and your baby will learn a lesson from every mistake as well as from every right action. You can always apologize when you slip up and make a mistake. Even with a small baby, the soul is listening.

I suggest you sit down with your husband and tell him your concerns. Agree to help each other along. And ask your guardian angels to help you to be your best selves with your child. If either of you is aware that you have a tendency to behave in a way that's hurtful or threatening, ask each other, the ascended masters and the angels to help you change that behavior. Invoke the violet flame to transmute the old behavior and choose a specific positive behavior to replace it. And remember, taking no action is better than taking a hurtful one. It's okay to walk out of the room and do nothing until you get yourself together.

My recipe for parenthood: One large measure of trust in the guidance of your guardian angels (who need to be asked to help!). Three cups of loving kindness, gentle touches and love hugs. Add a firm dash of limits and common sense. Mix and serve. *Bon appétit!*

Working Parents

Q: How can we make sure we are giving our children what they need when both my husband and I work long hours and the children are either in school or with a baby-sitter much of the time during the week?

A: Many families today find it necessary for both husband and wife to work. Yet parents can still give their children the love and support they need. Parenting is a labor of love, and it is the quality of the time you do spend with your children that makes the difference. Let me ask you some questions that suggest the more important dimensions of nurturing and meeting the needs of children.

Do you make it a point to take the time to listen with your heart and respond lovingly to your children when you are home? Do you spend family time together on the weekends? Do you and your husband show your love for your children physically—a touch on the shoulder, a loving hug, a kiss good-night? Do you support your children when they make mistakes by letting them know you love them, hearing them out and helping them to find a way to rectify the situation? Do you pray with your children and tuck them into bed?

If so, it's very likely that your children know you love them and are feeling nurtured. Attentive listening, kind words, physical expressions of love, family fun times, loving discipline, helpfulness when children need it—all of these seemingly small actions show your children that you care.

In one study where 1,500 school-age children were asked what they thought made a happy family, the answer most often given was "doing things together." Even such simple things as going for walks together, riding bikes together, popping corn and watching a good movie together, reading a book together. Note that the key word is "together."

Children need to express themselves and to be heard. They want to share their ideas, their accomplishments, their feelings, hopes and dreams with their parents. Sometimes simply turning off the TV and spending time talking about the day will be exactly what you and your children need. If dinner is a harmonious time in your home, it's a great time to share. Whatever time you choose, make sure everyone gets a turn and that each one receives a loving and appreciative response.

Rock Music

Q: My family and I disagree about rock music. Personally the rock beat jangles my nerves and gives me a headache. Our teenage son and daughter tell me rock is "cool," and our ten-year-old son is beginning to follow their lead. My husband says, "So what's the problem?" Any counsel for a frazzled mom?

A: Your teenagers are doing what teens do, separating out to become their own person, testing the limits, spreading their wings, and trying to fit in with friends. I'd take your husband's response as a challenge and get your information together. Your personal reaction actually squares with a lot of scientific research on the subject. You may wish to review

Your Body Doesn't Lie, by John Diamond, M.D., and *The Secret Power of Music,* by David Tame.[2]

Research shows that gentle sounds of nature and good music (classical music, especially music with the waltz rhythm, the best of folk music and ethnic music of various cultures) strengthen the body's energy and uplift one's emotional mood. On the other hand, detrimental music (rap music, heavy metal, techno rock, basically any music with the anapestic beat, the opposite of waltz rhythm) weakens the body's energy, agitates the heart and the emotions and may create frenzied passion or depressed, even suicidal, moods.

Energy-depleting music is frequently accompanied by lyrics that are violent, depressing, sexually explicit or encouraging of drug and alcohol use. This is not the message you want your youth to hear.

I suggest you keep the family communication lines open. A good opener might be to rent the excellent movie *Mr. Holland's Opus,* view it as a family and discuss it afterwards. Talk about different types of music and the thoughts, emotions and values they express and what kind of music stirs and strengthens you. Encourage your children to share their thoughts and feelings.

Ask each member of the family what their favorite songs mean to them? What do they think might be the effect of negative lyrics and jagged rhythms on one's thoughts, feelings, values or spirituality? What do they believe writers and musicians hope to accomplish by writing, playing and singing that kind of music?

Listen respectfully, nonjudgmentally, and openheartedly to your children's point of view. Listen to the music your children listen to, watch the media presentations your youngsters watch, discuss the content, and initiate a process of selective listening as a result of family discussions. Your goal is to teach your children to think actively and creatively instead of watching or listening passively.

The bottom line here is to tune into your children. Their choice of music is a clue to their inner world, their joys and hopes, fears and anxieties. Share their joy and hope. Take notice if they dwell on lyrics dealing with anger, hatred, violence or death. Encourage them to talk about it so they may resolve their worries in the safety of home and family. Give them love, respect, encouragement, appreciation—and viable choices.

As you and your husband express your ideas and values and encourage your children to do likewise, you foster youths' positive growth and development. Remember you have a parental right and responsibility to set limits. Just do so with a lot of love and understanding.

Drugs and Alcohol

Q: I have a family member who is falling back into drugs and alcohol. What can I do?

A: People who are alcohol or drug dependent are usually trying to get some kind of an inner boost through chemically inducing an extra surge of energy, an altered state of consciousness, or the relaxing of inhibitions. Most young people do alcohol to "fit in" with friends or to be popular with an "in crowd." Others drink to loosen up in social situations.

When it comes to street drugs, some young people foolishly try to expand or alter their state of consciousness that way. They think they will discover a higher meaning to life when in actuality they are on their way to addiction. And that takes years of painful resolution, if it ever gets resolved.

One of the most serious street drugs today is Ecstasy,

which surpasses the use of marijuana, cocaine and heroin. It is particularly popular among young adults at the huge, all-night "raves." They say it heightens their awareness, intensifies their emotions and makes them feel good. Research indicates that Ecstasy can damage brain cells. It appears to destroy the axons, which transmit nerve signals. Ask your kids, is it worth the risk?

Sometimes young people who get into drugs are indirectly asking for help. It works, to their detriment, because it gets the family's attention, but drug use is now in place. Psychologically, most people dependent on drugs or alcohol are seeking something outside of themselves to help them feel good, to function better socially or to get through difficult times.

Some years ago the Canadian government put out a little pamphlet, *Dependent Man and His Crutches*. I've always remembered it because it spelled out the psychological problem. Whether it is alcohol, drugs, nicotine, sex addiction, gambling or overeating (and you can probably add to the list), the underlying problem is resorting to a false high or false calm as a crutch to function in life.

Instead of depending on God-given talents and practical know-how to solve life's dilemmas, the person with an addictive disorder subconsciously depends on a so-called quick fix, a chemical altering of his or her perception of those dilemmas. The fact remains that the dilemma, whatever it is, still sits there waiting to be resolved.

The individual momentarily escapes by way of the false calm of alcohol or the false high of drugs. But once the high wears off, he's back in the bog. And looking for another fix.

How can you and your family and friends help? First, ask God and the angels to help your loved one mobilize the courage, strength and endurance to stand, face and conquer this dilemma. Next, do whatever it takes to get that person to a professional counselor skilled in treating chemical dependency and the accompanying emotional turmoil and physical impact of the addiction.

Once your loved one commits to treatment, encourage activities and interactions that provide a natural high: healthy exercise, the beauty of nature, uplifting music, art or literature, kind words, loving appreciation and heartfelt hugs. Such moments give emotional comfort and create relief from pain by stimulating the endorphins—our own inner analgesic found primarily in the pituitary and the brain.

Dos and Don'ts

Do give your prayers, dweller calls and violet-flame decrees for the alcohol and drug entities to be removed, the dweller to be bound and your family member to be cut free. *Do* call to Archangel Michael to help your loved one to conquer the addiction. *Do* be loving, kind and firm about getting professional help from a drug- or alcohol-addiction counselor and a support group like Alcoholics Anonymous (AA) or Narcotics Anonymous (NA).

Don't put up with unacceptable behavior. *Don't* protect your loved one from the consequences of negative actions, e.g., *don't* run after, bail out, give a place to crash or cover up, protect or rescue your family member. *Don't* give up— God loves both of you and is championing your victory!

Closeness to God

Q: I'm missing something in my life, and I know it's about not feeling close to God. I try to pray, but I don't see change. I feel stuck. Then I get angry with God for not helping me out. I end up feeling scared, lonely and guilty. What can I do?

A: Many people who seek counseling get angry at God for not solving their problems. I tell them it reminds me of a sign I saw once in an AA meeting room: "If you don't feel close to God, guess who moved?" God's love is like the sunshine, always beaming down upon us. Yet, when we are at odds with ourselves or surrounded by clouds of doubt and despair, we may not feel it. God loves you, dear one, and that love doesn't change when you make mistakes or get stuck. Surely there are tears in the eyes of the Divine Mother when one of her children is hurting.

Do you know that there is nearly always pain hidden under anger? Anger itself is often a feeble attempt at a show of strength, a protective shield to protect us from hurt. Real comfort comes from healing the underlying pain. How? Feel the pain, love yourself through it and ask God to help you understand its purpose. Love and forgive everyone concerned. As your heart opens, you will begin to feel inner resolution and comfort.

As the Aquarian age is moving on, many people on the spiritual path are seriously pursuing the bonding of their soul with their Holy Christ Self. They earnestly desire to fulfill their divine destiny on Earth and experience their mystical reunion with God. In this alchemical process they often contact painful memories surfacing from deep in the unconscious.

They become aware of the pain of their original separation from God when they left the heaven-world or the ancient mystery schools. They come to realize that this is the deeper underlying cause of their sense of separation from God and feelings of loneliness, fear, anger and guilt. As they seek to understand the lessons their soul is trying to learn, they restore their loving communion with the Father-Mother God.

Perhaps Jesus offered the story of the prodigal son to comfort us in these times. He knows that God is everlastingly loving and forgiving when we genuinely desire to return Home. How about talking to your Father and Mother God as though they were your best friends?

Tell God your troubles, how scared, lonely and guilty you feel. Share your burdens, call for the violet flame to transmute them, and ask your divine parents to forgive your mistakes. Tell them how much you love them and want them to be an integral part of your life. Step out into the sun and feel their love shining down upon you. Look up at the stars in the sky and imagine the twinkling presence of the angels.

As you share your burdens with Father-Mother God, remember to stay on the line to hear their counsel. Don't hang up! Listen with your heart and soul. Accept God's understanding and forgiveness, and forgive yourself. Let the warmth of the sun of God's Presence melt away any sense of separation. Allow comfort and hope to enter your heart and soul. Claim a new beginning and a close walk with God. Choose to win your victory as an adept of love. Your soul will rejoice with God and the angels!

Energizing and Purifying the Chakras

Each line of the cosmic clock is associated with a chakra. The term *chakra*, Sanskrit for "wheel," "disc" or "circle," refers to the centers of light anchored in the etheric body that govern the flow of energy to the four lower bodies. The seven major centers are shown on the illustration of Michelangelo's *David* on the following page.

An excellent way to energize and purify the chakras is to give violet-flame affirmations. We can visualize violet flame enveloping these sacred centers and see it dissolving any negative substance that may have collected around them. We can envision this for our loved ones as well as for ourselves.

Visualizations

Turn your attention to each individual chakra, starting with the base-of-the-spine chakra.

Visualize the base-of-the-spine chakra—four-petaled, pure white—and see the white-fire of the Mother light dissolving the energy of self pity, indecision, emotional instability and all misuse of the sacred fire in this chakra.

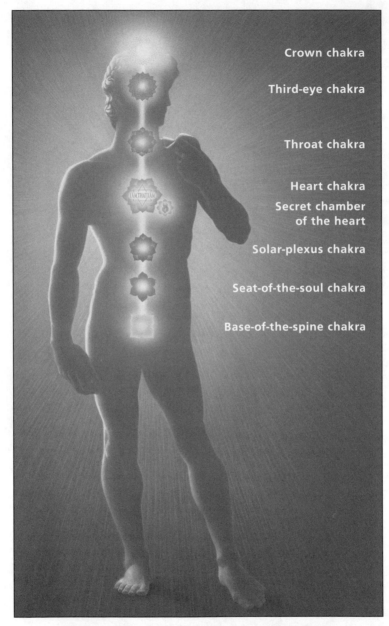

The Chakras as Shown on Michelangelo's *David*

Now visualize the seat-of-the-soul chakra—six-petaled, violet-purple-pink—and envision the light of the violet flame transforming all hardness of heart, ingratitude, thoughtlessness and spiritual blindness into love and forgiveness, gratitude and a sense of freedom.

Next visualize the solar-plexus chakra—ten-petaled, purple and gold with ruby flecks—and see the beautiful violet light transmuting all doubt, fear, sense of injustice, frustration and anxiety and enveloping you and your loved ones in God's justice and illumination's flame.

Focus on your heart chakra—twelve-petaled, a vibrant rose-pink—and envision the violet fire dissolving all hardness of heart and transforming the negative aspects of the human ego into light and love for your soul, your family, friends and neighbors.

See your throat chakra—sixteen petaled, an electric sapphire blue—and the violet flame transmuting all misuse of that power energy and replacing it with the perfect will of God for you, your loved ones, the nations and people worldwide.

Visualize your third-eye chakra—ninety-six-petaled, an intense emerald green—and the violet flame consuming all opposition to the light of God's vision and truth for the healing of yourself, family, friends and the world community.

Now envision your crown chakra—thousand-petaled, a brilliant yellow fire—and the energy and light of God's wisdom, enlightenment and illumination displacing all ignorance and darkness within and without for you, your loved ones, the nation and the world.

In conclusion, close your eyes and visualize your seven chakras. See the center of each chakra as a fiery sun of white light. And surrounding that brilliant sun, see the petals of each chakra in their vibrant, electric colors.

As you give the chakra affirmations that follow, hold in your mind's eye the image of powerful rays of light shooting out from the center of the chakras:

- brilliant white fire from the base of the spine

- beautiful violet light from the seat of the soul

- deep purple flecked with gold from the solar plexus

- radiant pink light from the heart

- intense blue fire from the throat

- emerald green rays from the third eye

- golden yellow radiating from the crown

CHAKRA AFFIRMATIONS

In the name I AM THAT I AM,
I invoke the violet flame to purify my chakras:

I AM a being of violet fire!
I AM the purity God desires!*

 My base chakra is a fount of violet fire,
My base chakra is the purity God desires!

I AM a being of violet fire!
I AM the purity God desires!

---

*Give this violet-flame affirmation three times each time it appears.

My soul chakra is a sphere of violet fire,
My soul is the purity God desires!

I AM a being of violet fire!
I AM the purity God desires!

My solar plexus is a sun of violet fire,
My solar plexus is the purity God desires!

I AM a being of violet fire!
I AM the purity God desires!

My heart is a chakra of violet fire,
My heart is the purity God desires!

I AM a being of violet fire!
I AM the purity God desires!

My throat chakra is a wheel of violet fire,
My throat chakra is the purity God desires!

I AM a being of violet fire!
I AM the purity God desires!

My third eye is a center of violet fire,
My third eye is the purity God desires!

I AM a being of violet fire!
I AM the purity God desires!

My crown chakra is a lotus of violet fire,
My crown chakra is the purity God desires!

I AM a being of violet fire!
I AM the purity God desires!

THE CHART OF YOUR DIVINE SELF

The Chart of Your Divine Self

The reason we can call to God and he will answer is because we are connected to him. We are his sons and daughters. We have a direct relationship to God and he has placed a portion of himself in us. In order to better understand this relationship, the ascended masters have designed the Chart of Your Divine Self.

The Chart of Your Divine Self is a portrait of you and of the God within you. It is a diagram of yourself and your potential to become who you really are. It is an outline of your spiritual anatomy.

The upper figure is your "I AM Presence," the Presence of God that is individualized in each one of us. It is your personalized "I AM THAT I AM." Your I AM Presence is surrounded by seven concentric spheres of spiritual energy that make up what is called your "causal body." The spheres of pulsating energy contain the record of the good works you have performed since your very first incarnation on Earth.

They are like your cosmic bank account.

The middle figure in the Chart represents the "Holy Christ Self," who is also called the Higher Self. You can think of your Holy Christ Self as your chief guardian angel and dearest friend, your inner teacher and voice of conscience. Just as the I AM Presence is the presence of God that is individualized for each of us, so the Holy Christ Self is the presence of the universal Christ that is individualized for each of us.

"The Christ" is actually a title given to those who have attained oneness with their Higher Self, or Christ Self. That's why Jesus was called "Jesus, the Christ." *Christ* comes from the Greek word *christos*, meaning "anointed"—anointed with the light of God.

What the Chart shows is that each of us has a Higher Self, or "inner Christ," and that each of us is destined to become one with that Higher Self—whether we call it the Christ, the Buddha, the Tao or the Atman. This "inner Christ" is what the Christian mystics sometimes refer to as the "inner man of the heart," and what the Upanishads mysteriously describe as a being the "size of a thumb" who "dwells deep within the heart."

We all have moments when we feel that connection with our Higher Self—when we are creative, loving, joyful. But there are other moments when we feel out of sync with our Higher Self—moments when we become angry, depressed, lost. What the spiritual path is all about is learning to sustain the connection to the higher part of ourselves so that we can make our greatest contribution to humanity.

The ribbon of white light descending from the I AM Presence through the Holy Christ Self to the lower figure in the Chart is the crystal cord (sometimes called the silver cord). It is the "umbilical cord," the lifeline, that ties you to Spirit.

Your crystal cord also nourishes that special, radiant flame of God that is ensconced in the secret chamber of your heart. It is called the threefold flame, or divine spark, because it is literally a spark of sacred fire that God has transmitted from his heart to yours. This flame is called "threefold" because it engenders the primary attributes of Spirit—power, wisdom and love.

The mystics of the world's religions have contacted the divine spark, describing it as the seed of divinity within. Buddhists, for instance, speak of the "germ of Buddhahood" that exists in every living being. In the Hindu tradition, the Katha Upanishad speaks of the "light of the Spirit" that is concealed in the "secret high place of the heart" of all beings.

Likewise, the fourteenth-century Christian theologian and mystic Meister Eckhart teaches of the divine spark when he says, "God's seed is within us." There is a part of us, says Eckhart, that "remains eternally in the Spirit and is divine.... Here God glows and flames without ceasing."

When we decree, we meditate on the flame in the secret chamber of our heart. This secret chamber is your own private meditation room, your interior castle, as Teresa of Avila called it. In Hindu tradition, the devotee visualizes a jeweled island in his heart. There he sees himself before a beautiful altar, where he worships his teacher in deep meditation.

Jesus spoke of entering the secret chamber of the heart when he said: "When thou prayest, enter into thy closet, and when thou hast shut thy door, pray to thy Father which is in secret; and thy Father which seeth in secret shall reward thee openly."

The lower figure in the Chart of Your Divine Self represents you as a soul on the spiritual path, surrounded by the violet flame and the protective white light of God known as the "tube of light." Your soul is the living potential of God— the part of you that is mortal but can become immortal. The high-frequency energy of the violet flame can help you reach that goal more quickly.

The purpose of your soul's evolution on Earth is to grow in self-mastery, balance your karma and fulfill your mission on Earth so that you can return to the spiritual dimensions that are your real home. When your soul at last takes flight and ascends back to God and the heaven-world, you will become an "ascended" master, free from the rounds of karma and rebirth.

Notes

Preface

1. Kahlil Gibran, *The Prophet* (New York: Alfred A. Knopf, 1923), p. 18.

Introduction

1. This picture of the Model T is in *The Dictionary of Cultural Literacy*, 2d ed., by E. D. Hirsch, Jr., Joseph F. Kett, and James Trefil (Boston: Houghton Mifflin Company, 1993), p. 442.
2. "Make Way for the 'Millennials,'" *Bits and Pieces*, May 2003, p. 20.

Chapter One • *Indigo, Crystal and Spirited Children*

1. See Nancy Ann Tappe, *Understanding Your Life through Color* (Carlsbad, Calif.: Starling Publishers, 1982).
2. Lee Carroll and Jan Tober, *The Indigo Children: The New Kids Have Arrived* (Carlsbad, Calif.: Hay House, 1999), pp. 1–2.
3. Lee Carroll and Jan Tober, *An Indigo Celebration: More Messages, Stories, and Insights from the Indigo Children* (Carlsbad, Calif.: Hay House, 1999), p. 69.
4. For excellent information on ADD and ADHD, see *Driven to Distraction: Recognizing and Coping with Attention Deficit Disorder from Childhood through Adulthood*, by

Edward M. Hallowell, M.D., and John J. Ratey, M.D. (New York: Simon and Schuster, Touchstone Book, 1995).

5. Doreen Virtue, *The Crystal Children* (Carlsbad, Calif.: Hay House, 2003).

6. For a memorable treatise on autism, written by a remarkable, autistic woman, see Temple Grandin's *Thinking in Pictures: And Other Reports from My Life with Autism* (New York: Vintage Books, 1995).

7. Christine Page, *Spiritual Alchemy: How to Transform Your Life* (Saffron Walden, Essex, U.K.: C.W. Daniel Company, 2003), pp. 28, 29–31.

8. Ibid., pp. 6–7.

9. Mary Sheedy Kurcinka, *Raising Your Spirited Child: A Guide for Parents Whose Child Is More Intense, Sensitive, Perceptive, Persistent, Energetic* (New York: HarperPerennial, 1992), pp. 7–8.

10. Ibid., pp. 8–9.

11. Ibid., p. 13.

12. Father Edward J. Flanagan, 1926, quoted in "Boys Town Education Model," by Patricia L. Wells (Boys Town, Nebr.: Father Flanagan's Boys Home, 1990), cover. Also see *Common Sense Parenting: A Proven Step-by-Step Guide for Raising Responsible Kids and Creating Happy Families*, 2d ed., by Raymond V. Burke, Ph.D., and Ronald W. Herron (Boys Town, Nebr.: Boys Town Press, 1996).

13. Wells, "Boys Town Education Model," p. 1.

Chapter Two • *The Child Is Father to the Man*

1. These classics—Frances Hodgson Burnett's *The Secret Garden* and A. J. Cronin's *The Keys of the Kingdom*—are readily available in several editions from publishers.

2. See "Girl Sends Thousands of Gifts to Foster Kids," Associated Press, December 12, 2003, at msnbc.msn.com.

3. See Erik H. Erikson, *Childhood and Society* (New York: W. W. Norton and Company, 1963) and Jane Middleton-Moz, *Children of Trauma: Rediscovering Your Discarded Self* (Deerfield Beach, Fla.: Health Communications, 1989), p. 23.

4. See Matt. 7:12; Luke 6:31.

5. Charles M. Sheldon, *In His Steps*, originally a series of Sheldon's sermons delivered in 1896 and published in many languages around the world since that time. A modern edition is published by Spire Books (Grand Rapids, Mich., 1984).

6. Judith Viorst, *Necessary Losses* (New York: Ballantine Books, Fawcett Gold Medal Book, 1987), p. 9.

7. For further information, see http://www.waterbirthinfo.com and Web pages for the Leboyer method of water birth.

8. Viorst, *Necessary Losses*, p. 15.

9. Ibid.

10. Ibid., p. 16.

11. This song came from a dictation of an ascended being, the God Meru, September 14, 1969.

12. Viorst, *Necessary Losses*, p. 73.

13. This quote is taken from a 1998 paper entitled "Grandparenthood," by Jack C. Westman, M.D., Professor Emeritus, Department of Psychiatry, University of Wisconsin-Madison; published on the Parenthood in America Web site: http://parenthood.library.wisc.edu/.

14. The movie *Rudy*, with Sean Astin as Rudy, was directed by David Anspaugh and produced in 1993 by Tri-Star Productions.

15. For Rudy's books, radio addresses and motivational material, type in the name Rudy Ruettiger in your Web search or go to Barnes & Noble.com.

Chapter Three • *The Family's Initiations: The Cosmic Clock and the Karmic Clock*

1. The understanding of the cosmic clock was given by dictation from the Blessed Mother to the messenger Elizabeth Clare Prophet.

2. This teaching on the cosmic clock is from Elizabeth Clare Prophet's lecture "The Freedom of the Child," given July 4, 1983.

3. Gal. 6:7.

4. For more information on the karmic clock, see Elizabeth Clare Prophet's book *Predict Your Future: Understand the Cycles of the Cosmic Clock* (Corwin Springs, Mont.: Summit University Press, 2004).

Chapter Four • *A Rapid Cycle of Self-Transformation*

1. The spiritual overseers are eight beings who comprise the Karmic Board. They dispense justice, adjudicating karma, mercy and judgment on behalf of every lifestream. All souls pass before the Karmic Board before and after each incarnation on Earth, receiving their assignment and karmic allotment for each lifetime beforehand and the review of their performance at its conclusion.

2. The kundalini is a powerful sacred fire that exists like a coiled serpent in the base-of-the-spine chakra and rises through spiritual purity and self-mastery to the crown chakra, quickening all of the spiritual centers (the chakras) on the way. This sacred fire is the precipitation of the Holy Spirit for purification, for alchemy and transmutation, and for the soul's realization of the ascension, the sacred ritual whereby the soul returns to the heaven-world.

3. Elizabeth Clare Prophet, *The Great White Brotherhood in the Culture, History and Religion of America* (Corwin Springs, Mont.: Summit University Press, 1987), p. 183.

Spiritual Formulas for Family Harmony and Soul Liberation

1. The mantras and decrees in this section are taken from Mark L. Prophet and Elizabeth Clare Prophet's *The Science of the Spoken Word* and *Prayers, Meditations and Dynamic Decrees for the Coming Revolution in Higher Consciousness*; published by Summit University Press.

Chapter Five • *The Psychology of the Soul*

1. This teaching was given by Elizabeth Clare Prophet in her lecture "The Psychology of Zailm: A Study of Reincarnation and Karma," Part II, December, 31, 1990.
2. For the scriptural story of Melchizedek, see Heb. 6:20; 7:1 22.
3. Elizabeth Clare Prophet, "The Psychology of Zailm."
4. For the full teaching on the mackerels, as well as the "ancestral tree," see Elizabeth Clare Prophet's *Predict Your Future*.
5. Ibid., chap. 10, "Psychology of Wholeness: The Karmic Clock."
6. Ibid.
7. See Rev. 22:2.
8. For a spiritually oriented astrological reading, I suggest you take a look at http://www.spiritualastrology.com or Edgar Cayce's astrological services.
9. See Mary Ann O'Roark, "The Miracle of Laughter," in the August 2003 issue of *Guideposts*, p. 66.

Chapter Six • *The Karmic Equation of Marriage and Family*

1. John Gray, Ph.D., *What Your Mother Couldn't Tell You and Your Father Didn't Know* (New York: HarperCollins Publishers, 1994), pp. 15, 16.
2. Ibid., pp. 42, 44.

3. Ibid., p. 26.

4. Ibid., p. 46.

5. See the Book of Job. The chief character, Job, despite great suffering and adversity, kept his faith in God.

Chapter Seven • The Impact of Today's Changing Culture

1. See the National Center for Health Statistics, National Vital Statistics Report, vol. 51, no. 10, 2003; and http://www .divorcereform.org/rates.html.

2. These 2001 statistics are listed on the National Institute of Mental Health Web site. See http://www.nimh.nih.gov/ research/ suifact.cfm.

3. See http://www.1-teenage-suicide.com. Also see *Wanting to Live: Overcoming the Seduction of Suicide*, by Dr. Neroli Duffy and Marilyn C. Barrick, Ph.D. (Corwin Springs, Mont.: Summit University Press, 2004). We have written this book for young people who are trying to withstand the pull of suicidal tendencies.

4. Doc Lew Childre, *A Parenting Manual: Heart Hope for the Family* (Boulder Creek, Calif.: Planetary Publications, 1995), p. 140.

5. CNN.com, "Survey: Teen Drug Use Falling," December 19, 2003.

6. NCHS, 2002 News Release, June 6, 2002, "HHS Report Shows Teen Birth Rate Falls to New Record Low in 2001," p. 1.

7. See the Good News Family Care Web site: http://www.gnfc .org.uk.

8. Kathleen Moorcroft, Ed.D., M.Ed., University of Toronto; B.A., Queen's University, Kingston.

9. Reported on the Web: "Media Use Statistics Resources on Media Habits of Children," March 2004.

10. This statistic was reported in the Knowledge Networks/SRI study, October 6, 2003.

11. Dr. Meg Meeker has written an excellent book on the subject of teen sex: *Epidemic: How Teen Sex Is Killing Our Kids* (Washington, D.C.: Lifeline Press, 2002).

12. Pam Stenzel can be reached through her Web site, http://www.pamstenzel.com.

13. Jack Kornfield, "Conscious Parenting," in the January-February 1993 issue of *Common Boundary*.

14. Marilyn C. Barrick, Ph.D., *Sacred Psychology of Change: Life as a Voyage of Transformation* (Corwin Springs, Mont.: Summit University Press, 2000).

15. Tom Brown, Jr., *Grandfather: A Native American's Lifelong Search for Truth and Harmony with Nature* (New York: Berkley Publishing Group, Berkley Books, 1993).

16. See James Redfield, *The Secret of Shambhala: In Search of the Eleventh Insight* (New York: Warner Books, 1999). Also see Redfield's *The Celestine Prophecy: An Adventure* (New York: Warner Books, 1994); *The Tenth Insight: Holding the Vision* (New York: Warner Books, 1998); and *The Celestine Vision: Living the New Spiritual Awareness* (New York: Warner Books, 1997).

17. From *Prayers, Meditations and Dynamic Decrees*, published by Summit University Press.

Chapter Eight • *The Inherent Genius of the Soul*

1. An excellent book on Montessori's work with young children is Lesley Britton's *Montessori Play and Learn: A Parent's Guide to Purposeful Play from Two to Six* (New York: Crown Publishers, 1992). This book is the source for much of the background on Maria Montessori.

2. Maria Montessori, *The Discovery of the Child* (reprint; New

York: Ballantine Books, 1972), p. 26.

3. Information on Mozart from the Island of Freedom Web site. References for biographical material on Mozart: *1996 Grolier Multimedia Encylopedia* and *Microsoft Encarta 98 Encyclopedia.*

4. The quotation comes from Emily Anderson, *The Letters of Beethoven*, vol. 3, as posted on the Island of Freedom Web site. References for biographical material on Beethoven: *1996 Grolier Multimedia Encyclopedia.*

5. See http://www.thekidshalloffame.com/CustomPage21.html.

6. Ibid.

7. This material is drawn from "Charlotte Mason in a Nutshell," by Deborah Taylor-Hough, editor of *The Charlotte Mason Monthly*; and "Who Is Charlotte Mason?" by Catherine Levison. Both articles are posted at http://www.christianity.com/cmason/.

8. This excerpt is from the October 18, 2002 letter from Ira Rubenzahl, Chair, and Rosanne Druckman, Executive Director, posted on the Hartford Consortium for Higher Education Web site: http://www.hartnet.org/hche. Click on "Partnerships with Public Schools."

9. This information comes from the Wake County Public School System's Web site: http://www.wcpss.net. Click on "Magnet Programs."

10. See "Cinderella," in *The Complete Grimm's Fairy Tales* (New York: Pantheon Books, 1972), pp. 121–28 for this classic version of the fairy tale.

11. See *The Gnostic Gospels,* by Elaine Pagels (New York: Vintage Books, 1979).

12. Prov. 22:6.

13. This address by Elizabeth Clare Prophet was given during "Freedom 1995: Soul Evolution: A Fusion of Mind and

Spirit," a conference hosted at the Royal Teton Ranch in Montana, June 24 through July 4, 1995.

14. Elizabeth Clare Prophet in her lecture "The Psychology of Zailm," Part II.

15. The ascended master Saint Germain describes the secret chamber within the heart: "Within it [the heart] there is a central chamber surrounded by a forcefield of such light and protection that we call it a 'cosmic interval.' It is a chamber separated from Matter and no probing could ever discover it. It occupies simultaneously not only the third and fourth dimensions but also other dimensions unknown to man." It serves "as the connecting point of the mighty crystal cord of light that descends from your God Presence to sustain the beating of your physical heart, giving you life, purpose, and cosmic integration." The secret chamber of the heart is a safe place for your soul and spirit. See *Saint Germain On Alchemy* (Corwin Springs, Mont.: Summit University Press, 1993), p. 350.

Chapter Nine • *The Care of Discipline Is Love's Fulfillment*

1. See *Emotions: Transforming Anger, Fear and Pain*, by Marilyn C. Barrick, Ph.D. (Corwin Springs, Mont.: Summit University Press, 2002) and *Emotional Intelligence*, by Daniel Goleman (New York: Bantam Books, 1995).

2. Page, *Spiritual Alchemy*, p. 176.

3. Adapted from "The Emperor's Seed," a story whose author is unknown. The story appears, with variations, on several Web sites on the Internet.

4. Paul the Venetian is the chohan of the ray of divine love. His etheric retreat, located in the heaven-world over southern France, is the Château de Liberté. He sponsors the ascended master culture for this age and works with all who desire to bring that culture forth on behalf of mankind.

In their book *The Masters and Their Retreats*, Mark L. Prophet and Elizabeth Clare Prophet state: "The seven color rays are the natural division of the pure white light emanating from the heart of God as it descends through the prism of manifestation. These are the subdivisions of the wholeness of Christ. Regardless of their color, all of the flames have a white-fire core of purity, which embodies all of the attributes of God and which may be invoked by those who desire to expand the Christ consciousness. The seven rays present seven paths to individual or personal Christhood. Seven masters have mastered identity by walking these paths, defined as the seven archetypes of Christhood. These seven masters are called the chohans of the rays, which means lords of the rays. *Chohan* is a Sanskrit term for lord, and lord is equivalent to law; hence the chohan is the action of the law of the ray. To be a chohan on one of the seven rays means that this master defines the law on that ray; through him that energy of the Christ and of God flows to mankind, to all who are evolving on that particular path" (Summit University Press, 2003, p. 5).

5. Mark L. Prophet and Elizabeth Clare Prophet explain: "Saint Germain holds a very important position in hierarchy in this age. Not only is he the chohan of the seventh ray of freedom, mercy, transmutation and ritual, he is also the hierarch of the Aquarian age. The pulsations of the violet flame can be felt from his retreat over the House of Rakoczy in Transylvania and from the Cave of Symbols in the United States" (*The Masters and Their Retreats*, p. 6).

6. The seven mighty Elohim and their feminine counterparts are the builders of form. Elohim is the name of God used in the first verse of the Bible, "In the beginning God created the heaven and the earth" (Gen. 1:1). The seven Elohim are "the seven Spirits of God" named in Revelation (Rev. 4:5) and the "morning stars" which sang together in the beginning as

the LORD revealed them to Job (Job 38:7). In the order of hierarchy, the Elohim and cosmic beings carry the greatest concentration, the highest vibration, of light that we can comprehend in our present state of evolution (see glossary in *Saint Germain On Alchemy*, p. 400).

7. The etheric retreats are temples and cities of light in the heaven-world, or etheric plane, where we can go in spiritual meditation and while our bodies sleep at night. For detailed information on the retreats see *The Masters and Their Retreats*, by Mark L. Prophet and Elizabeth Clare Prophet, compiled and edited by Annice Booth.

8. Paul the Venetian, "The Art of Living Love," in *Lords of the Seven Rays: Mirror of Consciousness*, by Mark L. Prophet and Elizabeth Clare Prophet (Corwin Springs, Mont.: Summit University Press, 1986), Book Two, pp. 97–98, 99–106, 110–11.

9. Dorothy Law Nolte as quoted in *Keeping Your Children Safe: A Practical Guide for Parents*, by Bettie B. Youngs (Louisville, Ky.: Westminster/John Knox Press, 1992), p. 34.

Chapter Ten • *The Education of the Heart*

1. The spiritual concepts in Rev Vosseler's presentation are based on the teachings of Mark L. Prophet and Elizabeth Clare Prophet and augmented by his many years of experience in youth and family ministry. For Elizabeth Clare Prophet's teaching on this subject, see "The Abortion of the Divine Plan of a Soul" (from the seminar "Life begets Life"), given March 30, 1991.

2. Ibid.

3. Joel L. Whitton and Joe Fisher, *Life between Life* (New York: Warner Books, 1986). For additional information on this topic, see Joe Fisher, *The Case for Reincarnation* (New York: Carol Publishing Group, Citadel Press Book, 1992).

4. Whitton and Fisher, *Life between Life*, p. 123.

5. Ibid., pp. 75–76.

6. Ibid., p. 76.

7. Ibid., p. 44.

8. Adapted from Elizabeth Clare Prophet, "The Key to Unlock the Genius of Your Child," given during the seminar "Family Designs for the Golden Age," June 16, 1974.

9. Elizabeth Clare Prophet, "The Discipline of the Four Lower Bodies," given July 2, 1991.

10. I Cor. 7: 3.

11. John 12:32.

12. Prophet, "The Discipline of the Four Lower Bodies."

13. Ibid.

14. Ibid.

15. Ibid.

16. Ibid.

17. Ibid.

18. *Watching America: What Television Tells Us about Our Lives*, by S. Robert Lichter, Linda S. Lichter, and Stanley Rothman (New York: Prentice-Hall, 1991).

19. Don Kowet, quoted in "The State of Education in America," an address by Elizabeth Clare Prophet, delivered June 29, 1991.

20. Marie Winn, *The Plug-In Drug: Television, Children, and the Family*, quoted in Prophet, "The State of Education in America."

21. Prophet, "The Discipline of the Four Lower Bodies."

22. Ibid.

23. Ibid.

Chapter Eleven • *Impartations of the Soul and Spirit*

1. This lecture, "The Challenge of Teaching an Adult Soul in a Child's Body," was given by Elizabeth Clare Prophet in a seminar entitled "Education in the Age of Aquarius," held in Minneapolis, Minnesota, October 4 and 5, 1975.

2. This touching story is based on events that happened some years ago. See Ina Hughs, February 3, 2004, "Happy Ending Didn't Need Added Drama," at http://www.knoxnews.com/kns/lifestyles_columnists. Click on her "Column Archives," then scroll down to the date.

3. See Marilyn C. Barrick, Ph.D., *Dreams: Exploring the Secrets of Your Soul* (Corwin Springs, Mont.: Summit University Press, 2001).

4. Statistics quoted in *The Teaching Church*, by Eugene C. Roehlkepartain (Nashville, Tenn.: Abingdon Press, 1993), p. 171.

5. Archeia Charity, "The Power of Love," a dictation delivered by the messenger Elizabeth Clare Prophet on Sunday, February 20, 1966.

Chapter Twelve • *The Soul's Restoration of Innocence*

1. Matt. 13:33; Luke 13:21.

2. See Luke 1:26–38.

3. This dictation of Jesus was delivered through the messenger Elizabeth Clare Prophet on June 16, 1974, during the two-day seminar "Family Designs for the Golden Age."

4. This quote from Mother Teresa was found on the Kindness Inc. Web site: http://www.kindnessinc.org/directory.htm. On October 19, 2003, beloved Mother Teresa was beatified by Pope John Paul II, the first step in becoming a saint in the Catholic Church.

Questions and Answers with Dr. Marilyn Barrick

1. *Nurturing Your Baby's Soul: A Spiritual Guide for Expectant Parents*, by Elizabeth Clare Prophet, compiled and edited by Nancy Hearn and Dr. Joye Bennett (Corwin Springs, Mont: Summit University Press, 1998).

2. *Your Body Doesn't Lie*, by John Diamond, M.D. (New York: Harper and Row, 1979) and *The Secret Power of Music*, by David Tame (Rochester, Vt.: Inner Traditions, Destiny Books, 1984).

Glossary

Ascended masters. Enlightened spiritual beings who once lived on Earth, fulfilled their reason for being and have reunited with God.

Ascension. A spiritual acceleration of consciousness that takes place at the natural conclusion of one's final lifetime on Earth whereby the soul reunites with God and is free from the rounds of karma and rebirth.

Astral plane. The lowest vibrating frequency of time and space; the repository of mankind's thoughts and feelings, conscious and unconscious.

Carnal mind. The lower aspects of the human ego, human intellect and human will; the animal nature of man.

Causal body. Interpenetrating spheres of light surrounding each one's I AM Presence at spiritual levels. The spheres of the causal body contain the records of the virtuous acts we have performed to the glory of God and the blessing of mankind.

Chart of Your Divine Self. *See* pp. 330–34.

Christ Self. *See* Holy Christ Self.

Decree. A dynamic form of spoken prayer used by students of the ascended masters to direct God's light into individual and world conditions.

Dictation. The messages of the ascended masters, archangels and other advanced spiritual beings delivered through the agency of the Holy Spirit by a messenger of the Great White Brotherhood.

Elementals. The nature spirits of earth, air, fire and water.

El Morya. The ascended master who is the teacher and sponsor of the messengers Mark L. Prophet and Elizabeth Clare Prophet and the founder of The Summit Lighthouse.

Four lower bodies. The four sheaths surrounding the soul; the vehicles the soul uses in her journey on Earth: the etheric, or memory, body; the mental body; the desire, or emotional, body; the physical body.

The etheric body houses the blueprint of the soul's identity and contains the memory of all that has ever transpired in the soul and all impulses she has ever sent out. The mental body is the vessel of the cognitive faculties; when purified, it can become the vessel of the mind of God. The desire body houses the higher and lower desires and records the emotions. The physical body is the miracle of flesh and blood that enables the soul to progress in the material universe.

Holy Christ Self. The Higher Self; our inner teacher, guardian, friend and advocate before God; the universal Christ individualized for each of us.

I AM Presence. The Presence of God, the I AM THAT I AM, individualized for each soul.

Karma. Sanskrit, meaning "act," "action," "work" or "deed." The consequences of one's thoughts, words and deeds of this life and previous lives; the law of cause and effect, which decrees that whatever we do comes full circle to our doorstep for resolution. The law of karma necessitates the soul's reincarnation so that she can balance her misuses of God's light, energy and consciousness.

Light. The universal radiance and energy of God.

Messenger. One trained by an ascended master to receive and deliver the teachings, messages and prophecies of the Great White Brotherhood.

Threefold flame. The divine spark, the flame of God ensconced within the secret chamber of the heart; the soul's point of contact with the I AM Presence and Holy Christ Self.

Bibliography

Barrick, Marilyn C., Ph.D. *Dreams: Exploring the Secrets of Your Soul.* Corwin Springs, Mont.: Summit University Press, 2001.

Barrick, Marilyn C., Ph.D. *Emotions: Transforming Anger, Fear and Pain.* Corwin Springs, Mont.: Summit University Press, 2002.

Barrick, Marilyn C., Ph.D. *Sacred Psychology of Change: Life as a Voyage of Transformation.* Corwin Springs, Mont.: Summit University Press, 2000.

Barrick, Marilyn C., Ph.D. *Sacred Psychology of Love: The Quest for Relationships That Unite Heart and Soul.* Corwin Springs, Mont.: Summit University Press, 1999.

Barrick, Marilyn C., Ph.D. *Soul Reflections: Many Lives, Many Journeys.* Corwin Springs, Mont.: Summit University Press, 2003.

Booth, Annice. *Memories of Mark: My Life with Mark Prophet.* Corwin Springs, Mont.: Summit University Press, 1999.

Britton, Lesley. *Montessori Play and Learn: A Parent's Guide to Purposeful Play from Two to Six.* New York: Crown Publishers, 1992.

Brown, Tom, Jr. *Grandfather: A Native American's Lifelong Search for Truth and Harmony with Nature.* New York: Berkley Publishing Group, Berkley Books, 1993.

Burke, Raymond V., Ph.D., and Ronald W. Herron. *Common Sense Parenting: A Proven, Step-by-Step Guide for Raising*

Responsible Kids and Creating Happy Families. Boys Town, Nebr.: Boys Town Press, 1996.

Burnett, Frances Hodgson. *The Secret Garden.*

Carroll, Lee, and Jan Tober. *An Indigo Celebration: More Messages, Stories, and Insights from the Indigo Children.* Carlsbad, Calif.: Hay House, 2001.

Carroll, Lee, and Jan Tober. *The Indigo Children: The New Kids Have Arrived.* Carlsbad, Calif.: Hay House, 1999.

Childre, Doc Lew. *A Parenting Manual: Heart Hope for the Family.* Boulder Creek, Calif.: Planetary Publications, 1995.

The Complete Grimm's Fairy Tales, trans. Margaret Hunt and James Stern. New York: Pantheon Books, 1972.

Cronin, A. J. *The Keys to the Kingdom.*

Diamond, John, M.D. *Your Body Doesn't Lie.* New York: Harper and Row, 1979.

Duffy, Neroli, Dr., and Marilyn C. Barrick, Ph.D. *Wanting to Live: Overcoming the Seduction of Suicide.* Corwin Springs, Mont.: Summit University Press, 2004.

Erikson, Erik H. *Childhood and Society.* New York: W. W. Norton and Company, 1963.

Fisher, Joe. *The Case for Reincarnation.* New York: Carol Publishing Group, Citadel Press Book, 1984.

Gibran, Kahlil. *The Prophet.* New York: Alfred A. Knopf, 1923.

Goleman, Daniel. *Emotional Intelligence.* New York: Bantam Books, 1995.

Grandin, Temple. *Thinking in Pictures: And Other Reports from My Life with Autism.* New York: Vintage Books, 1995.

Gray, John, Ph.D. *What Your Mother Couldn't Tell You and Your Father Didn't Know: Advanced Relationship Skills for Better Communication and Lasting Intimacy.* New York: HarperCollins Publishers, 1994.

Grolier Multimedia Encyclopedia, 1996. Grolier Interactive.

Hallowell, Edward M., M.D., and John J. Ratey, M.D. *Driven to Distraction: Recognizing and Coping with Attention Deficit Disorder from Childhood through Adulthood.* New York: Simon and Schuster, Touchstone Book, 1995.

Kurcinka, Mary Sheedy. *Raising Your Spirited Child: A Guide for Parents Whose Child Is More Intense, Sensitive, Perceptive, Persistent, Energetic.* New York: HarperPerennial, 1992.

Lichter, S. Robert; Linda S. Lichter; and Stanley Rothman. *Watching America: What Television Tells Us about Our Lives.* New York: Prentice-Hall, 1991.

Meeker, Meg, Dr. *Epidemic: How Teen Sex Is Killing Our Kids.* Washington, D.C.: Lifeline Press, 2002.

Microsoft Encarta 98 Encyclopedia. Microsoft Corporation.

Middleton-Moz, Jane. *Children of Trauma: Rediscovering Your Discarded Self.* Deerfield Beach, Fla.: Health Communications, 1989.

Montessori, Maria. *The Discovery of the Child*, trans. M. Joseph Costello. New York: Ballantine Books, 1972.

Page, Christine, Dr. *Spiritual Alchemy: How to Transform Your Life.* Saffron Walden, Essex, United Kingdom: C.W. Daniel Company, 2003.

Pagels, Elaine. *The Gnostic Gospels.* New York: Vintage Books, 1979.

Prayers, Meditations and Dynamic Decrees for the Coming Revolution in Higher Consciousness. Corwin Springs, Mont.: Summit University Press, 1984.

Prophet, Elizabeth Clare. *The Great White Brotherhood in the Culture, History and Religion of America.* Corwin Springs, Mont.: Summit University Press, 1987.

Prophet, Elizabeth Clare. *Nurturing Your Baby's Soul.* Corwin Springs, Mont.: Summit University Press, 1998.

Prophet, Elizabeth Clare. *Predict Your Future: Understand the Cycles of the Cosmic Clock.* Corwin Springs, Mont.: Summit University Press, 2004.

Prophet, Mark L., and Elizabeth Clare Prophet. *Lords of the Seven Rays: Mirror of Consciousness.* Corwin Springs, Mont.: Summit University Press, 1986.

Prophet, Mark L., and Elizabeth Clare Prophet. *The Masters and Their Retreats.* Corwin Springs, Mont.: Summit University Press, 2003.

Prophet, Mark L., and Elizabeth Clare Prophet. *The Science of the Spoken Word.* Corwin Springs, Mont.: Summit University Press, 1991.

Redfield, James. *The Celestine Prophecy: An Adventure.* New York: Warner Books, 1994.

Redfield, James. *The Celestine Vision: Living the New Spiritual Awareness.* New York: Warner Books, 1997.

Redfield, James. *The Secret of Shambhala: In Search of the Eleventh Insight.* New York: Warner Books, 1999.

Redfield, James. *The Tenth Insight: Holding the Vision.* New York: Warner Books, 1998.

Roehlkepartain, Eugene C. *The Teaching Church.* Nashville, Tenn.: Abingdon Press, 1993.

Saint Germain On Alchemy: Formulas for Self-Transformation. Corwin Springs, Mont.: Summit University Press, 1993.

Sheldon, Charles M. *In His Steps.* Grand Rapids, Mich.: Spire Books, 1984.

Stenzel, Pam, with Crystal Kirgiss. *Sex Has a Price Tag.* Grand Rapids, Mich.: Zondervan, Youth Specialties StudentWare Book, 2003. http://pamstenzel.com

Tame, David. *The Secret Power of Music.* Rochester, Vt.: Inner Traditions, Destiny Books, 1984.

Tappe, Nancy Ann. *Understanding Your Life through Color.*

Carlsbad, Calif.: Starling Publishers, 1982.

Viorst, Judith. *Necessary Losses*. New York: Ballantine Books, Fawcett Gold Medal Book, 1987.

Whitton, Joel L., M.D., Ph.D., and Joe Fisher. *Life between Life*. New York: Warner Books, 1986.

Youngs, Bettie B., Ph.D., Ed.D. *Keeping Your Children Safe: A Practical Guide for Parents*. Louiseville, Ky.: Westminster/ John Knox Press, 1992.

Credits

We gratefully acknowledge the following individuals and organizations for permission to reprint excerpts from their copyrighted material:

Excerpts from *Spiritual Alchemy: How to Transform Your Life*, by Dr. Christine Page, copyright © 2003 by Christine Page. Reprinted by permission of the C.W. Daniel Company Ltd.

Excerpts from Chapter 1 from *Raising Your Spirited Child*, by Mary Sheedy Kurcinka, copyright © 1992 by Mary Sheedy Kurcinka. Reprinted by permission of HarperCollins Publishers Inc.

Excerpt "Make Way for the 'Millennials,'" from *Bits & Pieces*, copyright © 2003 by Lawrence Ragan Communications Inc. Courtesy of Lawrence Ragan Communications Inc.

Excerpt from "Grandparenthood," by Jack C. Westman, M.D., Professor Emeritus of Psychiatry, University of Wisconsin Medical School, Madison, Wisconsin; copyright © 1998 by Jack C. Westman. Courtesy of Jack C. Westman.

Excerpt and statistics from the Good News Family Care Web site, copyright © 1998–2004 by Good News Family Care (Homes) Ltd. Courtesy of Good News Family Care.

Soul Reflections
Many Lives, Many Journeys

The journey of our soul has lasted many lifetimes...

As we move into the 21st century, many of us feel a yearning for spiritual awakening and divine guidance. We look to therapists, coaches and ministers for answers, but ultimately the healing of soul and spirit is an inner quest.

In *Soul Reflections: Many Lives, Many Journeys*, through intriguing studies of factual and legendary heroes, inspiring meditations and practical exercises, Dr. Barrick shows how love and compassion initiate a healing process for the soul. And she reveals alchemical formulas to enrich our quest for soul liberation.

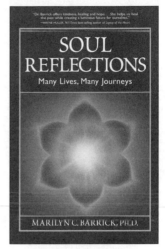

ISBN: 0-922729-83-2
Trade Paperback $14.95

"Marilyn Barrick fervently believes in the power of compassion as a potent tool for healing human sorrow and suffering. She offers us the possibility—nay, the promise—of spiritual companionship and support the moment we honor our brief time on earth as a gift to be opened, rather than as a problem to be solved."

—WAYNE MULLER, N.Y. *Times* best-selling author of
Legacy of the Heart

"Dr. Barrick has outlined a clear path for your soul's homeward journey, illumined by her many years of experience in guiding souls through life's difficult moments."

—DR. NEROLI DUFFY., author, lecturer and medical doctor

"This book is a must-read for any serious seeker who hungers for knowledge of the path that can lead to enlightenment and the ascension in the light."

—REV. E. GENE VOSSELER, public speaker, writer and spiritual counselor

Emotions
Transforming Anger, Fear and Pain

ISBN: 0-922729-77-8
Trade Paperback $14.95

Scientists have demonstrated the link between emotional balance and physical and mental well-being. When we learn how to handle our emotions, we can achieve balance in body, mind and soul. In *Emotions: Transforming Anger, Fear and Pain*, Dr. Marilyn Barrick, a transformational psychologist, takes the study of our emotions—and how to deal with them—to the next level.

In *Emotions*, you will discover how to release anger, guilt and grief in a healthy way to experience inner joy. The author shares techniques such as trauma-release therapy, peaceful self-observation and using nature as healer to help us realize loving-kindness, mindfulness and tolerance. She also shares successful spiritual techniques she has developed in her practice.

In these uncertain times, *Emotions: Transforming Anger, Fear and Pain* is an invaluable guide to creating heart-centeredness in a turbulent world.

"Marilyn Barrick is on the mark. While we search for the understanding of our physical, mental and spiritual selves, we often forget the source of the balance between all of them—our emotional self. This book addresses the issue magnificently. Read it and grow."

—DANNION BRINKLEY, *N.Y. Times* best-selling author of
Saved by the Light and *At Peace in the Light*

"*Emotions* is a wise, heartfelt and deeply spiritual path that can lead you from fear to courage, anger to joy, and helplessness to effectiveness—whatever challenges you may be facing. I have found it tremendously helpful."

—MARTIN L. ROSSMAN, M.D., author of *Guided Imagery for Self-Healing*

"Written in an easily understandable style, *Emotions: Transforming Anger, Fear and Pain* offers a wealth of information. Dr. Barrick provides excellent methods for freeing ourselves from some of our most destructive emotions—thus opening the door to improved health at all levels. This book is deserving of wide reading and rereading."

—RANVILLE S. CLARK, M.D., psychiatrist, Washington, D.C.

Dreams
Exploring the Secrets of Your Soul

Everyone and everything in our dreams is part of us . . . We spend one-third of our lives asleep—and most of that time we are dreaming. Dr. Marilyn Barrick's fascinating work shows that our dreams are not only meaningful and connected with events in our lives, but they also hold valuable keys to our spiritual and emotional development. In fact, our souls are great dramatists and teachers, and the scripts of our dreams often contain profound and valuable guidance.

ISBN: 0-922729-63-8
Trade Paperback $14.00

Dreams: Exploring the Secrets of Your Soul discusses Tibetan sleep and dream yoga, lucid dreaming and techniques to help you more clearly remember and understand your dreams. Learn how to interpret your dreams through the powerful insights in this book and the author's visionary analysis of actual dreams. And discover how to decode the metaphorical messages of your own soul.

"This unique book on dreams integrates the soul's development on the spiritual path with personal dream work. . . . It invites us to consider a greater potential of the self beyond life's ordinary conflicts and helps us open up to a greater understanding of the purpose of life."

—RALPH YANEY, M.D.,
psychiatrist/psychoanalyst and author of *10,001*

"Dreams. . . helps the reader unlock hidden secrets thereby opening new vistas to awareness, understanding, healing and finally, higher consciousness. . . . Dr. Barrick carefully, cogently and expertly enables the reader to understand the dream messages psychologically and spiritually."

—RICHARD FULLER, senior editor, *Metaphysical Reviews*

Sacred Psychology of Change

ISBN: 0-922729-57-3
Trade Paperback $14.95

Catch the vision of your role in the 21st century. *Sacred Psychology of Change* shows how you can welcome cycles of change and even chaos as transformational opportunities. It is jam-packed with helpful information from cutting-edge change theories, psychology and spirituality.

Dr. Marilyn Barrick teaches us how to envision and explore the future while living productively in the present. Discover the importance of a creative mind-set, an open heart and the maturing of soul to successfully navigate the waves of change. Learn how to meet the challenges of endings and beginnings and emerge from the darkness of grief and loss into a bright new day.

The storytelling chapters and exercises bring your personal journey to life and suggest practical approaches to the challenging scenarios of our fast-moving world.

"This book asks us to 'focus our attention on the higher intelligence of our heart' and then describes in loving detail ways of doing just that. Those interested in the heart's ability to heal will find encouragement in these pages."

–RUTH BLY, licensed psychologist, Jungian analyst, author

"A profound treasure of spiritual truths and their practical application based on the author's many successful years of personal and professional experience. Written in the language of the heart and with remarkable clarity and sensitivity, this book will lead you, chapter by chapter and step by step, to a profoundly healing dialogue with yourself—and through an exciting spiritual and psychological journey of change."

–KENNETH FRAZIER, L.P.C., D.A.P.A., A.C.P.E.

Sacred Psychology
of Love

Searching for your perfect love? *Sacred Psychology of Love* unfolds the hidden spiritual and psychological dramas inherent in friendships, love relationships and marriage. It tells the story of each one's inner beloved and offers tender ways to spark divine love in your relationships.

After 39 years as a clinical psychologist and relationship counselor, Dr. Barrick is uniquely qualified to reveal the impact of childhood experiences upon adult relationships and to awaken us to the benefits of the reflecting mirror of the beloved. She

ISBN: 0-922729-49-2
Trade Paperback $12.95

shows the key role your inner "other half" plays in the eternal dance of love and gives practical self-help exercises to guide you on your quest for relationships that unite heart and soul.

"A wonderful marriage of the mystical and practical,
this soul nourishing book is beautiful, healing and thought-provoking."

–SUE PATTON THOELE,
author of *Heart-Centered Marriage*

"In our search for the Beloved, whether inner or outer,
we seek that mysterious blend of beauty and practicality
which Dr. Marilyn Barrick masterfully conveys on every page.
Synthesizing her knowledge of sacred text, her clinical
expertise and her life's wisdom, she has written a book for
anyone seeking to love or to be loved. With compassion and humor,
she gives us an important tool for enriching relationships."

–ANNE DEVORE, Jungian analyst

Wanting to Live

ISBN: 0-922729-92-1
5 1/2 x 6 1/2 $8.95

Practical tools and priceless insights that will save lives...

In this unique and inspiring book, a minister and former medical doctor along with a clinical psychologist part the veil for a startling look beyond the physical world into a realm we usually don't see: malignant spirits coaxing depressed but beautiful people into suicide; a bleak, painful existence in a dark, frightening level of consciousness; and lost souls immediately coming back into a new lifetime to face the same test all over again.

Most important, *Wanting to Live: Overcoming the Seduction of Suicide*, by Dr. Neroli Duffy and Marilyn C. Barrick, Ph.D., tells us about powerful, life-changing partnerships with heavenly rescuers and offers priceless insights and practical tools for suicidal people and their loved ones. They shine the light of understanding to pierce the darkness and to bring hope to the despondent soul. This book is destined to save many lives.

The authors tell young people, "In reality there is no such thing as death. When we lay down the body, we do not die. Our soul and our spirit live on. The body is just a house, a temple for the spirit. If the near-death experience teaches us anything, it is the unreality of death and the reality of the continuity of the soul....

"In reality, your soul wants to live—not just in the finite sense of this earthly existence, but in the infinite sense of the great spiritual being that you are at inner levels."

FOR MORE INFORMATION

Summit University Press books are available at fine bookstores worldwide and at your favorite on-line bookseller.

For a free catalog of our books and products or to learn more about the spiritual techniques featured in this book, please contact:

Summit University Press
PO Box 5000
Corwin Springs, MT 59030-5000 USA
Telephone: 1-800-245-5445 or 406-848-9500
Fax: 1-800-221-8307 or 406-848-9555
E-mail: info@summituniversitypress.com
www.summituniversitypress.com

MARILYN C. BARRICK, Ph.D., minister, psychologist and transformational therapist, is the author of a valuable seven-book self-help series on spiritual psychology, six of which are already published and available in bookstores and on the Web:

A Spiritual Approach to Parenting:
Secrets of Raising the 21st
Century Child

Soul Reflections: Many Lives,
Many Journeys

Emotions: Transforming Anger,
Fear and Pain

Dreams: Exploring the Secrets
of Your Soul

Sacred Psychology of Change:
Life as a Voyage of Transformation

Sacred Psychology of Love:
The Quest for Relationships That
Unite Heart and Soul

In *A Spiritual Approach to Parenting: Secrets of Raising the 21st Century Child*, Dr. Barrick offers a unique approach of expert psychological advice and in-depth spiritual understanding, plus practical tips for families, children and youth. And Dr. Barrick's seventh book in the series—coming in 2005—will highlight energy therapy and past-life recall.

Dr. Barrick is also co-author with Dr. Neroli Duffy of *Wanting to Live: Overcoming the Seduction of Suicide*, a book written especially for today's teens and young adults.

In addition to her writing and private practice, Dr. Barrick conducts seminars and workshops in the U.S.A., Canada and Europe. Over her 39-year professional career, she has consulted as a psychological expert to schools, churches, government agencies, professional advisory boards and mental health facilities. She has also taught graduate psychology courses and served as a Peace Corps training development officer and field counselor.

Dr. Barrick's clinical practice includes individual, couple and family therapy, trauma release work, guided imagery, soul work and past-life analysis. For more information, visit Dr. Barrick's Web site: www.spiritualpsychology.com.